THE
100 BEST
STOCKS

TO OWN IN AMERICA

Fifth Edition

Gene Walden

Dearborn
Financial Publishing, Inc.®

TO LAURIE, WHITNEY, AND RYAN

Executive Editor: Cynthia A. Zigmund
Managing Editor: Jack Kiburz
Interior Design: Elizandro Carrington
Cover Design: S. Laird Jenkins Corporation
Typesetting: Elizabeth Pitts

Library of Congress Cataloging-in-Publication Data

Walden, Gene.
    The 100 best stocks to own in America / by Gene Walden. — 5th ed.
      p. cm.
    Includes index.
    ISBN 0-7931-2574-X (pbk.)
    1. Stocks—United States. I. Title
HG4963.W35 1997   97-28266
332.63′22′0973—dc21   CIP

Contents

Alphabetical Listing of the 100 Best Stocks

Abbott Laboratories (36)
Albertson's, Inc. (6)
American Home Products Corp. (74)
American International Group, Inc. (86)
Anheuser-Busch Cos., Inc. (49)
Automatic Data Processing (44)
Banc One Corp. (40)
Becton Dickinson (66)
Bemis Company, Inc. (19)
Bristol-Myers Squibb (67)
Cabletron Systems, Inc. (80)
Campbell Soup Co. (16)
Cardinal Health, Inc. (58)
Carlisle Cos., Inc. (53)
Carnival Corp. (87)
Cincinnati Financial Corp. (98)
Cintas Corp. (31)
Cisco Systems (78)
Clorox Co. (63)
Coca-Cola Company (7)
Colgate-Palmolive Co. (34)
Compaq Computer Corp. (81)
Computer Associates International, Inc. (70)
Computer Sciences Corp. (95)
ConAgra, Inc. (27)
CPC International, Inc. (59)
Crompton & Knowles Corp. (94)
Crown Cork & Seal Co. (99)
Danaher Corp. (83)
Walt Disney Co. (73)
Dollar General Corp. (14)
Donaldson Company, Inc. (45)

Dover Corp. (60)
Electronic Data Systems (51)
Emerson Electric Co. (65)
Equifax, Inc. (48)
Fannie Mae (2)
Federal Signal Corp. (13)
Fifth Third Bancorp (15)
First Empire State Corp. (23)
Fiserv, Inc. (84)
Franklin Resources, Inc. (9)
General Electric Co. (21)
Genuine Parts Co. (77)
Gillette Co. (3)
Grainger, W. W., Inc. (88)
Harley-Davidson, Inc. (11)
Heinz, H. J., Company (76)
Hershey Foods Corp. (54)
Hewlett-Packard Co. (61)
Home Depot (17)
Hubbell, Inc. (64)
International Flavors & Fragrances, Inc. (90)
Intel Corp. (28)
Interpublic Group of Cos., Inc. (22)
Jefferson-Pilot Corp. (52)
Johnson & Johnson (18)
Kellogg Co. (92)
Kimberly-Clark Corp. (35)
May Department Stores (55)
McDonald's Corp. (62)
Medtronic, Inc. (1)
Merck & Co., Inc. (12)
Microsoft Corp. (69)
Molex, Inc. (91)
Newell Co. (29)

Acknowledgments

There were several key contributors to this book who deserve a special thanks and a tip of the hat. As he has on other *100 Best* editions, Larry Nelson again assisted with the research and analysis—crunching numbers, compiling tables and graphs, double-checking facts, contacting companies, and helping keep the project organized and on schedule.

The editors and artists from Dearborn Financial Publishing also did another exceptional job of putting the book together in an attractive and professional format. Special thanks to Cynthia Zigmund and Jack Kiburz. And finally, thanks to the many corporate relations people who helped us track down the pertinent facts, figures, and financials on their companies.

Introduction

In a world where heart failure is the number one cause of death, it's little wonder that the world's number one manufacturer of heart pacemakers would ultimately become America's number one stock.

Medtronic's coin-sized implants have added years to the lives of millions of heart patients since the company was founded in 1949. The Minneapolis-based operation, which sells its devices in 120 countries, makes pacemakers for patients whose heartbeats are irregular, too slow, or too rapid. The company also makes a variety of related devices, such as blood pumps, catheters, and heart valves. Over the past ten years, Medtronic's shareholders have reaped an average annual return of 33 percent. That outstanding return, along with a steadily increasing dividend and 12 consecutive years of record sales and earnings, has helped make Medtronic America's number one stock.

Number two in this 5th Edition of *The 100 Best Stocks to Own in America* is Fannie Mae (the Federal National Mortgage Association), a corporation formed by Congress in 1938 as a government agency. Fannie Mae became a shareholder-owned company in 1968. Not only is it the nation's largest provider of residential mortgage funding, Fannie Mae is also the nation's largest corporation based on total assets. Its shareholders have enjoyed an average annual return over the past ten years of 32 percent.

The Gillette Company, which ranked number one in the last edition of this book, has continued its phenomenal performance as the world's best consumer products company. The maker of Gillette shaving products, Oral-B toothbrushes, Paper Mate pens, and Duracell batteries, has provided an average annual return for its shareholders of 30 percent per year over the past ten years.

Rounding out the top ten, from fourth through tenth respectively, are Norwest, a fast-growing Minnesota-based bank holding company; Schering-Plough, a leading pharmaceutical manufacturer and the parent company of Dr. Scholl's footcare products; Albertson's, the nation's fastest-growing supermarket chain; Coca-Cola, the world's leading soft drink maker; William Wrigley, the nation's leading gum maker; Franklin Resources, an investment management and mutual fund company; and Synovus Financial Corporation, a Georgia-based bank holding company.

This edition features 76 stocks that were also in the 4th Edition, 19 stocks that are new to the Best 100 list, and five stocks that were listed in previous editions but were not in the last edition (Campbell Soup, Nike, Kimberly-Clark, Hewlett-Packard, and Becton Dickinson).

Among the more notable new entries are Xerox, a company that soared through the 1970s, fell flat through the 1980s, and returned to financial prominence in the 1990s; Carnival, the world's largest cruise line operation; and Compaq Computer, one the most successful computer manufacturers in the world.

Only 29 companies have made the *Best 100* list in all five editions:

Abbott	Fifth Third Bancorp
PepsiCo	Tyson Foods
Albertson's	Genuine Parts
American Home Products	H. J. Heinz
Pitney Bowes	Valspar
Anheuser-Busch	Hershey Foods
RPM	Wal-Mart
Automatic Data Processing	Kellogg
Banc One	Walgreen
Sara Lee	McDonald's
Bemis	Walt Disney
Bristol-Myers Squibb	Merck
ConAgra	William Wrigley
Sherwin-Williams	Pall Corp.
Torchmark	

Six stocks that had appeared in each of the previous four editions were dropped from this edition. R. R. Donnelley & Sons, Shaw Industries, Rubbermaid, and A. Schuman were eliminated because of subpar financial performance. Tyson Foods, another perennial favorite, hung on by the skin of its teeth, ranking number 100 with a score of six points out of a possible 23.

Death by Gummy Bear

Two other stocks dropped from this edition that have rated among the top picks in all four previous editions are Philip Morris and UST.

Both companies continue to be financially sound, with solid earnings growth and promising stock growth potential. The problem is that both companies are involved in the increasingly controversial tobacco trade. Personally, I've never owned a tobacco stock, but I've always considered it my job to simply lay out the facts, and let readers make their own decisions on which stocks to buy and which to avoid. But some new developments involving the tobacco industry have prompted me to change my policy.

It's not the fact that cigarettes are addictive and deadly—we've known that for years, and so have consumers who have chosen to use tobacco products, and investors who have chosen to buy tobacco stocks. Consumers should be free to smoke if they choose, but new evidence suggests that tobacco companies may have gone so far as to juice up the ingredients of their cigarettes to make them even more addictive than they would have been using pure tobacco. In a recent court deposition, Philip Morris President James Morgan denied that cigarettes are "pharmacologically" addictive, comparing the smoker's craving for cigarettes to his own fondness for Gummy Bears. "I don't like it when I don't eat my Gummy Bears," said Morgan, "but I'm certainly not addicted to them." Nor is he likely to die from them. An industry that is that insensitive to the plight of the millions of consumers it methodically sends to early graves does not merit inclusion in the list of "America's Best."

FUTURE PROSPECTS

This book makes no pretense of projecting the future performance of any security. The rankings are based strictly on the past performance of the companies. I looked at several factors: Has the company had consistent earnings growth and consistent stock growth for the past ten years (or longer)? Is the company well diversified? Is it a leader in its market sector? Out of the approximately 2,000 stocks that I evaluated for positions in this book, the companies listed here have all passed with flying colors. They are the 100 major U.S. corporations that have fared the best over the past decade and given their shareholders the most.

While there is no assurance that any of these companies will outperform the market in the years to come, they do have a couple of strong points in their favor. For one, each company featured here has proven its ability to compete as a market leader in one or more areas. Their concepts are working. Their lines of products or services have made an impact in the marketplace, and have been highly profitable over the past 10 to 15 years. Each of these companies has a management team that has also proven capable of turning a buck on a consistent basis. They've ridden the ups and downs of the economy over the past decade, survived the rash of mergers and acquisitions (and probably made a few of their own), weathered the downtimes, and have still come away with an outstanding record of earnings and stock price growth. Presumably, most of these companies will continue their success throughout this decade.

While it is certainly possible that companies such as McDonald's (30 consecutive years of record earnings), Automatic Data Processing (47 consecutive years of double-digit growth in both earnings and revenues), and RPM (49 consecutive years of record sales and earnings) could slip into a sudden free fall, after decades of uninterrupted growth, the odds would seem to bode otherwise.

Traditionally, the type of top-quality stocks selected for this book tend to do very well compared with the overall market. For instance, a portfolio of the top 40 ranked stocks of the first edition of this book (published in 1989) would have grown 102 percent over the following five years—a record good enough to outperform 89 percent of all mutual funds for that period! If you had purchased the top ten ranked stocks in the first edition of this book in 1989 and held them through mid-1997, a $10,000 initial investment would have grown to about $40,000.

THE CASE FOR STOCKS

While an individual's first investment priority should be money in the bank—everyone needs a cash cushion to fall back on—stocks should be a key component of any well-balanced portfolio. Why buy stocks rather than collecting that safe, consistent flow of interest earnings a bank account would offer? Here are some numbers to reflect on:

On average, over the 70 years for which records are available—which includes both the stock market crash of 1929 and the crash of 1987—stocks have provided an average annual return of nearly 11 percent, roughly double the return of bonds and three times the return of money market funds. The difference is even more dramatic when put in inflation-adjusted terms. A dollar invested in a money market account in 1925 would have grown (inflation-adjusted) to about $2.60 by 1990. That same dollar invested in the broad stock market would have grown to about $77 (inflation-adjusted) during the same period. While stocks may have their ups and downs, if you can live with the volatility, you would be a far richer investor by keeping your money in the stock market.

Sometimes stock market investing requires great patience. Stock performance can vary dramatically from one ten-year period to another. An investor entering the market in 1965, for instance, would have experienced an agonizing 1.2 percent average annual return over the next ten years. But an investor in the market from 1949 to 1958 would have reaped a 20 percent average annual return.

STOCKS OR STOCK MUTUAL FUNDS?

The other issue for many investors is whether to invest in individual stocks or stock mutual funds. The fact is that mutual funds probably should be the investment of choice for many investors—particularly for those individuals who haven't the time, the expertise, or the resources to invest in a well-diversified selection of stocks.

But if you have an interest in the market, the time to spend researching it, and the money to diversify your portfolio, individual stocks can offer several advantages over mutual funds. First, buying stocks can be challenging, stimulating, and, at times, fulfilling. You pit your wits against the market and against the millions of other unseen investors who are also scouring the market for a bargain. It is a test of your insight, your shrewdness. At times it can also be a test of your endurance, or—during downturns in the market—a test of your courage as you hold fast to your position in anticipation of that next market rally.

When you pick a winner, the results can be exhilarating. You watch the price move up. You see the stock split two-for-one. Suddenly your 500 shares becomes 1,000. Your investment grows to a multiple of your initial outlay. You've won at the age-old game of picking stocks. And the victory is a boon not only to your pocketbook but to your ego as well. It's that psychological reward of picking a winner that motivates so many investors to set aside mutual funds and test their hand in the stock market.

There's also another important—though less publicized—reason to choose stocks over mutual funds. As they say, money is power. But it's only power if you use it as power. That means controlling it yourself and deciding exactly where each dollar is put to work. Socially conscious individuals who wouldn't dream of investing in companies that pollute the environment, produce tobacco products, or build weapons of mass destruction unwittingly invest in all those types of companies when they invest in stock mutual funds. Most mutual funds pay little heed to social concerns.

Of course, certain mutual funds take an ethical approach and avoid investing in companies with questionable ethical connections. The problem is that when you invest in those funds you're still letting someone else decide the fate of your money. After all, you may not necessarily agree with all the fund's ideals. You might, for instance, enjoy a beer on a hot afternoon and see no reason to avoid investing in alcoholic beverage producers. You may prefer not to invest in a weapons-manufacturing company, but you may think nuclear power is the best thing since windmills. So a mutual fund that invests according to all the popular ethical issues of our time may not be exactly the investment for you. Stocks give you the freedom to make those choices for yourself.

RATING THE COMPANIES

In selecting the 100 companies for this book, I looked at a wide range of financial factors, the most important of which was earnings performance. I wanted companies with a long history of annual increases in earnings per share, because if a company is able to raise its earnings year after year, the stock price will ultimately follow.

Other factors such as revenue growth, stock price performance, and dividend yield also played into the screening process, but none carried the same weight as earnings growth.

I made my selections after reviewing the financial histories of about 2,000 major U.S. companies.

After narrowing the list to the final 100, the next step was to rank them 1 to 100 based on a six-part rating system. Each category is worth up to four points (except shareholder perks, which is worth a maximum of three points) for a maximum of 23 points. The categories are *earnings-per-share growth, stock growth, dividend yield, dividend growth, consistency,* and *shareholder perks.*

I've also tried to bridge the long-term performance with the short-term performance. Stock growth was judged on ten-year performance, while earnings growth and dividend growth were rated based on the most recent five-year period. The dividend yield was rated based on the average yield over the past three years. And, finally, in the consistency category stocks were rated based on year-to-year earnings gains over a ten-year period. That gives the rating system a blend of the long term and the short term. Accompanying each company profile, you will see a ratings chart similar to the one on the following page.

ABCDE Corporation Ratings Box

Earnings Growth	★ ★ ★ ★	Dividend Growth	★ ★
Stock Growth	★ ★ ★	Consistency	★ ★ ★
Dividend Yield	★ ★ ★	Shareholder Perks	★ ★
NYSE—ABC		**Total**	**16 points**

Each star represents one ratings point. This company scored the maximum four points for stock growth and somewhat less for the other categories. The lower left indicates both where the stock is traded (e.g., NYSE—New York Stock Exchange) and the stock's ticker symbol (ABC). The lower right gives the total score.

The following charts offer an exact breakdown of the point system for each category:

Earnings-Per-Share Growth

5-Year Growth Rate	Average Annual Rate	Points Awarded
50–79%	9–12%	★ (1 point)
80–114%	13–16%	★ ★
115–139%	17–19%	★ ★ ★
140% and above	20% and above	★ ★ ★ ★

Stock Growth

10-Year Growth Rate	Average Annual Rate	Points Awarded
155–249%	10–13%	★ (1 point)
250–399%	14–17%	★ ★
400–599%	18–21%	★ ★ ★
600% and above	22% and above	★ ★ ★ ★

Dividend Yield

(Based on dividend yield average over past three years)

Dividend Yield Average	Points Awarded
0.5–1.4%	★
1.5–2.4%	★ ★
2.5–3.4%	★ ★ ★
3.5% and above	★ ★ ★ ★

Dividend Growth

In one sense, dividend growth may be even more important than the dividend yield. As the dividend grows, the current return on your original investment grows with it. Here's an example:

A stock yielding 2 percent when you bought it ten years ago at $10 a share may still be yielding a current return of only 2 percent, but if the stock has appreciated in value to $100 a share, then that 2 percent yield has now grown from its original 20 cents a share on a $10 stock to $2 per share on the $100 stock—the equivalent of a very generous 20 percent yield on your original $10 investment.

The rating scale is based on dividend growth over the most recent five-year period. However, a few factors can alter the score: If a company has raised its dividend fewer than five straight years, one point is subtracted from the total; if it has raised its dividend at least ten consecutive years, add a point (unless it is already at the four-point maximum). If the company pays a dividend of under 0.5 percent, the maximum score it can get in the dividend growth category is two points.

Dividend Growth

(Based on five-year growth)

Dividend Growth	Points Awarded
39–59%	★
60–99%	★ ★
100–149%	★ ★ ★
150% and above	★ ★ ★ ★

Consistency

A company that has had a flawless run of increases in earnings per share over the past ten years would score four points. The consistency of the stock price growth is not taken into account here because the volatility in a stock price can often be dictated by market factors beyond the control of the company. But if the company is strong and growing steadily, the stock price, over time, should reflect that.

- Score: four points. A company that has posted increased earnings at least ten consecutive years.
- Score: three points. A company that has had a nearly flawless run of earnings increases, with gains during nine of the past ten years.
- Score: two points. A company that has had a fairly consistent growth record, with earnings increases during eight of the past ten years.
- Score: one point. A company that has been somewhat inconsistent, with earnings increases during seven of the past ten years.

- Score: zero points. Theoretically, a company with a very volatile growth record would score no points here, although no company can make the top 100 list if it has had fewer than seven years of increased earnings out of the past ten.

Shareholder Perks

This category carries a maximum of three points. The grading in the perks category is very stringent. Most companies score two points or less. Only a handful scored a full three points. Without question, this has been both the most admired and the most questioned category of the rating system. Investment purists question its validity, while other investors looking for a little extra for their investment dollars have really taken the perks concept to heart.

But even investment purists should appreciate the investment value of the most common perk, a dividend reinvestment and stock purchase plan, which is offered by about 75 of the 100 companies in the book. These programs enable shareholders not only to reinvest their dividends in additional shares automatically but also to buy more stock in the company either commission-free or for a nominal fee (usually under $5).

For example, Coca-Cola shareholders may buy up to $60,000 a year in additional shares through the company plan, and McDonald's shareholders may make up to $75,000 a year in commission-free stock purchases. May Department Stores puts no upper limit on its program. The only drawback to such plans is that the shareholder has no control over when the stocks are purchased. Most companies have a date set each month or each quarter (depending on how the plan is set up) to make all shareholder stock purchases. You should also note that shareholders must pay income taxes on their dividends, even though the dividends are automatically reinvested in additional stock. These programs are perfect for investors who want to build a position in three or four companies at a time with relatively small monthly contributions (minimum contribution limits range from $10 to $50 per payment). The savings can be immense. For instance, normally commission costs even through a discount broker would run, on average, at least $40 per stock purchase per month—a total of $160 per month for four stocks. That adds up to $1,920 per year. With the free reinvestment plans, you can either put that $1,920 into your pocket or invest it in additional stock. Either way, the commission-free programs are a great perk and well worth the two points my system awards to each company that offers such a program.

Many companies offer other interesting perks as well. Some firms send welcome kits with free samples of their products to new shareholders of record. Others serve a free lunch at the annual meeting and give away a nice package of sample products. Anheuser-Busch shareholders who attend the annual meeting are welcome to sample the brewer's full line of beers and snacks. Shareholders are also offered a discount on admission to the company's amusement parks, including Busch Gardens, Sea World, Sesame Place, and Adventure Island. Each Christmas, the William Wrigley, Jr., Company sends shareholders several packs of Wrigley's gum.

Hershey is one of several companies that puts together Christmas gift boxes that their shareholders may buy (at discount prices) to send to friends or business clients. Shareholders simply send in their money along with the names and addresses of their friends, and the company does the rest.

While shareholder perks may not contribute to a company's investment performance, they can generate goodwill among shareholders. One investor called me to report that he had had great success with several stocks from a previous edition of the book, yet he saw his Marriott stock fall prey to hard times in the lodging industry. "But," he added, "I've used Marriott's 50 percent shareholder discount on lodging rates on several business trips, and it has already saved me a couple hundred dollars."

Breaking Ties

The 100 companies are ranked in order by points. The company with the most points is ranked first, and the company with the fewest points is ranked 100. To break ties between companies with identical point scores, the company with the higher average annual total return on shareholder value over the past ten years gets the higher ranking. If two companies tie on both total points and average annual return, the higher position goes to the company that has been listed in the *Best 100* the longest.

Performance Graphs

At the end of each profile, you will see a five-year financial "At a Glance" summary of the company's performance, including revenue, net income, earnings per share, dividend, dividend yield, and price-earnings (PE) ratio.

I have also included a "high-low-close" stock growth chart.

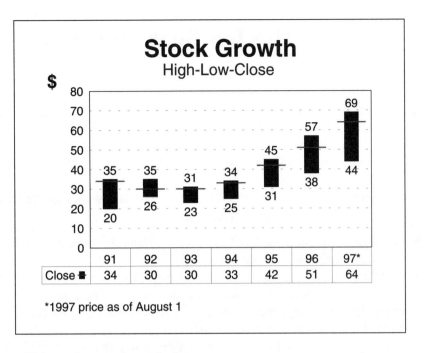

This stock growth graph shows:

- The yearly stock price range (all figures are adjusted for stock splits), including high price for the year, low price for the year, and closing price for the year.
- The graph shows the price range for 1991 through August 1, 1997. The price range indicated is for the 52-week period from August 1, 1996 to August 1, 1997.

Now you're ready to begin making this book work profitably for you.

How to Use This Book Profitably

Think of this book as a sales catalog for investment shoppers. You can page through it, look over the merchandise, and make your selections.

Let's assume that you have $20,000 to invest in stocks. Here is the process I recommend that you use to select the best stocks for you based on the entries in this book:

Begin by reading through the 100 profiles and narrowing your choices to 10 to 12 stocks by asking these questions:

- Are they companies you like? Are they involved in business activities that you think have a strong future?
- Are they located in your part of the country? This is not essential, but it is easier to follow companies based close to home because the local press tends to give those companies better coverage so you can stay better informed on your investment.
- Do they represent a diverse cross section of industries? Spread your choices around. You might select a food company, a medical products firm, a heavy manufacturer, perhaps a publisher, a retailer, or a computer or data-processing company. Choose no more than two or three companies from the same industrial segment. By making a broad selection, you can minimize your losses if one sector goes sour.

The next step is to narrow that list of 10 to 12 favorites to the four to six companies that you will ultimately invest in.

If you wish to use a stockbroker or financial adviser, call your adviser, read your list of choices, and ask if he or she has any current research on those stocks. If so, find out which ones the broker recommends, and buy the stocks through your broker. If you are interested in enrolling in the dividend reinvestment plan or in receiving the special perks your chosen companies might offer, instruct your broker to put your stocks in your name rather than holding them at the brokerage office in "street name." Most dividend reinvestment plans and perks programs are available only to shareholders of record.

GOING IT ALONE

If you have no broker, or wish to go it alone through a discount broker, here are some steps you can use to narrow your list to the four to six companies you will ultimately invest in:

1. Write or call those 10 to 12 companies to request their annual report and their 10-K report (which is a supplement to the annual report), then skim through the reports. (The phone numbers and addresses of each of the 100 companies are listed in this book along with their corporate profiles.)

2. Go to the library and look up the most recent articles on those stocks and request any other information the library may have on your selections. If it's a local company, there's a good chance your library will have an entire file on the firm. Make sure the company hasn't become involved in any major scandals or business problems.

   The library may also have two or three investment research books you can use to check up on your stock selections. *Value Line Investment Survey* and the Standard & Poor's report both offer up-to-date information and recommendations on hundreds of companies.

3. Keep an eye on the stock prices of the companies you are interested in. Find out what range each stock has been trading in over the past few months. Then select the four or five stocks that appear at present to be the best values. Timing can be very important in your overall success. All stocks fluctuate greatly in price, tugged along by the current of the overall market. But some stocks vacillate more than others. For instance, you could have bought Walt Disney stock in 1973 for $27 a share, and sold it for a mere $4 a share a year later. You could have reinvested in the stock in 1976 at $15 a share and sold out in disgust in 1984 at $11.50 a share. Or, on the other hand, you might have bought the stock for that same $11.50 a share in 1984 and sold out with a grin for more than ten times that price ($136 a share) in 1990. So even with stocks like Disney that qualify as a *Best 100* entry, timing can make a significant difference.

WHEN TO BUY

Volumes have been written on this topic. But the best advice may have come from Baron von Rothschild in the mid-1800s. He said, "Buy when the enemy is at the gate and sell when you hear your cavalry's bugle sounding charge."

Wall Street has a popular adage that reinforces that concept: "Pessimism is always most rampant just before the market hits bottom."

Two extraordinary buying opportunities have arisen in the past several years. The first came in 1987 following the October "Black Monday" crash. The crash frightened many investors out of the market, but those who bought when everyone else was selling got in on the bottom of a market that grew more than 50 percent over the next 18 months.

The second great opportunity came during Iraq's occupation of Kuwait, when oil prices were rising and the world was transfixed on the Middle East crisis. The market dropped about 15 percent in the months after Iraq invaded Kuwait, then roared back more than 20 percent in a three-month span that began the day the Allies started the bombing.

But barring war or disaster, the best strategy for most investors is a steady, persistent, long-term investment program.

In evaluating the *Best 100* stocks for my newsletter, *The Best 100 Update* (a twice-yearly report available for $12.95; 800-736-2970), I found that the stocks that tend to do the best are those that are trading at a lower price today than they were two years earlier. Often, their depressed price indicates that the stock and its segment have been out of favor on Wall Street, and it may be poised for a turnaround. In the in-depth evaluations I made of stocks in the first and third editions of this book, I found that the portfolio of *Best 100* stocks that were trailing their price of two years earlier grew during the succeeding year or two at a rate of more than double the Dow Jones Industrial Average.

While investors may strive to buy stocks while they are well below their peak prices, market experts advise against buying a stock on its way down. Or as they say in the brokerage business, "Don't fight the tape." Wait until a falling stock has bottomed out and shown some upward momentum before buying.

BENEFITS OF DOLLAR COST AVERAGING

One of the easiest and most effective investment strategies is called dollar cost averaging, and it's as simple as this: Pick a number, any number—$100 for instance—and invest that amount every month (or every quarter or every year) in the same stock. Period. It's that simple. Elementary as it sounds, however, the dollar cost averaging method is also a very effective technique for beating the market. The reason? By sticking to a set sum each time you invest, you automatically buy fewer shares when the stock price is high and more shares when the price is low.

The following table illustrates the advantages of dollar cost averaging. The table assumes that the stock price fluctuates somewhat each month (and lists the monthly price of the stock). The table compares the number of shares purchased through a dollar cost averaging strategy with the number of shares purchased through a method in which the investor buys a set number of shares each month.

Example of Dollar Cost Averaging

(Investing a set dollar amount each month versus buying a set number of shares each month.)

	Jan	Feb	Mar	Apr	May	June	July	Aug	Sept	Oct	Nov	Dec	Totals
Stock Price[1]	$ 10	9	12	13	9	10	8	7	9	12	10	11	
Investor A Dollar Cost Averaging[2] Investment:	$100	100	100	100	100	100	100	100	100	100	100	100	$1,200
Shares	10	11.1	8.3	7.7	11	10	12.5	14.3	11	8.3	10	9.1	123.5
Investor B Set Quantity[3] Investment:	$100	90	120	130	90	100	80	70	90	120	100	110	$1,200
Shares	10	10	10	10	10	10	10	10	10	10	10	10	120

1. Indicates average stock price each month.
2. Assumes investor invests $100 a month in the stock.
3. Assumes investor buys 10 shares of the stock per month.

As the table indicates, using the dollar cost averaging method, investor "A" would have purchased 3½ more shares than investor "B" who bought a set amount of shares each month, even though both spent a total of $1,200 during the year.

Tip: The dollar cost averaging method is most effective when you can make your purchases at no commission (or minimal commissions) through a company's dividend reinvestment and voluntary stock purchase plan. These plans are ideal for dollar cost averaging because they enable you to buy fractional shares and to make regular contributions (some companies offer stock purchase options once per month, others once per quarter). However, if the company you're interested in has no stock purchase plan, the brokerage commissions you would have to pay to make regular investments in the company's stock would greatly diminish the advantages of a dollar cost averaging plan. Most of the 100 top performers in this book offer a dividend reinvestment and voluntary stock purchase plan.

PICKING WINNERS

There is no infallible system for predicting tomorrow's market winners—only ratios and theories and computer-generated formulas that seem foolproof but aren't. For investors who trade actively in stocks, the key to beating the market is not so much which stocks to buy, but when to buy them and when to sell them. And that's about as easy to predict as next month's weather.

Even Wall Street's finest can't consistently outfox the market. Stock mutual funds offer an interesting example. Despite being actively managed by some of the sharpest, most well-supported analysts in the investment industry, the average rate of return of stock mutual funds traditionally trails the overall market averages. Generally speaking, history has shown that you can do better just buying and holding a representative sample of stocks—without ever making a single trade—than most mutual fund managers do with their wealth of investment research, their finely honed trading strategies, and all their carefully calculated market maneuvers.

Nor do investment newsletters, on average, fare any better than the mutual fund managers at timing their trade recommendations, according to Mark Hulbert, publisher of the *Hulbert Financial Digest* newsletter. "Most newsletters have not kept up with the Standard & Poor's 500," says Hulbert. In fact, in tracking the seven-year performance of a sampling of investment newsletters, Hulbert found that the ones that recommended the greatest number of buys and sells (switches) were the ones that did the worst.

"We've also conducted some studies that show that in the case of most newsletters, if you had bought and held the stocks they recommended at the first of the year, you would have done better than if you had followed all of their trading recommendations throughout the year," Hulbert adds.

The moral? For sustained, long-term growth, it's hard to beat a buy-and-hold strategy. Buy good companies with the intention of holding on to them for many years.

The Strategy of Benign Neglect

Most of us know someone who bought a few shares of a stock many years ago, stashed the certificates in a drawer, and then discovered years later that the stock had grown to a multiple of the original cost. Benign neglect is often the smartest policy for stock market investors. Besides avoiding the difficulties of making timely buying and selling decisions, the buy-and-hold approach offers some other excellent advantages:

No commission costs. Let's assume that you turn over your stock portfolio just once a year. You sell out all the stocks you own and buy new stocks that you think have greater short-term potential. Typically, you would incur about a 2 percent commission to sell the old stocks and a 2 percent commission to buy new ones—a total of 4 percent in round-trip commissions. That means, for instance, that a respectable 12 percent gain on your investments would suddenly shrink to 8 percent after you've paid off your broker. That commission may not seem like much at the time, but over the long term, it can add up to a significant amount. See the chart that follows, which illustrates the hidden costs of a buy-and-sell approach.

Tax-sheltered earnings. A buy-and-hold strategy is one of the best tax-advantaged investments available today. You pay no taxes on the price appreciation of your stocks until you sell them—no matter how long your keep them. (You are taxed, however, on any stock dividend income.) Every time you sell a stock, however, the federal government taxes you up to 33 percent on your gains (for most working professionals). And state taxes would very likely nibble away another 3 percent to 5 percent. That means each year Uncle Sam bites off more than a third of your investment profits. So you're looking at losing 36 percent of your gains, plus the brokerage house commission, every time you sell a stock at a profit. How does that translate into real dollars?

Let's assume that (1) you start with an investment of $10,000, (2) your stock portfolio appreciates at a rate of 12 percent per year, and (3) you sell your stocks, take the profit, and buy new stocks once a year. The following chart compares your performance with that of a buy-and-hold investor with an identical 12 percent compounded average annual appreciation rate:

The Hidden Costs of a Buy-and-Sell Approach

$10,000 investment @ 12% annual growth	Buy-and-hold (No commission and no taxes)	Buy-and-sell results[1]	
		With commission[2]	And with taxes[3]
After 1 year	$11,200	$10,800	$10,512
After 5 years	17,600	14,700	12,850
After 10 years	31,000	21,600	16,400
After 20 years	96,500	46,600	27,200
Total 20-year profit: (minus initial $10,000)	$86,500	$36,600	$17,200

1. Assumes investor sells all stocks in portfolio one time per year (and reinvests in new stocks).
2. Assumes commission of 2% to buy and 2% to sell (an annual total of 4% of total portfolio price).
3. Assumes 32% federal and 4% state tax (an annual total of 36% of profits).

As you can see, over a 20-year period, the buy-and-hold portfolio could earn five times the profit than with a buy-and-sell approach, even though both portfolios earn an average annual return of 12 percent.

Less emotional wear and tear.   By adhering to a buy-and-hold strategy you also avoid the high anxiety of trying to buy and sell stocks actively, of watching the financial pages each day to see how your stocks have fared, and of the inevitable disappointment of watching them rise and fall, then rise and fall again. Every stock goes through many ups and downs each year. There are no exceptions. The market moves like the tide of the ocean—it ebbs and flows—and every time it moves, it carries with it the broad market of individual stocks. Typically, about 70 percent of a stock's movement is attributable to the stock market itself. If the broad market is moving up, almost any stock you pick will also rise, but if the market is in a tailspin, almost any stock you pick—even those with record earnings—will fall with it. The remaining 30 percent of the movement of a stock is attributable to its industry group and to the performance of the company that issued the stock.

You skirt much of the emotional pressure the market inflicts if you invest with a buy-and-hold approach. You don't have to concern yourself with the inevitable daily ups and downs—or even the yearly ups and downs—of the market. Because over the long term, if you've bought stocks of good, solid, growing companies, the value of your portfolio will eventually reflect the strong performance of those companies. That's why it's crucial to select your stocks carefully. Because these are "one-decision stocks," that one decision takes on much greater importance.

When Not to Buy

Assuming that you've selected 10 to 12 prospective stocks, that you've researched the companies, and that you're ready to buy, what financial factors should you look at to decide which four to six of those 10 to 12 stocks represent the best value at the time?

The easiest way to select your finalists might be through the process of elimination: Weed out the stocks that appear to be overvalued and invest in the others.

To assist you with your elimination process, here are two of the most common "don'ts."

Don't buy when a stock is at an all-time high.   Stocks constantly rise and fall. A noteworthy adage in the securities industry goes like this: "The market always gives you a second chance." In almost every case, when a stock reaches an all-time high, it will eventually drop back in price, bounce back up, then drop back again. Nothing goes in a straight line. If you see that a stock is at its all-time high, it's probably not a very good value at that time. Prior to the October 1987 crash, many stocks were at or near their all-time highs, which is one reason why many investment experts claimed—correctly—that there were few good values in the market.

Don't buy when the price-earnings ratio is unusually high.   It sounds complicated, but the price-earnings (PE) ratio is actually a very simple formula that offers yet another barometer of a stock's relative value. And best of all, the PE ratio is listed along with the company's stock price in the financial section of most newspapers, so you don't have to calculate it yourself. Specifically, the ratio is the current price of the stock divided by the company's earnings per share.

Example:

ABC Corporation's stock price is $30.
Its earnings per share is $3.

$$\frac{\text{Stock price}}{\$30.00} \div \frac{\text{Earnings per share}}{\$3.00} = \frac{\text{PE ratio}}{10.0}$$

PE ratios are like golf scores—the lower the better. Generally, the PEs of most established companies are in the 10 to 20 range (although a handful of the stocks listed in this book have PEs over 20 and a few have PEs under 10). The real key, however, is not how the PE of one company compares to the PE of another, but how a company's current PE compares to its own previous PE ratios.

In this book, at the end of each company profile, you will see a financial summary, "At a Glance," that shows the PE ratio for the past six years. (The PE ratios in this book were calculated based on the earnings of the company's most recent four quarters, just as they are in the daily newspaper.) You might use that PE ratio as a guidepost to provide a relative point of comparison.

If you find in comparing the company's current PE (as listed in your morning newspaper) with its past PE range (as listed in this book) that the PE is near or above the high end of its past range, that could be an indication that the stock is relatively overvalued.

One More Way to Save

Once you've decided which stocks to buy, you may be able get more for your money by taking one more step.

Call around to several discount brokerage firms to find out which firm has the lowest minimum. Then buy your stocks through the discounter with the lowest minimum and have the broker put the stocks in your name (rather than "street name") and mail you the certificates. Buy a few shares—whatever you feel comfortable with—enroll in the company's dividend reinvestment and stock purchase plan, and make your subsequent stock purchases through the company. You may never have to pay commissions again!

WHEN TO SELL

Probably the most common mistakes investors make in selling their stocks is that they tend to sell their winners to take a (fully taxable) profit and to hold on to their losers in hopes that those stocks will someday rebound. That's an excellent way to assemble a portfolio full of losers. Prevailing wisdom in the investment business—for what it's worth—calls for just the opposite approach: "Cut your losses and let your profits run."

With that in mind, you might consider following a couple of basic strategies for selling stocks:

When news is grim.   If a company you own stock in comes under legal siege or becomes involved in some type of disaster or health controversy, take your lumps and get out as fast as you can dial up your broker.

Sell when the stock price drops relative to the market.   Barring disaster, you might also want to set up some other type of safety valve for your stocks. For instance, if the stock drops 10 percent to 20 percent while the market in general is moving up, it might be time to move on to something more promising. Some investors use a 10 percent/10 percent rule in which they sell a stock when it (1) drops 10 percent from its recent high and (2) drops 10 percent relative to the market. For example, if your stock drops 10 percent from $100 to $90, it meets the first criterion. But if the market has also gone down with it, then the stock still hasn't met the second criterion. If, on the other hand, the broad market has stayed the same or moved up while your stock dropped 10 percent, then it's time to sell—based on the 10 percent/10 percent rule.

More patient investors might lean toward a modified version of this: call it the 20 percent/20 percent rule. If your stock drops 20 percent and drops 20 percent relative to the market, sell it and move on to something more promising.

Sell when earnings drop.   Investment professionals sometimes call it the "cockroach theory." When you see one disappointing earnings report, that may mean more bad periods loom around the corner—just as the sight of a single cockroach usually means that other bugs are in hiding under the sink or behind the cupboard. Money managers who follow the cockroach theory get out of a stock at the first sign of trouble—even if it means taking a small loss—to avoid taking a bigger loss later should the bad news continue.

Sell when the company no longer meets your investment objectives.
If you bought a stock because the company had enjoyed 40 consecutive
years of record earnings, you should continue to hold the stock as long as
the company continues to pile up record earnings. But if it hits a slump,
and earnings stop growing, that company no longer meets your objectives. That's a time to sell. Weeding out your portfolio every two or three
years can help make you a more successful investor.

But timing is a tricky business. As Mark Hulbert puts it, "You need
to approach those decisions realizing that more than half the time you're
inclined to sell you would be better off holding than selling. So you'd better make sure there's a preponderance of evidence in your favor before
you sell."

That's why your buying decision is so important. This guide can help
steer you to 100 of the best stocks of the past ten years. Here's hoping you
can cull from this collection some of the all-star stocks of the next ten
years.

1

Medtronic, Inc.

7000 Central Avenue, N.E.
Minneapolis, MN 55432
612-574-4000

Chairman and CEO: William W. George
President: Arthur D. Collins

Earnings Growth	★ ★ ★ ★	Dividend Growth	★ ★ ★ ★
Stock Growth	★ ★ ★ ★	Consistency	★ ★ ★ ★
Dividend Yield	★	Shareholder Perks	★ ★
NYSE—MDT		**Total**	**19 points**

Medtronic hasn't missed a beat in 12 years. Year in and year out, the world's largest manufacturer of pacemakers and other implantable biomedical devices has racked up record sales, earnings, and book value per share.

The Minneapolis-based manufacturer sells its pacemakers and implantable devices in 120 countries. About 44 percent of its sales come from outside the United States.

Medtronic designs and manufactures pacing devices for patients whose heartbeats are irregular or too slow, as well as for patients whose hearts beat too rapidly. Medtronic's pacing devices can adjust electrical pulse intensity, duration, rate, and other characteristics.

Medtronic's pacemakers are small, coin-sized, implantable pulse generators with extended battery life. The implantable pacemaker is among a growing line of biomedical devices that Medtronic manufactures as part of its mission to "alleviate pain, restore health, and extend life."

The company's pacing business accounts for about 68 percent of its $2.2 billion in annual sales.

Cardiovascular products such as blood pumps, heart valves, oxygenators, and catheters contribute about 24 percent of the company's sales. In addition to its line of cardiovascular products, Medtronic provides such value-added services as physician education programs.

Medtronic's neurological device business, which offers therapies for treating pain and controlling movement disorders, accounts for about 8 percent of the company's sales.

Medtronic pioneered the pacemaker 39 years ago when Dr. C. Walton Lillehei of the University of Minnesota Medical School identified a medical need for young heart-block patients. Working with Earl Bakken, an electrical engineer, Dr. Lillehei developed the first wearable, external, battery-generated pulse generator.

Medtronic has about 10,500 employees and 26,000 shareholders.

EARNINGS-PER-SHARE GROWTH   ★ ★ ★ ★

Past 5 years: 236 percent (27 percent per year)
Past 10 years: 470 percent (24 percent per year)

STOCK GROWTH   ★ ★ ★ ★

Past 10 years: 1,500 percent (32 percent per year)
Dollar growth: $10,000 over 10 years (including reinvested dividends) would have grown to $165,000
Average annual compounded rate of return (including reinvested dividends): 33 percent

DIVIDEND YIELD   ★

Average dividend yield in the past 3 years: 0.6 percent

DIVIDEND GROWTH   ★ ★ ★ ★

Increased dividend: 10 consecutive years
Past 5-year increase: 160 percent (21 percent per year)

CONSISTENCY   ★ ★ ★ ★

Increased earnings per share: 12 consecutive years
Increased sales: 12 consecutive years

SHAREHOLDER PERKS   ★ ★

Good dividend reinvestment and stock purchase plan: voluntary stock purchase plan allows contributions of $25 to $4,000 per month.

MEDTRONIC AT A GLANCE

Fiscal year ended: April 30
Revenue and net income in $ millions

| | 1991 | 1992 | 1993 | 1994 | 1995 | 1996 | 5-Year Growth | |
							Avg. Annual (%)	Total (%)
Revenue ($)	1,021.4	1,176.9	1,328.2	1,390.9	1,742.4	2,169.1	16	112
Net income ($)	133.4	161.5	197.2	232.4	294	437.8	27	228
Earnings/share ($)	.56	.68	.83	1.01	1.28	1.88	27	236
Div. per share ($)	.10	.12	.14	.17	.21	.26	21	160
Dividend yield (%)	.7	.7	.9	.8	.5	.5	—	—
Avg. PE ratio	26	25	18	20	26	27	—	—

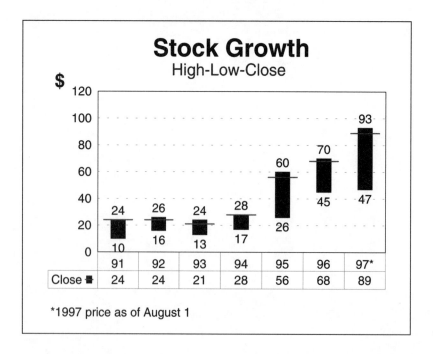

Stock Growth
High-Low-Close

	91	92	93	94	95	96	97*
Close ■	24	24	21	28	56	68	89

*1997 price as of August 1

2

Fannie Mae

3900 Wisconsin Avenue, N.W.
Washington, DC 20016
202-752-7115

Chairman and CEO: James A. Johnson

Earnings Growth	★ ★	Dividend Growth	★ ★ ★ ★
Stock Growth	★ ★ ★ ★	Consistency	★ ★ ★ ★
Dividend Yield	★ ★ ★	Shareholder Perks	★ ★
NYSE—FNM		**Total**	**19 points**

Known formerly as the Federal National Mortgage Association, Fannie Mae is the nation's largest provider of residential mortgage funding.

Fannie Mae was created by Congress in 1938 as a U.S. government agency to supplement the mortgage market in order to help low-, moderate-, and middle-income American families buy new homes. Since then, the company has helped about 25 million families afford homes.

Fannie Mae became a shareholder-owned company in 1968. In terms of total assets, Fannie Mae is the nation's largest company. It is also the largest investor in home mortgage loans in the United States. The company has posted ten consecutive years of record earnings.

The company buys mortgages from lenders, such as banks, mortgage banks, and savings and loan associations, thereby replenishing their funds for additional lending. That leaves more money available for institutions to lend to other homebuyers.

Fannie Mae's primary business is buying mortgages that it funds by issuing debt securities on the global capital markets. Its profit comes on the spread between the yield on the mortgages and the cost of the debt. The company holds a mortgage portfolio in excess of $250 billion. Fannie Mae is committed to provide $1 trillion in targeted lending for ten million homes by the end of this decade.

The company is also active in the mortgage-backed securities business. It guarantees the timely payment of principal and interest on securities backed by pools of mortgages, earning a guaranty fee on the amount of mortgage-backed securities outstanding.

The Washington, D.C., operation has about 3,500 employees and 175,000 stockholders.

EARNINGS-PER-SHARE GROWTH ★ ★

Past 5 years: 89 percent (14 percent per year)
Past 10 years: 1,100 percent (28 percent per year)

STOCK GROWTH ★ ★ ★ ★

Past 10 years: 1,294 percent (30 percent per year)
Dollar growth: $10,000 over 10 years (including reinvested dividends) would have grown to $165,000
Average annual compounded rate of return (including reinvested dividends): 32 percent

DIVIDEND YIELD ★ ★ ★

Average dividend yield in the past 3 years: 2.7 percent

DIVIDEND GROWTH ★ ★ ★ ★

Increased dividend: 11 consecutive years
Past 5-year increase: 192 percent (24 percent per year)

CONSISTENCY ★ ★ ★ ★

Increased earnings per share: 10 consecutive years

SHAREHOLDER PERKS

Excellent dividend reinvestment and stock purchase plan: voluntary stock purchase plan allows contributions of $10 to $5,000 per month.

FANNIE MAE AT A GLANCE

Fiscal year ended: Dec. 31
Mortgage loans and net income in $ millions

	1991	1992	1993	1994	1995	1996	5-Year Growth Avg. Annual (%)	5-Year Growth Total (%)
Mortgage loans ($)	128,983	156,021	189,892	220,525	252,588	286,259	17	122
Net income ($)	1,455	1,649	1,873	2,132	2,144	2,754	14	89
Earnings/share ($)	1.33	1.50	1.86	1.95	1.96	2.52	14	89
Div. per share ($)	.26	.35	.46	.60	.68	.76	24	192
Dividend yield (%)	2.0	2.1	2.3	2.9	2.9	2.3	—	—
Avg. PE ratio	10	11	12	11	12	14	—	—

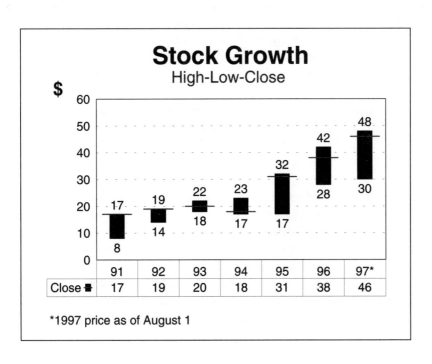

Stock Growth
High-Low-Close

Close ■	91	92	93	94	95	96	97*
	17	19	20	18	31	38	46

*1997 price as of August 1

The Gillette Company

Prudential Tower Building
Boston, MA 02199
617-421-7000

Chairman and CEO: Alfred M. Zeien
President and COO: Michael C. Hawley

Earnings Growth	★ ★ ★	Dividend Growth	★ ★ ★ ★
Stock Growth	★ ★ ★ ★	Consistency	★ ★ ★ ★
Dividend Yield	★ ★	Shareholder Perks	★ ★
NYSE—G		**Total**	**19 points**

Every night the world over, beards are growing, and so is business for the Gillette Company. The Boston operation is the dominant producer in the razor blade market both in the United States and around the world. But Gillette means more than just a close shave. With its Oral-B and Paper Mate brands, Gillette is also the world leader in toothbrushes and writing instruments.

Gillette has also added a new powerhouse product to its battery of offerings. In 1996, Gillette acquired Duracell International, Inc., the maker of the world's top-selling alkaline battery. Duracell, which had fiscal 1996 sales of $2.3 billion, sells its products in about 150 countries.

Duracell should be a good fit for Gillette, which relies on international sales for 70 percent of its $8.2 billion in annual revenue. The company has 50 manufacturing plants in 24 countries. Its products are sold in more than 200 countries and territories.

Razors and blades make up Gillette's largest segment, accounting for 39 percent of its total revenue, and 69 percent of the company's total operating profit (prior to the Duracell acquisition). The company controls about 65 percent of the U.S. razor blade market. Gillette's leading razor brands include the Sensor, Good News, CustomPlus, Atra, and Trac II razors.

Gillette's other key segments include:

- **Toiletries and cosmetics** (18 percent of revenue). Gillette manufactures Right Guard, Gillette, and Soft & Dri deodorants; White Rain shampoo; Epic Wave home permanents; Jafra skin care products; and Gillette shaving creams and gels.
- **Stationery products** (13 percent of revenue). Gillette is the world's leading manufacturer of writing instruments and correction fluid. It makes Paper Mate, Parker, Flair, Flexigrip, and Waterman pens, and Liquid Paper correction fluid.
- **Braun products** (24 percent of revenue). Gillette's German subsidiary is one of the leading manufacturers of electric shavers in both Europe and North America. The company also makes toasters, clocks, coffeemakers, food processors, and other household appliances.
- **Oral-B products** (6 percent of revenue). Oral-B is the leading marketer of toothbrushes in the United States and in several international markets. It also manufactures dental floss and other dental care products.

Gillette was founded in 1903 by King C. Gillette, who introduced a safety razor with a compact brass shaving head and a sleek wooden handle. It came with 20 steel blades and sold for $5.

The company has about 34,000 employees and 27,000 shareholders.

EARNINGS-PER-SHARE GROWTH   ★ ★ ★

Past 5 years: 135 percent (19 percent per year)
Past 10 years: 533 percent (20 percent per year)

STOCK GROWTH   ★ ★ ★ ★

Past 10 years: 1,105 percent (28 percent per year)
Dollar growth: $10,000 over 10 years (including reinvested dividends) would have grown to $138,000
Average annual compounded rate of return (including reinvested dividends): 30 percent

DIVIDEND YIELD

Average dividend yield in the past 3 years: 1.4 percent

DIVIDEND GROWTH

Increased dividend: 19 consecutive years
Past 5-year increase: 132 percent (19 percent per year)

CONSISTENCY

Increased earnings per share: 11 consecutive years
Increased sales: 14 straight years

SHAREHOLDER PERKS

Good dividend reinvestment and stock purchase plan: voluntary stock purchase plan allows contributions of $100 to $120,000 a year.

Shareholders who attend the annual meeting receive an excellent selection of products. At a recent meeting, the shareholder's gift bag included Gillette Satin Care Skin Replenishing Cream, SensorExcel razor, Gillette Series Body Wash, Right Guard Clear Stick Antiperspirant, Oral-B Advantage toothbrush, Paper Mate Comfort Mate pens, Durabeam flashlight batteries, and a four-pack of Duracell AA PowerCheck batteries.

GILLETTE AT A GLANCE

Fiscal year ended: Dec. 31
Revenue and net income in $ millions

	1991	1992	1993	1994	1995	1996	5-Year Growth Avg. Annual (%)	Total (%)
Revenue ($)	4,683.9	5,162.8	5,410.8	6,070.2	6,794.7	8,226.9	12	76
Net income ($)	427.4	513.4	591	698.3	823.5	1,095	21	156
Earnings/share ($)	0.97	1.16	1.33	1.57	1.85	2.28	19	135
Div. per share ($)	.31	.36	.42	.50	.60	.72	19	132
Dividend yield (%)	1.6	1.4	1.5	1.5	1.4	1.2	—	—
Avg. PE ratio	20	23	21	22	24	28	—	—

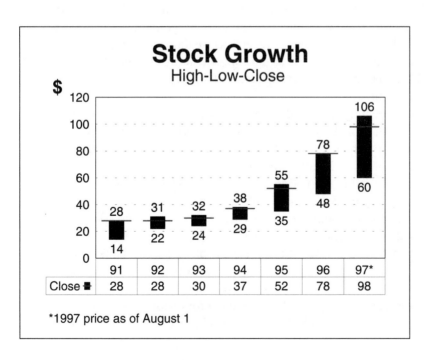

Stock Growth
High-Low-Close

Close ■	28	28	30	37	52	78	98
	91	92	93	94	95	96	97*

*1997 price as of August 1

Norwest Corp.

Norwest Center
Sixth and Marquette
Minneapolis, MN 55479
612-667-1234

President and CEO: Richard M. Kovacevich

Earnings Growth	★ ★ ★	Dividend Growth	★ ★ ★ ★
Stock Growth	★ ★ ★ ★	Consistency	★ ★ ★
Dividend Yield	★ ★ ★	Shareholder Perks	★ ★
NYSE—NOB		**Total**	**19 points**

Based in the northern city of Minneapolis, Norwest Corporation (formerly Northwest Bank) may have to change its name again soon to "Souwest." Thanks to a series of recent acquisitions, more than half of Norwest's branches (or "stores" as the company terms its banking offices) are now located in the southwestern states of Arizona, Colorado, Nevada, New Mexico, and Texas.

Norwest recently acquired several Texas banks, including Central Bancorporation, which has 21 offices in the Fort Worth area; Franklin Federal Bancorp, which has ten offices in the Austin area, and Texas Bancorporation, which has locations in Odessa and Austin.

Norwest, which is the nation's 13th largest bank holding company, has become big by thinking small. "We're focused on the retail customer, small business, and agriculture," says Norwest President and CEO Richard M. Kovacevich. "That's our emphasis."

The company also takes a unique view of its branch bank system. "We view ourselves more as a retailer than as a traditional bank," adds Kovacevich. "We deal with stores—not branches."

In Norwest's "stores," the focus is on "cross-selling"—selling customers multiple services such as savings, checking, CDs, consumer loans, mortgages, credit cards, and investment services. A high percentage of Norwest's customers use several of its banking services.

Norwest's banking division now boasts about 850 branches in 16 states. The bank offers a wide range of traditional services, including community and corporate banking, trust, capital management, and credit card services.

Along with the traditional banking operation, the company operates several related subsidiaries, including investment services, insurance, and venture capital companies.

Norwest's mortgage division, which has offices in all 50 states, funded $51.5 billion in mortgages in 1996.

The company's consumer finance subsidiary, which offers installment loans and related services, has about 1,300 offices in 47 states, Guam, and all ten Canadian provinces.

In all, Norwest has about 3,400 stores throughout North America.

The company's banking segment is its most profitable, accounting for 66 percent of its $1.15 billion in annual earnings. Mortgage banking makes up 11 percent of its income and consumer finance accounts for 23 percent.

Founded in 1929, Norwest has 54,000 employees and 32,000 shareholders.

EARNINGS-PER-SHARE GROWTH ★ ★ ★

Past 5 years: 129 percent (18 percent per year)
Past 10 years: 403 percent (18 percent per year)

STOCK GROWTH ★ ★ ★ ★

Past 10 years: 650 percent (22 percent per year)
Dollar growth: $10,000 over 10 years (including reinvested dividends) would have grown to $100,000
Average annual compounded rate of return (including reinvested dividends): 26 percent

DIVIDEND YIELD   ★ ★ ★

Average dividend yield past 3 years: 3.0 percent

DIVIDEND GROWTH   ★ ★ ★ ★

Increased dividend: 10 consecutive years
Past 5-year increase: 123 percent (17 percent per year)

CONSISTENCY   ★ ★ ★

Increased earnings per share: 9 consecutive years

SHAREHOLDER PERKS   ★ ★

Excellent dividend reinvestment and stock purchase plan: voluntary stock
purchase plan allows contributions of $25 to $30,000 per quarter.

NORWEST AT A GLANCE

Fiscal year ended: Dec. 31
Total assets and net income in $ millions

	1991	1992	1993	1994	1995	1996	5-Year Growth Avg. Annual (%)	Total (%)
Total assets ($)	38,502	44,557	50,782	59,316	72,134	80,175	16	108
Net income ($)	418.3	394	613.1	800.4	956	1,153.9	22	176
Earnings/share ($)	1.34	1.44	1.89	2.45	2.76	3.07	18	129
Div. per share ($)	0.47	0.54	0.64	0.77	0.90	1.05	17	123
Dividend yield (%)	3.3	2.8	2.6	3.1	3.2	2.8	—	—
Avg. PE ratio	10	11	12	10	10	12	—	—

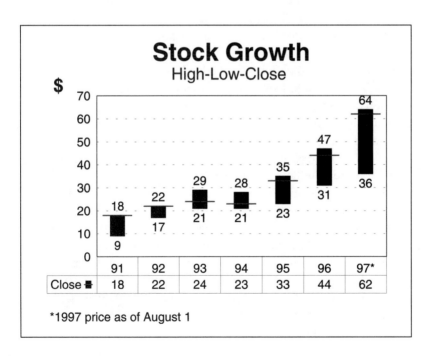

Stock Growth
High-Low-Close

	91	92	93	94	95	96	97*
Close	18	22	24	23	33	44	62

*1997 price as of August 1

5

Schering-Plough Corp.

One Giralda Farms
Madison, NJ 07940
201-822-7000

Chairman and CEO: Robert P. Luciano
President: Richard J. Kogan

Earnings Growth	★ ★ ★	Dividend Growth	★ ★ ★
Stock Growth	★ ★ ★ ★	Consistency	★ ★ ★ ★
Dividend Yield	★ ★ ★	Shareholder Perks	★ ★
NYSE—SGP		**Total**	**19 points**

Schering-Plough can thank runny noses for much of its recent commercial success. The company's Claritin antihistamine, now sold in more than 90 countries, is the world's best-selling antihistamine brand with worldwide sales of nearly $1 billion a year.

Although respiratory medications are the leading product segment of Schering-Plough, the Madison, New Jersey, operation is well diversified in the prescription and over-the-counter medication markets.

The company's Dr. Scholl's brand is the number one foot care company in North America, Lotramin AF is the leading athlete's foot medication, and (fast-acting) Tinactin antifungal medication and Dr. Scholl's Bunion Guard are leaders in their respective markets.

Schering-Plough, with its Coppertone, Solarcaine, and Tropical Blend brands, also leads in every segment of the U.S. sun care industry. And the company continues to introduce new sunscreen products as medical evidence mounts over the dangers of exposure to the sun.

Other leading over-the-counter products include Afrin and Duration nasal decongestants, Chlor-Trimeton antihistamine, Coricidin and Drixoral cold and decongestant products, Correctol laxative, and Di-Gel antacid.

While its over-the-counter products are most familiar to consumers, Schering-Plough's line of pharmaceuticals is what powers the company's balance sheet. In addition to its respiratory medications, the company makes drugs for cancer and infectious diseases, skin disorders, and cardiovascular disorders.

The company also has an animal health business and a vision care business operated under the Wesley-Jessen name. Its line of soft contact lenses is the second-leading U.S. brand.

Respiratory products account for 36 percent of the company's $5.6 billion in annual sales. Its second leading segment, anti-infective and anticancer medications, accounts for about 20 percent. Other segments include dermatologicals (10 percent), cardiovasculars (8 percent), other pharmaceuticals (10 percent), over-the-counter medications (5 percent), foot care (5 percent), animal care (4 percent), and sun care (2 percent).

Schering-Plough generates about 45 percent of its revenue in foreign markets. Europe is its leading overseas market, although the company also has substantial sales in Latin America, Canada, Asia, and Africa.

The company has about 20,000 employees and 34,000 shareholders.

EARNINGS-PER-SHARE GROWTH ★ ★ ★

Past 5 years: 119 percent (17 percent per year)
Past 10 years: 513 percent (20 percent per year)

STOCK GROWTH ★ ★ ★ ★

Past 10 years: 619 percent (22 percent per year)
Dollar growth: $10,000 over 10 years (including reinvested dividends) would have grown to $89,000
Average annual compounded rate of return (including reinvested dividends): 24.5 percent

DIVIDEND YIELD ★ ★ ★

Average dividend yield in the past 3 years: 2.5 percent

DIVIDEND GROWTH

Increased dividend: 10 consecutive years
Past 5-year increase: 100 percent (15 percent per year)

CONSISTENCY

Increased earnings per share: 15 consecutive years
Increased sales: 17 consecutive years

SHAREHOLDER PERKS ★ ★

Good dividend reinvestment and stock purchase plan: voluntary stock purchase plan allows contributions of $25 to $36,000 per year.

Schering-Plough also hands out a sample packet of newer products to shareholders at its annual meetings. It recently handed out foot care and sun care products.

SCHERING-PLOUGH AT A GLANCE

Fiscal year ended: Dec. 31
Revenue and net income in $ millions

	1991	1992	1993	1994	1995	1996	5-Year Growth Avg. Annual (%)	Total (%)
Revenue ($)	3,615.6	4,055.7	4,341.3	4,536.6	5,104.4	5,655.8	9	56
Net income ($)	646	720	825	926	1,053	1,213	14	88
Earnings/share ($)	1.51	1.80	2.09	2.42	2.85	3.31	17	119
Div. per share ($)	0.64	0.75	0.87	0.99	1.13	1.28	15	100
Dividend yield (%)	2.2	2.4	2.6	2.9	2.3	2.1	—	—
Avg. PE ratio	18	16	15	14	16	18	—	—

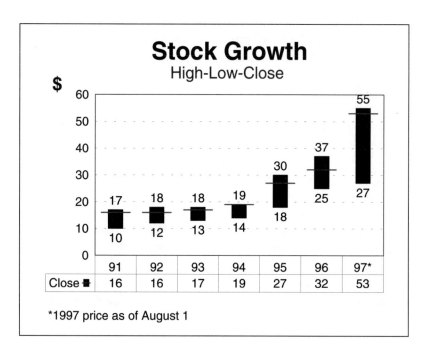

Stock Growth
High-Low-Close

Close ■	16	16	17	19	27	32	53
	91	92	93	94	95	96	97*

*1997 price as of August 1

6

Albertson's, Inc.

250 Parkcenter Blvd.
P. O. Box 20
Boise, ID 83726
208-395-6200

Chairman and CEO: Gary G. Michael
President: Richard L. King

Earnings Growth	★ ★ ★	Dividend Growth	★ ★ ★ ★
Stock Growth	★ ★ ★ ★	Consistency	★ ★ ★ ★
Dividend Yield	★ ★	Shareholder Perks	★ ★
NYSE—ABS		Total	**19 points**

This is a company that puts a lot of food on a lot of tables. As the nation's fourth largest grocery store chain, Albertson's has sales of more than $13 billion a year. The company has posted 27 consecutive years of record sales and earnings.

The Boise, Idaho, grocer operates more than 800 stores in 19 Western, Midwestern, and Southern states. That's up from about 500 stores in 1990. The company opens about 85 new stores per year. And to keep its supermarkets up-to-date, it remodels about 50 stores per year.

Albertson's largest concentration of stores is in Texas (146 stores), California (165 stores), Florida (85 stores), and Washington State (73 stores).

The company has been successful in increasing its sales and earnings by expanding its stores both in size and in number. Most of its stores are combination food stores and drugstores that average about 50,000 square feet. It also operates about 75 conventional supermarkets that range in size from 15,000 to 35,000 square feet, and it runs 39 Max Food and Drug warehouse-style stores that range in size from 17,000 to 73,000 square feet. Max stores offer substantial discounts over other groceries, with special emphasis on discounted meat and produce.

The firm has 11 distribution centers across the country.

The company's five-year plan calls for the opening of an additional 388 stores, as well as the remodeling of 265 stores and the expansion of 22 stores.

Many of the larger Albertson's stores provide not only the standard offering of grocery items, but they also include floral centers, pharmacies, video rentals, delis, and full-service bakeries.

In addition to its standard grocery offerings, many of Albertson's larger stores have five special service departments:

1. **Pharmacy.** Grocery customers can pick up prescription drugs at low-cost pharmacies in many of the Albertson's stores.
2. **Lobby departments.** Most Albertson's stores offer a variety of special services for customers such as money orders, bus passes, lottery tickets, stamps, camera supplies, film developing, and video rental.
3. **Service deli.** Delicatessens in about 500 of its stores offer take-home foods, meats, cheeses, fresh salads, and fried chicken. Salad bars have been added to many of the Albertson's stores.
4. **Service fish and meat departments.** Most of the larger Albertson's stores have specialty departments with a full array of fresh fish, shellfish, premium cuts of meat, and semiprepared items such as stuffed pork chops.
5. **Bakeries.** The company offers a full range of baked goods in its in-store bakeries.

The company was founded in 1939 by the late Joe Albertson, who opened his first grocery in Boise, Idaho, in 1939. Although he retired from management in 1976, Albertson remained a director of the company's executive committee until his death in 1993 at age 86. Albertson's has 87,000 employees and 18,000 shareholders.

EARNINGS-PER-SHARE GROWTH   ★ ★ ★

Past 5 years: 102 percent (15 percent per year)
Past 10 years: 416 percent (18 percent per year)

STOCK GROWTH   ★ ★ ★ ★

Past 10 years: 613 percent (22 percent per year)

Dollar growth: $10,000 over 10 years (including reinvested dividends) would have grown to $79,000
Average annual compounded rate of return (including reinvested dividends): 23 percent

DIVIDEND YIELD

Average dividend yield in the past 3 years: 1.6 percent

DIVIDEND GROWTH   ★ ★ ★ ★

Increased dividend: 26 consecutive years
Past 5-year increase: 114 percent (16 percent per year)

CONSISTENCY   ★ ★ ★ ★

Increased earnings per share: 27 consecutive years
Increased sales: 27 consecutive years

SHAREHOLDER PERKS

Good dividend reinvestment and stock purchase plan: for stockholders owning at least 15 shares allows contributions of $30 to $30,000 per quarter.

Shareholders who attend the annual meeting receive coupons for a myriad of free grocery items. The coupons, which are valued in the range of $20 to $30 in all, are redeemable at any Albertson's store for one year.

ALBERTSON'S AT A GLANCE

Fiscal year ended: Feb. 1
Revenue and net income in $ millions

	1991	1992	1993	1994	1995	1996	5-Year Growth Avg. Annual (%)	Total (%)
Revenue ($)	8,680.5	10,173	11,283	11,894	12,585	13,777	10	59
Net income ($)	257.8	276.1	339.7	417.4	465	493.8	14	92
Earnings/share ($)	0.97	1.04	1.34	1.58	1.84	1.96	15	102
Div. per share ($)	.28	.32	.36	.44	.52	.60	16	114
Dividend yield (%)	1.4	1.4	1.4	1.5	1.7	1.6	—	—
Avg. PE ratio	21	21	19	17	17	20	—	—

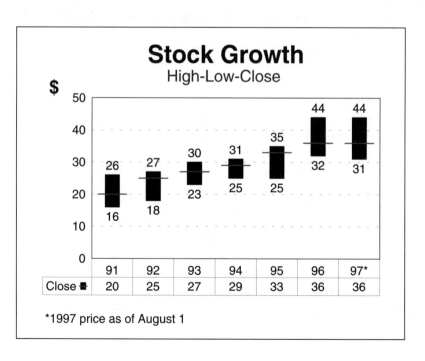

Stock Growth
High-Low-Close

	91	92	93	94	95	96	97*
Close ■	20	25	27	29	33	36	36

*1997 price as of August 1

The Coca-Cola Company

The Coca-Cola Company

One Coca-Cola Plaza, N.W.
Atlanta, GA 30313
404-676-2121

Chairman and CEO: Roberto C. Goizueta

Earnings Growth	★ ★ ★	Dividend Growth	★ ★ ★ ★
Stock Growth	★ ★ ★ ★	Consistency	★ ★ ★ ★
Dividend Yield	★	Shareholder Perks	★ ★
NYSE—KO		**Total**	**18 points**

The Coca-Cola Company quenches thirsts in nearly 200 countries around the globe. But nowhere do people drink more Coke products than they do here in America. On average, Americans drink 363 eight-ounce servings of Coca-Cola Company beverages per year—about one serving per day.

Mexico is a close second at 332 servings per year per capita, followed by Australia at 308 servings, Chile at 291, Norway at 266, and Israel at 253.

Not only is Coca-Cola the world's leading soft drink maker, it is also the world's largest distributor of juices and juice products, primarily through its Minute Maid subsidiary. In all, Coke sells about 14 billion unit cases per year.

The company draws about one third of its $18.5 billion in annual revenue from the North American market and another third from Europe. The Middle and Far East account for about 22 percent, Latin America accounts for 11 percent, and Africa generates about 2 percent.

In addition to Coke and Diet Coke, the company produces a broad range of other beverages, including Cherry Coke, Fanta, Sprite, diet

Sprite, Mr Pibb, Mellow Yello, Tab, Fresca, Barq's root beer, Surge, Powerade, Fruitopia, and other products developed for specific countries. Through Coke's Minute Maid division, Coke produces a variety of Minute Maid juices and soft drinks, Five Alive, Bright & Early, Bacardi brand tropical fruit mixers, and Hi-C fruit drinks.

Coca-Cola is the world's most recognized trademark. It commands about a 60 percent share of the worldwide cola market and 43 percent of the U.S. cola market.

One of Coke's fastest growing markets is China, where the company recently began construction of its 23rd bottling plant. The company now sells more than 200 million cases a year in China.

The Coca-Cola Company was founded in 1886. The firm has about 32,000 employees and 225,000 shareholders.

EARNINGS-PER-SHARE GROWTH   ★ ★ ★

Past 5 years: 130 percent (18 percent per year)
Past 10 years: 438 percent (18 percent per year)

STOCK GROWTH   ★ ★ ★ ★

Past 10 years: 1,096 percent (28 percent per year)
Dollar growth: $10,000 over 10 years (including reinvested dividends) would have grown to $130,000
Average annual compounded rate of return (including reinvested dividends): 29.5 percent

DIVIDEND YIELD   ★

Average dividend yield in the past 3 years: 1.4 percent

DIVIDEND GROWTH   ★ ★ ★ ★

Increased dividend: 35 consecutive years
Past 5-year increase: 108 percent (15 percent per year)

CONSISTENCY   ★ ★ ★ ★

Increased earnings per share: 18 consecutive years
Increased sales: 10 consecutive years

SHAREHOLDER PERKS   ★ ★

Good dividend reinvestment and stock purchase plan: voluntary stock purchase plan allows contributions of $10 to $60,000 per year.

COCA-COLA AT A GLANCE

Fiscal year ended: Dec. 31
Revenue and net income in $ millions

	1991	1992	1993	1994	1995	1996	5-Year Growth Avg. Annual (%)	Total (%)
Revenue ($)	11,572	13,074	13,963	16,181	18,018	18,546	10	60
Net income ($)	1,618	1,883	2,188	2,554	2,986	3,492	17	116
Earnings/share ($)	0.61	0.72	0.84	0.99	1.18	1.40	18	130
Div. per share ($)	.24	.28	.34	.39	.44	.50	15	108
Dividend yield (%)	1.6	1.5	1.6	1.7	1.4	1.1	—	—
Avg. PE ratio	24	29	25	23	27	33	—	—

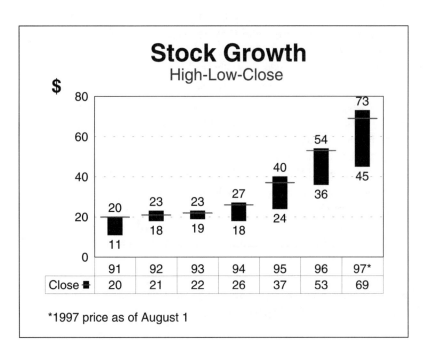

Stock Growth
High-Low-Close

	91	92	93	94	95	96	97*
Close ■	20	21	22	26	37	53	69

*1997 price as of August 1

8

William Wrigley, Jr., Company

410 North Michigan Avenue
Chicago, IL 60611
312-644-2121

President and CEO: William Wrigley

Earnings Growth	★ ★	Dividend Growth	★ ★ ★
Stock Growth	★ ★ ★ ★	Consistency	★ ★ ★ ★
Dividend Yield	★ ★	Shareholder Perks	★ ★ ★
NYSE—WWY		**Total**	**18 points**

Consumers around the world are getting a taste of Wrigley's Spearmint, Doublemint, and Juicy Fruit gums, and they're coming back for more.

In China, where Wrigley has been operating a manufacturing facility since 1993, sales are climbing at a rate of 50 percent per year. In India, the world's other massive population nation, Wrigley launched a marketing campaign in 1997 to distribute its three leading brands nationwide. And in St. Petersburg, Russia, Wrigley is building a $25-million, 70,000-square-foot production plant.

The growing global popularity of Wrigley's gum couldn't have come at a better time, with the U.S. gum market posting flat returns in recent years. But Wrigley's foreign sales growth has helped keep its overall earnings on the upswing.

The company has had 15 consecutive years of record sales and earnings, and has seen its stock price establish new highs for 14 consecutive years from 1983 to 1996.

William Wrigley is the world's leading gum manufacturer. The 104-year-old Chicago operation markets its gum in about 120 countries and territories, and has operations in 28 foreign countries. Foreign sales account for about 47 percent of the company's $1.84 billion in annual sales.

The company's largest markets outside the United States are Australia, Canada, Germany, the Philippines, Taiwan, the United Kingdom, the Czech and Slovak Republics, France, Russia, and China.

In the United States, Wrigley is the leading gum producer, with a 50 percent share of the total gum market.

Brand extension has paid big dividends for Wrigley. The company has added about 15 new brands in recent years. Wrigley's top grossing brands continue to be Spearmint, Doublemint, Juicy Fruit, Big Red, and Winterfresh. Its Extra sugar-free gum (available in several flavors and as bubble gum) is the nation's top selling sugar-free brand. The sugar-free line is also beginning to sell well in European markets, thanks to the company's marketing emphasis on the "dental benefits" of sugar-free gum.

Other Wrigley brands include Freedent, Orbit, Hubba Bubba, and Sugarfree Hubba Bubba (original and grape).

Wrigley also owns Amurol Products, which manufactures children's novelty bubble gum and other confectionery products, including Big League Chew, Bubble Tape gum, and Reed's hard-roll candies.

Wrigley was founded in 1891 by William Wrigley, Jr., the late grandfather of current president William Wrigley, 63. Wrigley was a baking soda salesman who first offered gum as a premium to customers who bought his baking soda. The gum quickly became more in demand than the baking soda, so Wrigley did what any smart marketer would do—he switched products. In 1893, he introduced his first flavors of Wrigley's gum, Spearmint and Juicy Fruit, and an American institution was born.

As Will Rogers once put it, "All Wrigley had was an idea. He was the first man to discover that American jaws must wag, so why not give them something to wag against." Now jaws all over the world are wagging with Wrigley's.

The Wrigley Company has about 7,800 employees and 35,000 shareholders.

EARNINGS-PER-SHARE GROWTH ★ ★

Past 5 years: 91 percent (14 percent per year)
Past 10 years: 388 percent (17 percent per year)

STOCK GROWTH

Past 10 years: 746 percent (24 percent per year)
Dollar growth: $10,000 over 10 years (including reinvested dividends) would have grown to $128,000
Average annual compounded rate of return (including reinvested dividends): 26.5 percent

DIVIDEND YIELD

Average dividend yield in the past 3 years: 2.0 percent

DIVIDEND GROWTH

Increased dividend: 16 consecutive years
Past 5-year increase: 85 percent (13 percent per year)

CONSISTENCY

Increased earnings per share: 15 consecutive years
Increased sales: 15 consecutive years

SHAREHOLDER PERKS

Good dividend reinvestment and stock purchase plan: voluntary stock purchase plan allows contributions of $50 to $5,000 per month. Some 17,500 shareholders participate in the company's dividend reinvestment program.

Wrigley also sends out a gift package to all of its shareholders each Christmas that includes several packs of Wrigley's gum, personally selected by Company Chairman and President William Wrigley.

WRIGLEY AT A GLANCE

Fiscal year ended: Dec. 31
Revenue and net income in $ millions

	1991	1992	1993	1994	1995	1996	5-Year Growth Avg. Annual (%)	5-Year Growth Total (%)
Revenue ($)	1,148.9	1,286.9	1,428.5	1,596.6	1,754.9	1,840.4	10	60
Net income ($)	128.7	148.6	174.9	230.5	223.7	243.3	14	89
Earnings/share ($)	1.10	1.27	1.50	1.98	1.93	2.10	14	91
Div. per share ($)	0.55	0.63	0.75	0.90	0.96	1.02	13	85
Dividend yield (%)	2.7	2.2	2.0	1.9	2.1	1.8	—	—
Avg. PE ratio	19	23	25	27	24	27	—	—

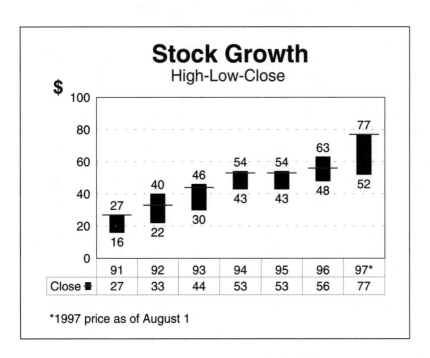

Stock Growth
High-Low-Close

	91	92	93	94	95	96	97*
Close	27	33	44	53	53	56	77

*1997 price as of August 1

Franklin Resources, Inc.

777 Mariners Island Boulevard
San Mateo, CA 94404
415-312-3000

President and CEO: Charles B. Johnson

Earnings Growth	★ ★ ★ ★	Dividend Growth	★ ★ ★
Stock Growth	★ ★ ★ ★	Consistency	★ ★ ★ ★
Dividend Yield	★	Shareholder Perks	★ ★
NYSE—BEN		**Total**	**18 points**

Investment legend John Templeton was one of the first to extol the virtues of investing in overseas markets. As the founder of Templeton Funds, Templeton searched the world for promising stocks.

Now Franklin Resources, which acquired the Templeton family of funds in 1992, is reaping the rewards of going global with its broad line of investment services and products. The company has offices in 17 foreign countries, including Australia, Canada, Hong Kong, India, Russia, Singapore, South Africa, Taiwan, Vietnam, the United Kingdom, and several European and South American cities.

In all, Franklin provides management and servicing for $151.6 billion in mutual funds and institutional separate accounts. The company operates more than 100 mutual funds. Franklin recently added five more funds with the acquisition of Michael F. Price's Mutual Series Funds.

The Franklin funds are marketed nationwide through a network of brokers, financial planners, and investment advisers. The company owns the Franklin Bank (formerly the Pacific Union Bank & Trust Company), which has about $152 million in assets.

The firm also operates real estate and insurance services and a capital corporation that specializes in auto loans, although those services account for less than 1 percent of the company's $1.5 billion in annual revenue.

Franklin, which was founded in New York City in 1947, has about 2,000 shareholders and 4,900 employees.

EARNINGS-PER-SHARE GROWTH ★ ★ ★ ★

Past 5 years: 200 percent (25 percent per year)
Past 10 years: 833 percent (25 percent per year)

STOCK GROWTH ★ ★ ★ ★

Past 10 years: 785 percent (24 percent per year)
Dollar growth: $10,000 over 10 years (including reinvested dividends) would have grown to $93,000
Average annual compounded rate of return (including reinvested dividends): 25 percent

DIVIDEND YIELD ★

Average dividend yield in the past 3 years: 0.9 percent

DIVIDEND GROWTH ★ ★ ★

Increased dividend: 10 consecutive years
Past 5-year increase: 93 percent (14 percent per year)

CONSISTENCY ★ ★ ★ ★

Increased earnings per share: 10 consecutive years
Increased sales: 8 consecutive years

SHAREHOLDER PERKS ★ ★

Good dividend reinvestment and stock purchase plan: voluntary stock purchase plan allows minimum contribution of $100 and a maximum of $50,000 a month.

FRANKLIN RESOURCES AT A GLANCE

Fiscal year ended: Sept. 30
Revenue and net income in $ millions

	1991	1992	1993	1994	1995	1996	5-Year Growth Avg. Annual (%)	Total (%)
Revenue ($)	318.4	370.9	656	1,342.1	1,257.8	1,522.6	36	379
Net income ($)	98.2	124.1	175.5	251.3	268.9	314.7	26	220
Earnings/share ($)	0.84	1.06	1.41	2.00	2.16	2.52	25	200
Div. per share ($)	.15	.17	.19	.21	.27	.29	14	93
Dividend yield (%)	1.4	1.0	.7	.8	1.0	.8	—	—
Avg. PE ratio	13	16	18	14	13	15	—	—

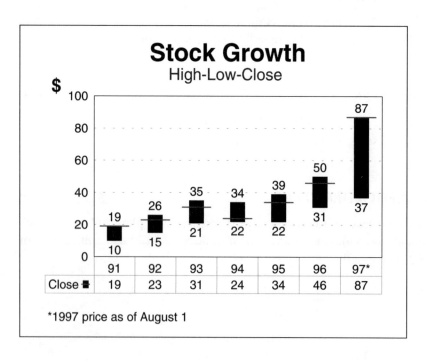

Stock Growth
High-Low-Close

	91	92	93	94	95	96	97*
Close	19	23	31	24	34	46	87

*1997 price as of August 1

Synovus Financial Corp.

One Arsenal Place
901 Front Avenue, Suite 301
P. O. Box 120
Columbus, GA 31902-0120
706-649-2387

Chairman and CEO: James H. Blanchard
President: Stephen L. Burts, Jr.

Earnings Growth	★ ★ ★	Dividend Growth	★ ★ ★ ★
Stock Growth	★ ★ ★	Consistency	★ ★ ★ ★
Dividend Yield	★ ★	Shareholder Perks	★ ★
NYSE—SNV		**Total**	**18 points**

Synovus Financial operates a group of about 34 banks scattered across five Southern states, but the company's biggest growth during the past few years has come through a sideline business. Synovus has seen its data-processing subsidiary double its income in just three years.

Total System Services (of which Synovus holds an 81 percent share) is one of the world's largest credit, debit, and private label card-processing companies. The firm saw its income climb from $148 million in 1993 to $296 million in 1996.

Total System provides a variety of bank card and private label card data-processing services, including card production, international and domestic electronic clearing, cardholder statement preparation, customer service support, merchant accounting, and management information and reporting. The company primarily processes cardholder accounts for customers issuing Visa, MasterCard, and Diners Club credit cards along with corporate cards, private label cards, and automated teller machine cards. Among its leading customers are BankAmerica and NationsBank.

Synovus Financial's banking business has grown quickly through a series of mergers and buyouts. The firm has acquired more than 20 banks in the past five years. Most are in smaller cities and towns throughout Georgia, Alabama, Florida, and South Carolina.

But rather than turning its new acquisitions into branch banks that operate under the same name, Synovus preserves each bank's original name, and keeps its management and board of directors intact. Only the back-office duties such as auditing and data processing are rolled into the home office operations to cut costs.

The company's unique hands-off management strategy has worked well. Synovus has posted 14 consecutive years of record earnings.

Synovus has about 6,300 employees and 16,000 shareholders.

EARNINGS-PER-SHARE GROWTH

Past 5 years: 133 percent (19 percent per year)
Past 10 years: 1,090 percent (27 percent per year)

STOCK GROWTH

Past 10 years: 449 percent (19 percent per year)
Dollar growth: $10,000 over 10 years (including reinvested dividends) would have grown to $66,000
Average annual compounded rate of return (including reinvested dividends): 21 percent

DIVIDEND YIELD

Average dividend yield in the past 3 years: 2.1 percent

DIVIDEND GROWTH

Increased dividend: 17 consecutive years
Past 5-year increase: 133 percent (19 percent per year)

CONSISTENCY

Increased earnings per share: 14 consecutive years

SHAREHOLDER PERKS

Good dividend reinvestment and stock purchase plan: voluntary stock purchase plan allows contributions of up to $2,500 per month.

SYNOVUS AT A GLANCE

Fiscal year ended: Dec. 31
Total assets and net income in $ millions

	1991	1992	1993	1994	1995	1996	5-Year Growth Avg. Annual (%)	5-Year Growth Total (%)
Total assets ($)	4,070	5,183.8	5,627.4	6,115.4	7,927.6	8,612.3	16	112
Net income ($)	48.6	61.2	77.5	89.5	114.6	139.6	23	187
Earnings/share ($)	0.51	0.61	0.74	0.79	1.00	1.19	19	133
Div. per share ($)	.18	.21	.25	.30	.36	.42	19	133
Dividend yield (%)	2.4	2.2	2.1	2.5	2.2	1.7	—	—
Avg. PE ratio	14	15	16	14	15	20	—	—

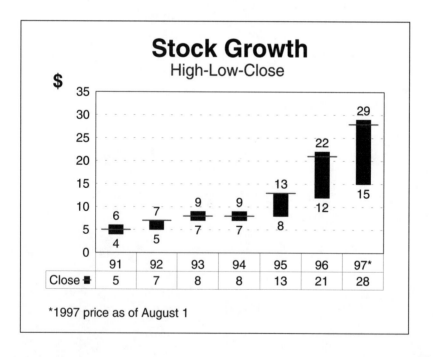

Stock Growth
High-Low-Close

	91	92	93	94	95	96	97*
Close	5	7	8	8	13	21	28

*1997 price as of August 1

11

Harley-Davidson, Inc.

3700 West Juneau Avenue
P. O. Box 653
Milwaukee, WI 53201
414-342-4680

Chairman and CEO: Richard F. Teerlink

Earnings Growth	★ ★ ★ ★	Dividend Growth	★ ★ ★
Stock Growth	★ ★ ★ ★	Consistency	★ ★ ★
Dividend Yield	★	Shareholder Perks	★ ★
NYSE—HDI		**Total**	**17 points**

High demand, low supply—it's every manufacturer's dream. But for Harley-Davidson, it's not just a dream. The Milwaukee-based operation is years away from being able to meet the growing global demand for its popular motorcycles.

In the United States, Harley buyers face about a six-month wait for its entry-level Harley Sportster model and about a two-year wait for its higher-end Road King model. Foreign buyers generally must wait even longer.

With its emphasis on quality, Harley refuses to speed up production just to meet demand. Like a fine wine, no Harley hog is ready before its time. But the company is building a new production plant in Kansas City that should be ready for operation in 1998. A new engine and transmission manufacturing plant is currently under construction in Menomonee Falls, Wisconsin.

The company sells 23 models of touring and custom heavyweight motorcycles, with suggested retail prices ranging from $5,100 to $18,200. Its touring bikes are equipped for long-distance travel with fairings, windshields, saddlebags, and Harley Tour Paks. The custom bikes have distinctive styling, with customized trim and accessories. The company manufactures all of its chassis and engines itself. The bikes are based on four chassis variations and are powered by one of three air-cooled, twin cylinder engines of "V" configurations with engine displacements of 883cc, 1200cc, and 1340cc.

The typical Harley buyer is a male, in his early 40s, with a household income of $66,000. Only 9 percent of Harley buyers are women. About a third of Harley riders are college graduates. Harley buyers are also extremely loyal. The company's riders club, The Harley Owners Group (HOG), has about 300,000 members worldwide.

Harley-Davidson, in its present incarnation, was incorporated in 1981 by a private investment group that purchased Harley-Davidson Motorcyle from AMF, Inc., and took it public in 1986. The reputation of the bikes—and the profits of the company—have been rising ever since. From a net profit of $4.5 million in 1986, the company's profits have soared to $143 million (in 1996).

Overseas sales are also on the rise. Foreign sales account for about 30 percent of Harley's $1.53 billion in annual revenue. Harleys enjoy their greatest popularity in Germany, Japan, Canada, and Australia, which account for about 60 percent of export sales.

Founded in 1903, Harley-Davidson has about 5,000 employees and 35,000 shareholders.

EARNINGS-PER-SHARE GROWTH   ★ ★ ★ ★

Past 5 years: 265 percent (29 percent per year)
Past 10 years: 1,800 percent (35 percent per year)

STOCK GROWTH   ★ ★ ★ ★

Past 10 years: 3,515 percent (43 percent per year)
Dollar growth: $10,000 over 9 years (including reinvested dividends) would have grown to $370,000
Average annual compounded rate of return (including reinvested dividends): 43 percent

DIVIDEND YIELD   ★

Average dividend yield in the past 3 years: 0.6 percent

DIVIDEND GROWTH

Increased dividend: 3 consecutive years
Past 3-year increase: 267% (30% per year). (The company has only paid a dividend for 4 years.)

CONSISTENCY

Increased earnings per share: 9 of the past 10 years
Increased sales: 10 consecutive years

SHAREHOLDER PERKS ★ ★

Good dividend reinvestment and stock purchase plan: voluntary stock purchase plan allows contributions of $30 to $5,000 per quarter.

HARLEY-DAVIDSON AT A GLANCE

Fiscal year ended: Dec. 31
Revenue and net income in $ millions

	1991	1992	1993	1994	1995	1996	5-Year Growth Avg. Annual (%)	Total (%)
Revenue ($)	939.9	1,105.3	933.3	1,158.9	1,350.5	1,531.2	10	63
Net income ($)	37	54.2	76.3	96.2	111.1	143.4	31	288
Earnings/share ($)	0.52	0.75	1.01	1.26	1.48	1.90	29	265
Div. per share ($)	—	—	.06	.14	.18	.22	30	267 3-Yr.
Dividend yield (%)	—	—	.3	.5	.6	.5	—	—
Avg. PE ratio	18	19	20	18	18	22	—	—

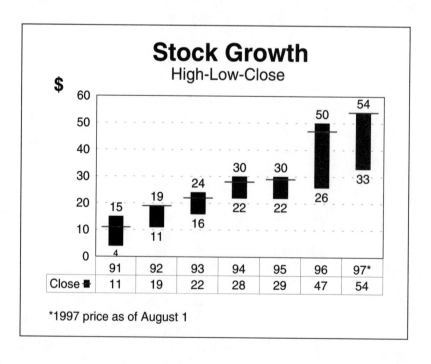

Stock Growth
High-Low-Close

	91	92	93	94	95	96	97*
Close	11	19	22	28	29	47	54

*1997 price as of August 1

Merck & Company, Inc.

One Merck Drive
P. O. Box 100
Whitehouse Station, NJ 08889-0100
908-423-1000

Chairman, President, and CEO:
Raymond V. Gilmartin

Earnings Growth	★	Dividend Growth	★ ★ ★
Stock Growth	★ ★ ★ ★	Consistency	★ ★ ★ ★
Dividend Yield	★ ★ ★	Shareholder Perks	★ ★
NYSE—MRK		**Total**	**17 points**

Osteoporosis has troubled aging women for generations, but Merck has recently developed a new medication called Fosamax that builds healthy bones and reduces by nearly half the risk of spinal fractures in postmenopausal women.

Fosamax is one of dozens of innovative drugs developed and marketed by Merck and Company, the world's largest pharmaceutical maker. Its six leading drugs all gross in excess of $500 million a year. Cholesterol medications Mevacor and Zocor each gross more than $1 billion a year, and Vasotec, a heart and blood pressure medication, grosses more than $2 billion per year. Merck's other leading drugs include Primaxin, an antibiotic; Pepcid, an ulcer medication; and Ivermectin, an antiparasitic for animals.

The company's biggest market is cardiovascular medications, which account for 37 percent of Merck's $19.8 billion in annual revenue. Other leading drug groups include:

- **Antibiotics** (5 percent of sales), including Primaxin, Noroxin, and Mefoxin
- **Antiulcerants** (6 percent of sales), including Pepcid and Prilosec
- **Ophthalmologicals** (3 percent), including Timoptic

- **Vaccines** (3 percent), including the M-M-RII (measles, mumps, and rubella virus vaccine live) and hepatitis B vaccines
- **Other human health** (38 percent), including antiparkinsonism products, psychotherapeutics, and muscle relaxants
- **Animal health and crop protection products** (6 percent)

Merck has operations in about 20 countries, with sales in more than 100 countries. Sales outside of North America account for about 26 percent of the company's total revenue.

Merck spends about $1.3 billion a year on research and development. The firm, which was founded in 1881, has about 45,000 employees and 243,000 shareholders.

EARNINGS-PER-SHARE GROWTH ★

Past 5 years: 75 percent (12 percent per year)
Past 10 years: 494 percent (20 percent per year)

STOCK GROWTH ★ ★ ★ ★

Past 10 years: 627 percent (22 percent per year)
Dollar growth: $10,000 over 10 years (including reinvested dividends) would have grown to $86,000
Average annual compounded rate of return (including reinvested dividends): 24 percent

DIVIDEND YIELD ★ ★ ★

Average dividend yield in the past 3 years: 2.7 percent

DIVIDEND GROWTH ★ ★ ★

Increased dividend: 13 consecutive years
Past 5-year increase: 84 percent (13 percent per year)

CONSISTENCY ★ ★ ★ ★

Increased earnings per share: 15 consecutive years
Increased sales: 16 consecutive years

SHAREHOLDER PERKS ★ ★

Good dividend reinvestment and stock purchase plan: voluntary stock purchase plan allows contributions of $50 to $50,000 per year.

MERCK AT A GLANCE

Fiscal year ended: Dec. 31
Revenue and net income in $ millions

	1989	1990	1991	1992	1993	1994	5-year Growth Avg. Annual (%)	Total (%)
Revenue ($)	8,602.7	9,662.5	10,498	14,969	16,681	19,828	19	131
Net income ($)	2,121.7	2,446.6	2,166.2	2,997	3,335.2	3,881.3	13	83
Earnings/share ($)	1.83	2.12	1.87	2.38	2.70	3.21	12	75
Div. per share ($)	.77	.92	1.03	1.14	1.24	1.42	13	84
Dividend yield (%)	1.6	2.0	2.9	3.3	2.5	2.1	—	—
Avg. PE ratio	22	23	15	14	18	21	—	—

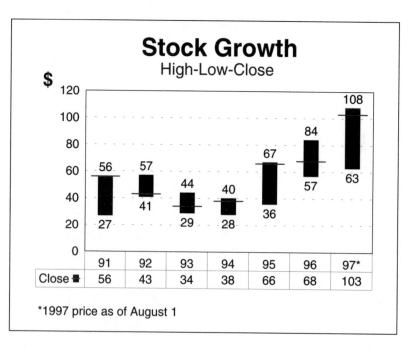

Stock Growth
High-Low-Close

	91	92	93	94	95	96	97*
Close	56	43	34	38	66	68	103

*1997 price as of August 1

13

Federal Signal Corp.

1415 West 22nd Street
Oak Brook, IL 60521-9945
630-954-2000

Chairman, President, and CEO:
Joseph J. Ross

Earnings Growth	★ ★	Dividend Growth	★ ★ ★ ★
Stock Growth	★ ★ ★	Consistency	★ ★ ★ ★
Dividend Yield	★ ★	Shareholder Perks	★ ★
NYSE—FSS		**Total**	**17 points**

Accidents happen—around the world—and when they do, Federal Signal often has a presence at the scene. The Oak Brook, Illinois, operation is a leading manufacturer of fire trucks, ambulances, sirens, signals, and communications equipment.

The company is well diversified in other areas as well. It manufactures signs, specialized tools, and a wide range of municipal sanitation equipment.

Federal Signal has been expanding internationally in recent years, with sales in Europe, Asia, North and South America, and Africa. Foreign sales account for about 23 percent of the company's $896 million in annual revenue.

Federal Signal's largest division is its vehicle group, which accounts for 55 percent of the company's total revenue. Along with its line of fire apparatus and fire trucks, airport rescue vehicles and ambulances, the company also makes air and mechanical street-sweeping equipment, municipal sewer and catch basin cleaner vehicles, vacuum street sweepers, catch basin cleaners, and submersible pumping systems.

Federal Signal markets its products primarily to municipalities, airports, the military, and fire and medical emergency services agencies.

The firm's other key divisions include:

- **Safety products** (20 percent of revenue). Federal Signal makes warning, signaling, and communications products, and parking, revenue and access control systems for airports, parking lots, toll roads, and related applications. It is also a leading manufacturer of hazardous waste storage containers.
- **Tools** (16 percent). The company produces carbide cutting tools, die components, and precision parts for a wide range of manufacturers.
- **Signs** (9 percent). The company builds and installs a variety of commercial signs, both illuminated and nonilluminated.

Founded in 1901, Federal Signal has enjoyed solid, consistent growth, including 12 consecutive years of record sales and earnings. Federal Signal has about 6,000 employees and 16,000 shareholders.

EARNINGS-PER-SHARE GROWTH ★ ★

Past 5 years: 101 percent (15 percent per year)
Past 10 years: 440 percent (23 percent per year)

STOCK GROWTH ★ ★ ★

Past 10 years: 581 percent (21 percent per year)
Dollar growth: $10,000 over 10 years (including reinvested dividends) would have grown to $82,000
Average annual compounded rate of return (including reinvested dividends): 23.5 percent

DIVIDEND YIELD ★ ★

Average dividend yield in the past 3 years: 2.3 percent

DIVIDEND GROWTH ★ ★ ★ ★

Increased dividend: 9 consecutive years
Past 5-year increase: 115 percent (17 percent per year)

CONSISTENCY

Increased earnings per share: 10 consecutive years
Increased sales: 14 consecutive years

SHAREHOLDER PERKS ★ ★

Good dividend reinvestment and stock purchase plan: voluntary stock purchase plan allows contributions of $25 to $3,000 per quarter.

FEDERAL SIGNAL AT A GLANCE

Fiscal year ended: Dec. 31
Revenue and net income in $ millions

	1991	1992	1993	1994	1995	1996	5-Year Growth Avg. Annual (%)	Total (%)
Revenue ($)	467	518.2	565.2	677.2	816.1	896.4	14	92
Net income ($)	31	34.5	39.8	46.8	51.6	62	15	100
Earnings/share ($)	0.67	0.75	0.86	1.02	1.13	1.35	15	101
Div. per share ($)	.27	.31	.36	.42	.50	.58	17	115
Dividend yield (%)	2.0	2.0	1.8	2.2	2.3	2.3	—	—
Avg. PE ratio	19	20	22	19	19	19	—	—

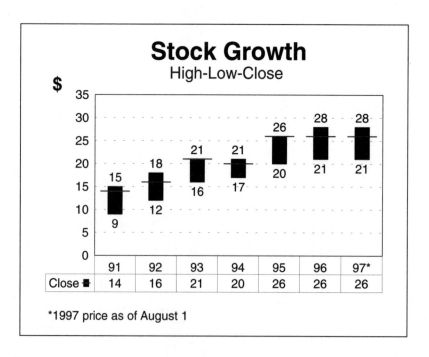

Stock Growth
High-Low-Close

	91	92	93	94	95	96	97*
Close ■	14	16	21	20	26	26	26

*1997 price as of August 1

14

Dollar General Corp.

104 Woodmont Blvd., Suite 500
Nashville, TN 37205
615-783-2000

Chairman, President, and CEO:
Cal Turner, Jr.

Earnings Growth	★ ★ ★ ★	Dividend Growth	★ ★ ★ ★
Stock Growth	★ ★ ★ ★	Consistency	★ ★ ★ ★
Dividend Yield	★	Shareholder Perks	
NYSE—DG		**Total**	**17 points**

Dollar General has stolen a page from the Wal-Mart marketing plan. Like the early days of Wal-Mart, Dollar General has been putting its stores in small, rural markets, far from the discount superstores of the metropolitan areas. The result for Dollar has been an explosive rate of growth that, in recent years, has exceeded even Wal-Mart's.

The Nashville-based retail chain began business in 1939 as a distributer of merchandise for retailers in rural Kentucky and Tennessee. Originally known as J. L. Turner and Son, the company opened its first store in 1945 and its first Dollar General Store in 1955 in Springfield, Kentucky. Its marketing slogan, "nothing over a dollar," helped pack the aisles with curious bargain-hunters.

Since then, the Dollar General chain has grown to 2,700 stores in 24 states. It still sells hundreds of items for just $1. A deck of cards, a box of lightbulbs, a can of Spanish peanuts, a bottle of dish soap, a broom, a mop, a pair of socks—all for just a buck. But unlike the old days, the stores also carry some $2, $3, $5, $10, and even $20 items. You'll find headphones and vitamins for $2, shoes, hats, and towels for $5, telephones for $8, and pants, curtains, and sheets for $10.

The company's stores are located in the South, East, Midwest, and Southwest. There are 277 stores in Texas, 175 in Tennessee, 157 in

Kentucky, 156 in Florida, and 149 in Missouri. Most of its stores are located in smaller towns and cities with populations of under 25,000.

The company adds 300 to 400 new stores per year.

Dollar General targets low-, middle-, and fixed-income consumers through its everyday low prices. It offers a wide variety of household merchandise, such as health and beauty aids, cleaning supplies, housewares, stationery, seasonal goods, non–fashion apparel, shoes, and domestics.

The company has about 22,000 employees and 3,300 shareholders.

EARNINGS-PER-SHARE GROWTH   ★ ★ ★ ★

Past 5 years: 373 percent (36 percent per year)
Past 10 years: 2,500 percent (39 percent per year)

STOCK GROWTH   ★ ★ ★ ★

Past 10 years: 642 percent (22 percent per year)
Dollar growth: $10,000 over 10 years (including reinvested dividends) would have grown to $83,000
Average annual compounded rate of return (including reinvested dividends): 23.5 percent

DIVIDEND YIELD   ★

Average dividend yield in the past 3 years: 0.7 percent

DIVIDEND GROWTH   ★ ★ ★ ★

Increased dividend: 4 consecutive years
Past 5-year increase: 200 percent (25 percent per year)

CONSISTENCY   ★ ★ ★ ★

Increased earnings per share: 10 consecutive years
Increased sales: 10 consecutive years

SHAREHOLDER PERKS   (no points)

The company offers no dividend reinvestment and stock purchase plan.

DOLLAR GENERAL AT A GLANCE

Fiscal year ended: Dec. 31
Revenue and net income in $ millions

	1991	1992	1993	1994	1995	1996	5-Year Growth Avg. Annual (%)	5-Year Growth Total (%)
Revenue ($)	754.4	920.7	1,133	1,448.6	1,764.2	2,134.4	23	183
Net income ($)	21.5	35.6	48.6	73.6	87.8	115.1	40	435
Earnings/share ($)	0.22	0.34	0.46	0.68	0.80	1.04	36	373
Div. per share ($)	.05	.07	.08	.10	.13	.15	25	200
Dividend yield (%)	1.5	.9	.7	.8	1.0	.5	—	—
Avg. PE ratio	16	18	21	19	22	28	—	—

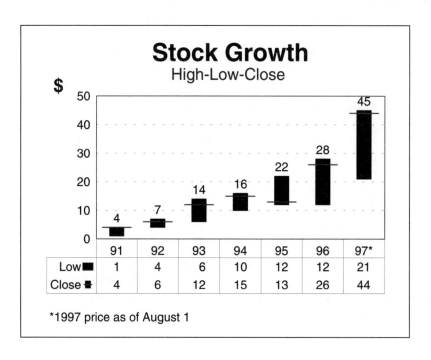

Stock Growth
High-Low-Close

	91	92	93	94	95	96	97*
Low	1	4	6	10	12	12	21
Close	4	6	12	15	13	26	44

*1997 price as of August 1

15

Fifth Third Bancorp

Fifth Third Center
Cincinnati, OH 45263
513-579-5300

President and CEO: George A. Schaefer, Jr.

Earnings Growth	★ ★	Dividend Growth	★ ★ ★ ★
Stock Growth	★ ★ ★	Consistency	★ ★ ★ ★
Dividend Yield	★ ★	Shareholder Perks	★ ★
NYSE—FITB		**Total**	**17 points**

After 139 years in the business, Fifth Third Bancorp is a company you can bank on. The Cincinnati-based institution has posted 23 consecutive years of record earnings.

Fifth Third has branches throughout Ohio, Kentucky, Indiana, and Florida. It has grown rapidly the past few years through a series of acquisitions, including more than 35 acquisitions of other financial institutions in its core region of Ohio, Kentucky, Indiana, and Florida.

The institution has consistently ranked in the top 1 percent of all publicly traded companies based on dividend growth. Its growth has come through aggressive new product development, increasing market share in existing markets, and geographic expansion into new markets.

Fifth Third acquired its improbable-sounding name in the early part of the century through the merger of the Fifth National and Third National Banks of Ohio. The company continues to bill itself as "the only bank you'll ever need."

Fifth Third has a reputation for quick response to credit problems, high credit standards, a strong sales culture, and strict cost control measures. The bank is also noted for eagerness to extend loans to businesses and consumers in the local markets it serves.

The company has won customers over the years through its mix of convenience and personal service delivered along with a comprehensive package of banking services. In addition to its regular branch offices, the bank operates seven-day-a-week banking centers in grocery stores throughout its four-state market area. The bank pioneered the use of automatic teller machines more than 20 years ago and continues to operate the Jeanie system, one of the premier ATM networks, with about 800 machines currently in operation.

About 31 percent of Fifth Third's loan portfolio is commercial loans, 27 percent are consumer loans; 17 percent are residential mortgages, and 13 percent are consumer leases, with the balance divided between construction loans, commercial mortgage loans, and commercial lease financing.

Fifth Third is the parent company of Midwest Payment Systems, the nation's largest third-party provider of electronic funds transfer services. The subsidiary processes Visa and MasterCard transactions for more than 20,000 retail outlets throughout the country.

Fifth Third has about 6,400 employees and 15,000 shareholders.

EARNINGS-PER-SHARE GROWTH ★ ★

Past 5 years: 106 percent (16 percent per year)
Past 10 years: 262 percent (14 percent per year)

STOCK GROWTH ★ ★ ★

Past 10 years: 493 percent (20 percent per year)
Dollar growth: $10,000 over 10 years (including reinvested dividends) would have grown to $72,000
Average annual compounded rate of return (including reinvested dividends): 22 percent

DIVIDEND YIELD ★ ★

Average dividend yield in the past 3 years: 2.3 percent

DIVIDEND GROWTH ★ ★ ★ ★

Increased dividend: More than 21 consecutive years
Past 5-year increase: 112 percent (16 percent per year)

CONSISTENCY ★ ★ ★ ★

Increased earnings per share: 23 consecutive years

SHAREHOLDER PERKS ★ ★

Good dividend reinvestment and stock purchase plan: voluntary stock purchase plan allows contributions of $25 to $2,500 per month.

FIFTH THIRD AT A GLANCE

Fiscal year ended: Dec. 31
Total assets and net income in $ millions

	1991	1992	1993	1994	1995	1996	5-Year Growth Avg. Annual (%)	Total (%)
Total assets ($)	8,826.1	10,213	11,966	14,957	17,053	20,549	19	133
Net income ($)	143	172	206.2	244.5	287.7	335.1	19	134
Earnings/share ($)	1.56	1.84	2.19	2.53	2.91	3.22	16	106
Div. per share ($)	0.52	0.60	0.68	0.80	0.96	1.10	16	112
Dividend yield (%)	2.3	1.9	1.9	2.4	2.5	2.0	—	—
Avg. PE ratio	14	17	16	13	13	18	—	—

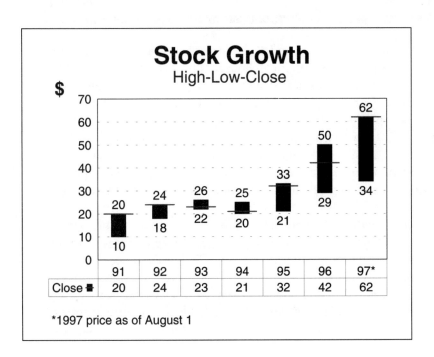

Stock Growth
High-Low-Close

	91	92	93	94	95	96	97*
Close	20	24	23	21	32	42	62

*1997 price as of August 1

Campbell Soup Company

Campbell Soup Company

Campbell Place
Camden, NJ 08103-1799
609-342-4800

Chairman, President, and CEO: David W. Johnson

Earnings Growth	★ ★	Dividend Growth	★ ★ ★ ★
Stock Growth	★ ★ ★	Consistency	★ ★ ★
Dividend Yield	★ ★ ★	Shareholder Perks	★ ★
NYSE—CPB		**Total**	**17 points**

With a dominating position in the U.S. soup market—cans of Campbell's are found in 93 percent of American households—where do you turn to soup up profits? Campbell's has been pushing aggressively into the international market in recent years, with a series of acquisitions, joint ventures, and new product introductions.

Campbell's recently acquired Erasco, which is Germany's leading soup company, and entered joint ventures in Malaysia, Japan, and Indonesia. International sales account for about 19 percent of the company's $7.68 billion in annual sales. In all, the company has about 100 facilities in 22 countries, with sales on six continents.

In the U.S. market, the company continues to introduce a barrage of new soups and other products. The company introduced 19 new soups in 1996 alone. And its three biggest sellers—Chicken Noodle, Cream of Mushroom, and Tomato—continue to generate increasing sales. Americans consume about 2 billion bowls of these three soups per year.

Many of Campbell's other products are leaders in their categories, including V8 vegetable juice, Vlasic pickles, Pace Mexican sauces,

Swanson canned poultry, Franco-American gravy, Pepperidge Farm premium biscuits and crackers, and Godiva super-premium chocolates.

The company is also a producer of specialty products for the food-service industry. Campbell's food-service division recently began producing soups for Sysco (the nation's largest food-service distributor), chicken pot pies for KFC, and soup for McDonald's.

Campbell's U.S. foods segment accounts for 59 percent of its total revenue, and its bakery and confectionery division generates 19 percent of the company's revenue.

Campbell's condensed soups were first introduced a century ago in 1897. The first year, the company sold only about ten cans per week of the new soups. But by 1905, the company was selling 40,000 cases per week, and Campbell's was on its way to becoming an American staple.

The Campbell Soup Company has 41,000 employees and 43,000 shareholders.

EARNINGS-PER-SHARE GROWTH

Past 5 years: 104 percent (15 percent per year)
Past 10 years: 274 percent (14 percent per year)

STOCK GROWTH ★ ★ ★

Past 10 years: 471 percent (19 percent per year)
Dollar growth: $10,000 over 10 years (including reinvested dividends) would have grown to $68,000
Average annual compounded rate of return (including reinvested dividends): 21 percent

DIVIDEND YIELD

Average dividend yield in the past 3 years: 2.6 percent

DIVIDEND GROWTH   ★ ★ ★ ★

Increased dividend: 22 consecutive years
Past 5-year increase: 139 percent (19 percent per year)

CONSISTENCY   ★ ★ ★

Increased earnings per share: 9 of the past 10 years
Increased sales: 9 of the past 10 years

SHAREHOLDER PERKS   ★ ★

Good dividend reinvestment and stock purchase plan: voluntary stock purchase plan allows contributions of $25 to $25,000 per year.

The company also often hands out bags of freebies at the annual meeting, including a variety of soups and other Campbell's products.

CAMPBELL SOUP AT A GLANCE

Fiscal year ended: July 31
Revenue and net income in $ millions

	1991	1992	1993	1994	1995	1996	5-Year Growth Avg. Annual (%)	5-Year Growth Total (%)
Revenue ($)	6,204.1	6,263.2	6,586	6,664	7,250	7,678	4	24
Net income ($)	401.5	490.5	557.2	630	698	802	15	100
Earnings/share ($)	0.79	0.97	1.10	1.26	1.40	1.61	15	104
Div. per share ($)	.28	.36	.46	.55	.61	.67	19	139
Dividend yield (%)	1.7	1.9	2.2	2.8	2.7	2.3	—	—
Avg. PE ratio	20	19	19	16	16	18	—	—

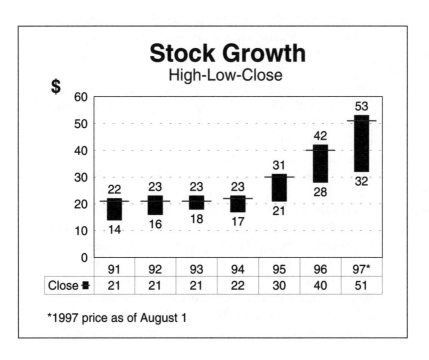

Stock Growth
High-Low-Close

$	91	92	93	94	95	96	97*
Close	21	21	21	22	30	40	51

*1997 price as of August 1

The Home Depot

2727 Paces Ferry Road, N.W.
Atlanta, GA 30339-4089
770-433-8211

Chairman and CEO: Bernard Marcus
President: Arthur M. Blank

Earnings Growth	★ ★ ★ ★	Dividend Growth	★ ★
Stock Growth	★ ★ ★ ★	Consistency	★ ★ ★ ★
Dividend Yield		Shareholder Perks	★ ★
NYSE—HD		**Total**	**16 points**

Over a four-year period from 1992 to 1996, hardware superstore Home Depot doubled its store count and tripled its earnings. Despite the growth, however, its stock price closed lower in 1996 than it did in 1992 ($33.42 versus $33.76).

Blame it on the retail segment's sagging stock syndrome. Sears, Kmart, JC Penney, and even Wal-Mart all enjoyed early stock market success, but as their markets became saturated and their profit margins tightened, investors quickly lost interest in the stock.

So far, however, Home Depot is still growing rapidly, adding about 100 new stores per year. The Atlanta-based operation has about 470 stores in 36 states, plus 24 stores in three Canadian provinces. It plans to have 800 stores by the end of fiscal 1998. For three consecutive years, the company has been ranked by *Fortune* magazine as America's most admired retailer. The Home Depot is the world's largest home improvement retailer. Each of the company's cavernous warehouse-style outlets, which average about 100,000 square feet, stocks 40,000 to 50,000 home improvement products, including nuts, bolts, brushes, boards, carpets, screens, saws, spades, power tools, appliances, and lawn and garden supplies. The newer stores also include 25,000-square-foot garden centers.

Home Depot has built its business by offering its vast selection of merchandise at low prices. The company avoids special sales, but it routinely offers wholesale-type prices on all of its merchandise. In addition to the aisles and aisles of hardware, most stores also feature a small stage and bleachers for how-to clinics.

One of the secrets to Home Depot's success is its well-trained sales force. Store employees are cross-trained in all departments, and many have a background in the building industry. Customers with questions about home projects can usually learn all they need to know by talking with sales clerks. About 95 percent of the company's 77,000 employees are full-time, and the company offers above-average salaries and benefits to keep its employees in the fold.

The Home Depot's primary customers are do-it-yourself homeowners, although many remodeling contractors and building maintenance professionals also buy supplies at Home Depot stores.

Of the company's $19.5 billion in annual revenue, 28 percent comes from plumbing, heating, lighting, and electrical supplies; 34 percent from building materials, lumber, and floor and wall coverings; 13 percent from hardware and tools; 15 percent from seasonal and specialty items; and 10 percent from paint and other products.

The Home Depot was founded in 1978 by Bernard Marcus (who still serves as the company's chairman and CEO), Arthur Blank (Home Depot president), and Kenneth G. Langone (a company board of directors member). The company has about 61,000 shareholders.

EARNINGS-PER-SHARE GROWTH ★ ★ ★ ★

Past 5 years: 242 percent (28 percent per year)
Past 10 years: 5,033 percent (48 percent per year)

STOCK GROWTH ★ ★ ★ ★

Past 10 years: 3,033 percent (40 percent per year)
Dollar growth: $10,000 over 10 years (including reinvested dividends) would have grown to $315,000
Average annual compounded rate of return (including reinvested dividends): 41 percent

DIVIDEND YIELD   (no points)

Average dividend yield in the past 3 years: 0.3 percent

DIVIDEND GROWTH

Increased dividend: 9 consecutive years
Past 5-year increase: 375 percent (37 percent per year)

CONSISTENCY   ★ ★ ★ ★

Increased earnings per share: 10 consecutive years
Increased sales: 16 consecutive years

SHAREHOLDER PERKS

Good dividend reinvestment and stock purchase plan: voluntary stock
purchase plan allows contributions of $10 up to $4,000 monthly.

HOME DEPOT AT A GLANCE

Fiscal year ended: Jan. 31
Revenue and net income in $ millions

	1991	1992	1993	1994	1995	1996	5-Year Growth Avg. Annual (%)	Total (%)
Revenue ($)	5,136.7	7,148.4	9,238.8	12,476	15,470	15,470	25	201
Net income ($)	163.4	249.2	362.9	457.4	604.5	731.5	35	348
Earnings/share ($)	0.45	0.60	0.81	1.01	1.33	1.54	28	242
Div. per share ($)	.04	.06	.08	.11	.15	.19	37	375
Dividend yield (%)	.3	.2	.3	.3	.4	.6	—	—
Avg. PE ratio	41	47	42	33	28	20	—	—

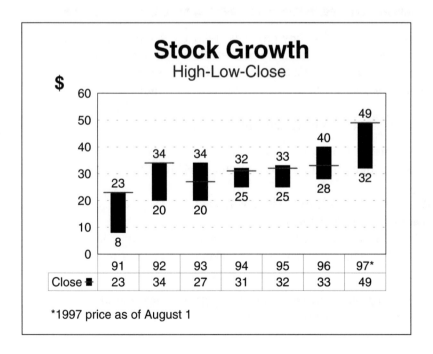

Stock Growth
High-Low-Close

	91	92	93	94	95	96	97*
Close ■	23	34	27	31	32	33	49

*1997 price as of August 1

Johnson & Johnson

Johnson&Johnson

One Johnson & Johnson Plaza
New Brunswick, NJ 08933
908-524-0400

Chairman and CEO: Ralph S. Larsen

Earnings Growth	★ ★	Dividend Growth	★ ★ ★
Stock Growth	★ ★ ★	Consistency	★ ★ ★ ★
Dividend Yield	★ ★	Shareholder Perks	★ ★
NYSE—JNJ		**Total**	**16 points**

Long known mostly for its baby products, Johnson & Johnson continues to turn out a vast array of innovative new medical products. Its long-term success in the medical products field earned the company the National Medal of Technology in 1996, which is the highest honor for technological innovation.

Among its most promising new products are:

- **The Ultracision Harmonic Scalpel** that vibrates at a rate of 55,000 times per second, enabling it to cut and seal blood vessels simultaneously.
- **Topamax antiepileptic medicine,** which reduces the frequency of seizures among epileptic patients.
- **The Nicotrol Patch,** the first nicotine patch available for sale without a prescription. The patch can help smokers quit smoking in about six weeks.

The New Brunswick, New Jersey, operation has manufacturing plants in about 50 countries and sales in more than 150 countries. Approximately 50 percent of the firm's $21.6 billion in annual revenue is generated in foreign markets.

The company turns out a number of well-known consumer brands, including Johnson & Johnson baby powders, lotions, and related products; Band-Aids; Tylenol; Mylanta antacid; Imodium A-D antidiarrheal medicine; Carefree Panty Shields, Stayfree and Sure and Natural sanitary protection products; Pediacare cold and allergy medications for children; Prevent and Reach toothbrushes; Serenity incontinence products; and Piz Bun and Sundown sun care products. Consumer products account for about 29 percent of the company's annual revenue.

The company also has operations in two other key segments:

1. **Pharmaceutical products** (33 percent of revenue). The company's principal areas of treatment include allergy and asthma medications, antifungals, central nervous system medications, contraceptives, gastrointestinal treatments, and skin care formulas.
2. **Professional medical products** (38 percent of revenue). The company produces sutures, mechanical wound closure products, endoscopic products, dental products, diagnostic products, medical equipment and devices, ophthalmic products, and surgical instruments and medical supplies used by physicians, dentists, therapists, hospitals, and clinics.

Johnson & Johnson has 89,000 employees and 70,000 shareholders.

EARNINGS-PER-SHARE GROWTH ★★

Past 5 years: 97 percent (15 percent per year)
Past 10 years: 843 percent (20 percent per year)

STOCK GROWTH ★★★

Past 10 years: 563 percent (21 percent per year)
Dollar growth: $10,000 over 10 years (including reinvested dividends) would have grown to $79,000
Average annual compounded rate of return (including reinvested dividends): 23 percent

DIVIDEND YIELD   ★ ★

Average dividend yield in the past 3 years: 1.9 percent

DIVIDEND GROWTH   ★ ★ ★

Increased dividend: 31 consecutive years
Past 5-year increase: 90 percent (14 percent per year)

CONSISTENCY   ★ ★ ★ ★

Increased earnings per share: 10 consecutive years
Increased sales: 21 consecutive years

SHAREHOLDER PERKS   ★ ★

Good dividend reinvestment and stock purchase plan: voluntary stock
purchase plan allows contributions of up to $50,000 per year.

JOHNSON & JOHNSON AT A GLANCE

Fiscal year ended: Dec. 31
Revenue and net income in $ millions

	1991	1992	1993	1994	1995	1996	5-Year Growth Avg. Annual (%)	Total (%)
Revenue ($)	12,447	13,753	14,138	15,734	18,842	21,620	12	74
Net income ($)	1,461	1,625	1,787	2,006	2,403	2,887	15	98
Earnings/share ($)	1.10	1.23	1.37	1.56	1.86	2.17	15	97
Div. per share ($)	.39	.45	.51	.56	.64	.74	14	90
Dividend yield (%)	1.5	1.8	2.4	2.4	1.9	1.5	—	—
Avg. PE ratio	21	20	15	15	19	22	—	—

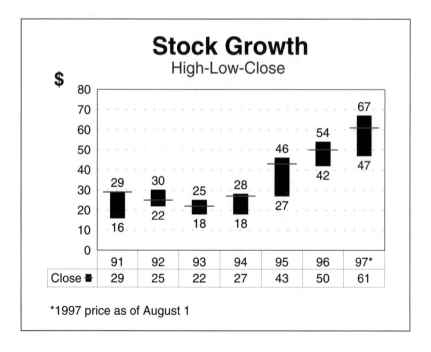

Stock Growth
High-Low-Close

	91	92	93	94	95	96	97*
Close	29	25	22	27	43	50	61

*1997 price as of August 1

Bemis Company, Inc.

222 South Ninth Street, Suite 2300
Minneapolis, MN 55402-4099
612-376-3000

President and CEO: John H. Roe

Earnings Growth	★ ★	Dividend Growth	★ ★ ★
Stock Growth	★ ★ ★	Consistency	★ ★ ★ ★
Dividend Yield	★ ★	Shareholder Perks	★ ★
NYSE—BMS		**Total**	**16 points**

Bemis makes the wrappers, bags, and boxes for hundreds of products from foods and pharmaceuticals to fertilizer, soaps, seeds, and cement.

Flexible packaging accounts for about 73 percent of the company's $1.66 billion in total annual revenue. Its flexible packaging includes:

- **Coated and laminated film packaging.** The company does resin manufacturing, extruding, coating, laminating, metallizing, printing, and converting for packaging for processed meats, cheese, coffee, condiments, potato chips, candy, and related products.
- **Polyethylene packaging products.** Bemis makes preformed bags, extruded products, and printed roll packaging for items such as bakery goods, seeds, lawn and garden products, ice, and produce.
- **Industrial and consumer paper bags.** The firm makes multiwall and small paper bags, balers, printed paper roll stock, and bag-closing materials for industrial and consumer packaging products such as pet foods, chemicals, dairy products, fertilizers, feed, flour, and sugar.
- **Packaging machinery.** Bemis manufactures packaging systems that provide automated bag handling, weighing, filling, closing, and sealing.

The company's other leading segment is its specialty-coated and graphics products, which account for 27 percent of its total sales.

Founded in 1858 as a grain bag manufacturer, the Minneapolis-based operation has sales offices and plants throughout the United States, Canada, Great Britain, Europe, Scandinavia, Australia, and South Central America. About 14 percent of the company's annual revenue comes from its foreign operations. Bemis has about 8,500 employees and 5,700 shareholders.

EARNINGS-PER-SHARE GROWTH ★ ★

Past 5 years: 84 percent (13 percent per year)
Past 10 years: 313 percent (15 percent per year)

STOCK GROWTH ★ ★ ★

Past 10 years: 485 percent (19 percent per year)
Dollar growth: $10,000 over 10 years (including reinvested dividends) would have grown to $73,000
Average annual compounded rate of return (including reinvested dividends): 22 percent

DIVIDEND YIELD ★ ★

Average dividend yield in the past 3 years: 2.3 percent

DIVIDEND GROWTH ★ ★ ★

Increased dividend: 13 consecutive years
Past 5-year increase: 71 percent (11 percent per year)

CONSISTENCY ★ ★ ★ ★

Increased earnings per share: 14 consecutive years
Increased sales: 14 consecutive years

SHAREHOLDER PERKS

Good dividend reinvestment and stock purchase plan: voluntary stock purchase plan allows contributions of up to $10,000 per quarter.

BEMIS AT A GLANCE

Fiscal year ended: Dec. 31
Revenue and net income in $ millions

	1991	1992	1993	1994	1995	1996	5-Year Growth Avg. Annual (%)	Total (%)
Revenue ($)	1,141.6	1,181.3	1,203.5	1,390.5	1,523.4	1,655.4	8	45
Net income ($)	53	57.3	46.1	72.8	85.2	101.1	14	91
Earnings/share ($)	1.03	1.11	0.89	1.40	1.63	1.90	13	84
Div. per share ($)	.42	.46	.50	.54	.64	.72	11	71
Dividend yield (%)	2.4	1.9	2.2	2.3	2.4	2.2	—	—
Avg. PE ratio	17	22	20	17	17	18	—	—

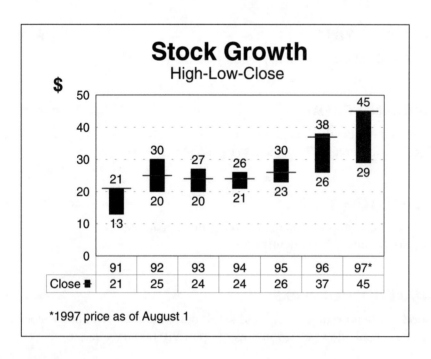

Stock Growth
High-Low-Close

	91	92	93	94	95	96	97*
Close	21	25	24	24	26	37	45

*1997 price as of August 1

20

Pfizer, Inc.

235 East 42nd Street
New York, NY 10017-5755
212-573-2323

Chairman and CEO: William C. Steere, Jr.

Earnings Growth	★ ★ ★	Dividend Growth	★ ★ ★
Stock Growth	★ ★ ★	Consistency	★ ★ ★
Dividend Yield	★ ★	Shareholder Perks	★ ★
NYSE—PFE		**Total**	**16 points**

For many of Pfizer's most successful new medications, the research doesn't end when the initial product launch begins. The company, which spends about $2 billion per year on research and development, continues to test new applications for its existing medications to extend their life cycles and bolster their profits.

For instance, in 1991 Pfizer introduced the antibiotic Zithromax for treatment of respiratory and skin infections. Through further research the company also found Zithromax to be effective in treating otitis media and pharyngitis in children, as well as several other types of ailments. The result has been a steady increase in the sales of Zithromax. The company reported sales of $619 million in 1996, a 53 percent increase over 1995.

Pharmaceuticals and health care products account for 85 percent of the company's $11.3 billion in annual revenue. Three of its medications had annual sales in excess of $1 billion, including the antidepressant Zoloft and the cardiovascular medications, Norvasc and Procardia XL. Its other leading pharmaceuticals include the antifungal Diflucan ($910 million in annual sales), the antibiotic Zithromax, the cardiovascular medication Cardura ($533 million), and the allergy drug Zyrtec ($146 million).

Pfizer also has a line of animal health care products to treat livestock, poultry, and household pets. Animal health care products account for about 11 percent of the company's annual revenue. Consumer health care products account for the other 4 percent of its revenue. Leading products include Reactine antiallergy medication, Hemorid, Bain de Soleil sun lotion, and Cortizone anti-itch cream.

Pfizer has sales in more than 150 countries. Foreign sales account for about 47 percent of the company's total revenue. The New York–based operation has about 44,000 employees and 63,000 shareholders.

EARNINGS-PER-SHARE GROWTH   ★ ★ ★

Past 5 years: 120 percent (17 percent per year)
Past 10 years: 205 percent (12 percent per year)

STOCK GROWTH   ★ ★ ★

Past 10 years: 457 percent (19 percent per year)
Dollar growth: $10,000 over 10 years (including reinvested dividends) would have grown to $70,000
Average annual compounded rate of return (including reinvested dividends): 21.5 percent

DIVIDEND YIELD   ★ ★

Average dividend yield in the past 3 years: 2.2 percent

DIVIDEND GROWTH   ★ ★ ★

Increased dividend: 30 consecutive years
Past 5-year increase: 82 percent (13 percent per year)

CONSISTENCY   ★ ★ ★

Increased earnings per share: 9 of the past 10 years
Increased sales: 47 consecutive years

SHAREHOLDER PERKS

Excellent dividend reinvestment and stock purchase plan: voluntary stock purchase plan allows contributions of $25 to $10,000 per month.

PFIZER AT A GLANCE

Fiscal year ended: Dec. 31
Revenue and net income in $ millions

	1991	1992	1993	1994	1995	1996	5-Year Growth Avg. Annual (%)	Total (%)
Revenue ($)	6,580	6,871	7,162	7,977	10,021	11,306	12	72
Net income ($)	722	811	658	1,298	1,573	1,929	21	167
Earnings/share ($)	1.36	1.63	1.84	2.05	2.47	2.99	17	120
Div. per share ($)	0.66	0.74	0.84	0.94	1.04	1.20	13	82
Dividend yield (%)	2.2	2.0	2.6	2.9	2.1	1.6	—	—
Avg. PE ratio	22	23	18	16	20	25	—	—

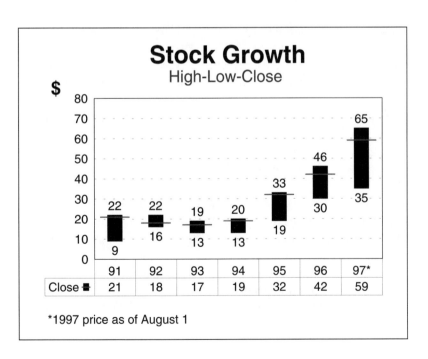

Stock Growth
High-Low-Close

	91	92	93	94	95	96	97*
Close	21	18	17	19	32	42	59

*1997 price as of August 1

General Electric Company

3135 Easton Turnpike
Fairfield, CT 06431
203-373-2211

Chairman and CEO: John F. Welch, Jr.

Earnings Growth	★	Dividend Growth	★ ★ ★
Stock Growth	★ ★ ★	Consistency	★ ★ ★ ★
Dividend Yield	★ ★ ★	Shareholder Perks	★ ★
NYSE—GE		**Total**	**16 points**

With a total market capitalization of $173 billion, General Electric has become the world's most valuable company. The firm reached that position by posting record earnings for 21 consecutive years, with double-digit earnings growth the past four years—no small feat for a conglomerate the size of GE.

The Fairfield, Connecticut, operation has been focusing recently on building its service maintenance business. The company is beginning to offer maintenance contracts for the broad range of electrical and medical equipment it manufactures (as well as for some equipment from other manufacturers).

GE breaks its business into several key segments. Its largest manufacturing segment is its industrial division that accounts for about 15 percent of its $79.2 billion in annual revenue. The company manufactures factory automation products, motors, electrical equipment, transportation systems (including locomotives and transit propulsion equipment), lightbulbs, and other types of lighting products.

GE's other leading divisions include:

- **Power generation** (9 percent of total revenue). The company builds power generators (primarily steam-turbine generators) and transmitters for worldwide utility, industrial, and government customers.
- **Aircraft engines** (9 percent). It is a leading manufacturer of jet engines and engine parts for short-, medium-, intermediate-, and long-range commercial aircraft and military aircraft and helicopters.
- **Broadcasting** (6 percent). GE owns the National Broadcasting Company (NBC), which serves more than 200 affiliated stations throughout the United States. NBC also owns the cable channel CNBC and television stations in Chicago, Philadelphia, Los Angeles, Miami, New York, and Washington, D.C.
- **Major appliances** (9 percent of revenue). The company is known for its GE, Hotpoint, and Monogram appliances including refrigerators, ranges, microwaves, freezers, dishwashers, clothes washers and dryers, and room air conditioners.
- **Materials** (10 percent of revenue). The company makes high-performance plastics for such uses as automobile bumpers, computer casings, and other office equipment. It also produces silicones, superabrasives, and laminates.
- **Technical products and services** (6 percent of revenue). The company manufactures a variety of medical instruments, including scanners, X rays, nuclear imaging, ultrasound, and other diagnostic equipment. It also manufactures communications systems.
- **GE Financial Services** (37 percent of revenue). GE owns a number financial and insurance subsidiaries. Its largest division is GE Capital, a financing institution that specializes in revolving credit, credit cards, and inventory financing for retail merchants.

GE traces its roots to the Edison Electric Company, which was founded in 1878 by Thomas Edison. The company has about 220,000 employees and 460,000 shareholders.

EARNINGS-PER-SHARE GROWTH ★

Past 5 years: 73 percent (12 percent per year)
Past 10 years: 222 percent (12 percent per year)

STOCK GROWTH

Past 10 years: 410 percent (18 percent per year)
Dollar growth: $10,000 over 10 years (including reinvested dividends) would have grown to $66,000
Average annual compounded rate of return (including reinvested dividends): 21 percent

DIVIDEND YIELD

Average dividend yield in the past 3 years: 2.7 percent

DIVIDEND GROWTH

Increased dividend: 21 consecutive years
Past 5-year increase: 77 percent (12 percent per year)

CONSISTENCY

Increased earnings per share: 21 consecutive years
Increased sales: 9 of the past 10 years

SHAREHOLDER PERKS ★ ★

Good dividend reinvestment and stock purchase plan: voluntary share purchase plan allows contributions of up to $10,000 per month.

GENERAL ELECTRIC AT A GLANCE

Fiscal year ended: Dec. 31
Revenue and net income in $ millions

	1991	1992	1993	1994	1995	1996	5-Year Growth Avg. Annual (%)	5-Year Growth Total (%)
Revenue ($)	51,300	53,100	55,700	60,100	70,000	79,200	9	54
Net income ($)	4,435	4,725	5,177	5,915	6,573	7,280	10	64
Earnings/share ($)	2.55	2.75	3.03	3.46	3.90	4.41	12	73
Div. per share ($)	1.04	1.16	1.31	1.49	1.69	1.84	12	77
Dividend yield (%)	2.8	2.9	2.8	3.0	2.9	2.2	—	—
Avg. PE ratio	14	16	16	14	15	19	—	—

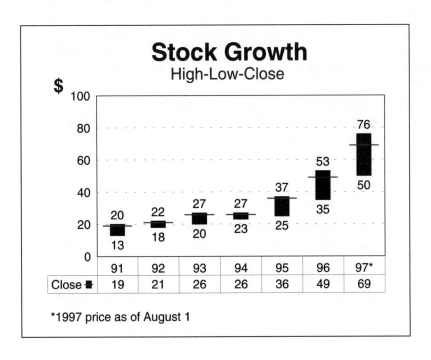

Stock Growth
High-Low-Close

	91	92	93	94	95	96	97*
Close	19	21	26	26	36	49	69

*1997 price as of August 1

The Interpublic Group of Companies, Inc.

1271 Avenue of the Americas
New York, NY 10020
212-399-8000

Chairman, President, and CEO: Philip H. Geier, Jr.

Earnings Growth	★ ★	Dividend Growth	★ ★ ★
Stock Growth	★ ★ ★	Consistency	★ ★ ★ ★
Dividend Yield	★ ★	Shareholder Perks	★ ★
NYSE—IPG		**Total**	**16 points**

McCann-Erickson Worldwide is the largest and most developed advertising agency system in the world, with operations in more countries with far more global accounts than any other agency.

And yet McCann-Erickson, which counts among its clients Microsoft, General Motors, Unilever, Nestlé, and L'Oreal, is just one of several major agencies that make up the advertising mega-agency, The Interpublic Group.

In all, the Interpublic Group has more than 4,000 advertising clients and offices in more than 100 countries. The New York–based operation is the world's second largest organization of advertising agencies.

About 64 percent of its $2.54 billion in total revenue comes from its foreign operations.

Interpublic's other leading agencies include Ammirati Puris Lintas, The Lowe Group, Campbell Mithun Esty, Daily and Associates, and Western International Media. Among its clients are Levi-Strauss, Nestlé, GMAC, Camel cigarettes, L'Oreal, Gillette, Mennen, Black & Decker, Delta faucets, Johnson & Johnson, Maybelline, Goodyear, Exxon, Casio, and Del Monte fruits. Interpublic gave Chevrolet the "Heartbeat of America," deemed Coke "the Real Thing," and made UPS the "tightest ship in the shipping business."

Interpublic was founded in 1902 by A. W. Erickson (and in 1911 by Harrison K. McCann). It was first incorporated in 1930 as McCann-

Erickson and has been operating under the name Interpublic Group since 1961. The New York–based agency has about 20,000 employees and 3,500 shareholders.

EARNINGS-PER-SHARE GROWTH   ★ ★

Past 5 years: 97 percent (15 percent per year)
Past 10 years: 313 percent (15 percent per year)

STOCK GROWTH   ★ ★ ★

Past 10 years: 452 percent (19 percent per year)
Dollar growth: $10,000 over 10 years (including reinvested dividends) would have grown to $67,000
Average annual compounded rate of return (including reinvested dividends): 21 percent

DIVIDEND YIELD   ★ ★

Average dividend yield in the past 3 years: 1.6 percent

DIVIDEND GROWTH   ★ ★ ★

Increased dividend: 13 consecutive years
Past 5-year increase: 63 percent (10 percent per year)

CONSISTENCY   ★ ★ ★ ★

Increased earnings per share: 15 consecutive years
Increased sales: 11 of the past 12 years

SHAREHOLDER PERKS   ★ ★

Good dividend reinvestment and stock purchase plan: voluntary stock purchase plan allows contributions of $10 to $3,000 per month.

INTERPUBLIC GROUP AT A GLANCE

Fiscal year ended: Dec. 31
Revenue and net income in $ millions

	1991	1992	1993	1994	1995	1996	5-Year Growth Avg. Annual (%)	Total (%)
Revenue ($)	1,677.5	1,856	1,793.9	1,984.3	2,179.7	2,537.5	9	51
Net income ($)	94,557	87,273	124,767	93,467	129,812	205,089	17	117
Earnings/share ($)	1.30	1.50	1.67	1.53	1.66	2.56	15	97
Div. per share ($)	.41	.45	.49	.55	.61	.67	10	63
Dividend yield (%)	1.8	1.5	1.6	1.7	1.6	1.5	—	—
Avg. PE ratio	17	20	18	16	17	19	—	—

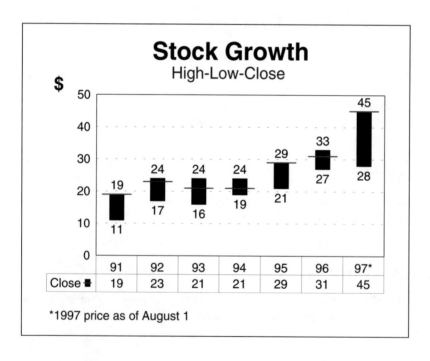

Stock Growth
High-Low-Close

	91	92	93	94	95	96	97*
Close	19	23	21	21	29	31	45

*1997 price as of August 1

First Empire State Corp.

One M&T Plaza
Buffalo, NY 14240
716-842-5445

Chairman, President, and CEO:
Robert G. Wilmers

Earnings Growth	★ ★ ★	Dividend Growth	★ ★ ★ ★
Stock Growth	★ ★ ★	Consistency	★ ★ ★
Dividend Yield	★	Shareholder Perks	★ ★
NYSE—FES		**Total**	**16 points**

First Empire State is steadily expanding its banking empire beyond the Empire State. The Buffalo, New York, institution has banking operations in a total of eight states, including Pennsylvania, Ohio, Oregon, Utah, Colorado, Massachusetts, Washington, and New York.

The company does most of its business through two wholly-owned banking subsidiaries, Manufacturers and Traders Trust Company and the East New York Savings Bank.

Manufacturers and Trust Bank (M&T) has about 150 banking offices located throughout New York State and one branch office in Nassau, the Bahamas. M&T offers the standard banking services such as savings, checking, and loan services for consumers, businesses, and other clients.

M&T also conducts business through a number of subsidiaries, including M&T Capital Corp., which provides equity capital and long-term credit to small businesses; M&T Credit Corp., which offers credit services for consumers; M&T Mortgage, which has offices in several states and specializes in residential home mortgage loans and mortgage services; M&T Financial, which specializes in capital equipment leasing; M&T Real Estate, which specializes in commercial real estate lending and servicing; and M&T Securities, which provides securities brokerage and advisory services for bank customers.

First Empire's East New York Savings Bank subsidiary operates 16 banking offices in New York City and Long Island. The bank offers the standard banking services for its business and consumer customers.

First Empire has about 5,000 employees and 3,800 shareholders.

EARNINGS-PER-SHARE GROWTH ★ ★ ★

Past 5 years: 129 percent (18 percent per year)
Past 10 years: 344 percent (16 percent per year)

STOCK GROWTH ★ ★ ★

Past 10 years: 585 percent (19 percent per year)
Dollar growth: $10,000 over 10 years (including reinvested dividends) would have grown to $67,000
Average annual compounded rate of return (including reinvested dividends): 21 percent

DIVIDEND YIELD ★

Average dividend yield in the past 3 years: 1.3 percent

DIVIDEND GROWTH ★ ★ ★ ★

Increased dividend: More than 16 consecutive years
Past 5-year increase: 100 percent (15 percent per year)

CONSISTENCY ★ ★ ★

Increased earnings per share: 9 consecutive years

SHAREHOLDER PERKS

Dividend reinvestment and stock purchase plan: voluntary stock purchase plan allows contributions of $10 to $1,000 per quarter.

FIRST EMPIRE STATE AT A GLANCE

Fiscal year ended: Dec. 31
Total assets and net income in $ millions

	1991	1992	1993	1994	1995	1996	5-Year Growth Avg. Annual (%)	Total (%)
Total assets ($)	9,171	9,588	10,365	10,529	11,956	12,944	7	41
Net income ($)	67.2	97.9	102	117.3	131	151.1	18	125
Earnings/share ($)	9.32	13.41	13.87	16.35	18.79	21.31	18	129
Div. per share ($)	1.40	1.60	1.90	2.20	2.50	2.80	15	100
Dividend yield (%)	1.5	1.3	1.3	1.6	1.3	1.1	—	—
Avg. PE ratio	9	10	10	9	9	12	—	—

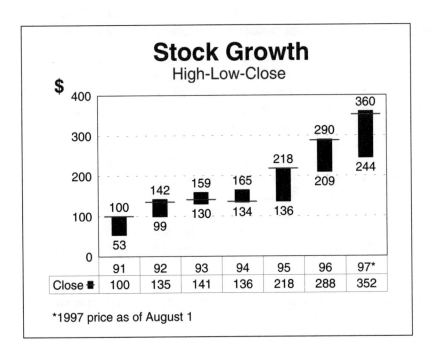

Stock Growth
High-Low-Close

Close ■	91	92	93	94	95	96	97*
	100	135	141	136	218	288	352

*1997 price as of August 1

24

State Street Boston Corp.

225 Franklin Street
Boston, MA 02110
617-786-3000

Chairman and CEO: Marshall N. Carter
President: David A. Spina

Earnings Growth	★ ★	Dividend Growth	★ ★ ★
Stock Growth	★ ★ ★	Consistency	★ ★ ★ ★
Dividend Yield	★ ★	Shareholder Perks	★ ★
NYSE—STT		**Total**	**16 points**

State Street Boston has taken its growing array of investment products and financial management services to the international market. Since opening its first foreign office in Munich, Germany, in 1970, the company has added offices in 15 other countries and sales or services in 72 markets.

Since 1990, State Street's foreign assets under management have jumped from $3 billion to $26 billion and its foreign assets under custody have climbed from $30 billion to $186 billion. The Boston-based institution has offices in Canada, Hong Kong, Japan, Australia, New Zealand, Taiwan, the United Kingdom, France, Belgium, Luxembourg, Germany, and several other overseas locations.

State Street is a banking organization that traces its roots back two centuries to the Union Bank, which opened shortly after the American Revolution in 1792.

Although the company does offer many traditional banking services, its main source of revenue comes from the managing and servicing of assets for mutual funds, pension funds, and other large asset pools. The company offers a broad range of services including accounting, recordkeeping, custody of securities, information services and recordkeeping, investment management, foreign exchange trading, and cash management.

State Street, which began offering mutual fund services in 1924, now has more than $1 trillion in mutual fund assets under custody. It is the leading mutual fund custodian in the United States, servicing 41 percent of the registered funds. The company also provides services for more than 250 collective investment funds registered outside the United States.

The firm's mutual fund custodial services include safekeeping portfolio assets, settling trades, collecting and accounting for income, monitoring corporate actions, and reporting investable cash.

State Street is also a leader in the pension asset segment, servicing about $1 trillion in assets for North American customers. State Street ranks as the nation's largest servicer of tax-exempt assets for corporations and public funds.

The company also provides traditional commercial lending services such as corporate banking, specialized lending, and international banking for businesses and financial institutions.

The company's financial asset services accounted for 62 percent of its $293 million in annual net profit, commercial lending generated 23 percent, and investment management accounted for 15 percent.

State Street has 11,000 employees and 6,000 shareholders.

EARNINGS-PER-SHARE GROWTH ★ ★

Past 5 years: 92 percent (14 percent per year)
Past 10 years: 290 percent (15 percent per year)

STOCK GROWTH ★ ★ ★

Past 10 years: 439 percent (18 percent per year)
Dollar growth: $10,000 over 10 years (including reinvested dividends) would have grown to $61,000
Average annual compounded rate of return (including reinvested dividends): 20 percent

DIVIDEND YIELD

Average dividend yield in the past 3 years: 1.6 percent

DIVIDEND GROWTH

Increased dividend: 18 consecutive years
Past 5-year increase: 90 percent (14 percent per year)

CONSISTENCY ★ ★ ★ ★

Increased earnings per share: 20 consecutive years

SHAREHOLDER PERKS ★ ★

Good dividend reinvestment and stock purchase plan: voluntary stock purchase plan allows contributions of $10 to $1,000 per quarter.

STATE STREET BOSTON AT A GLANCE

Fiscal year ended: Dec. 31
Fee revenue and net income in $ millions

	1991	1992	1993	1994	1995	1996	5-Year Growth Avg. Annual (%)	Total (%)
Fee revenue ($)	596.4	743.5	865.6	1,017.3	1,119.1	1,302	17	118
Net income ($)	151.3	170.1	189.4	220.3	247.1	293	14	94
Earnings/share ($)	1.87	2.07	2.30	2.66	2.98	3.59	14	92
Div. per share ($)	.39	.45	.52	.60	.68	.74	14	90
Dividend yield (%)	1.6	1.3	1.4	1.6	1.9	1.4	—	—
Avg. PE ratio	14	17	16	14	12	15	—	—

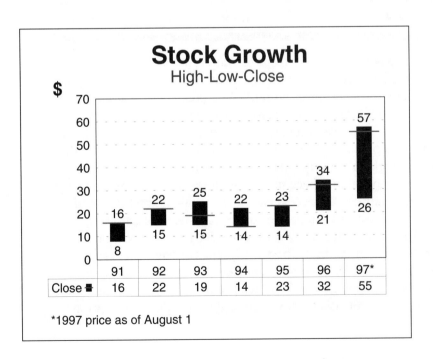

Stock Growth
High-Low-Close

Close	91	92	93	94	95	96	97*
	16	22	19	14	23	32	55

*1997 price as of August 1

Walgreen Company

𝒲𝒶𝓁𝑔𝓇𝑒𝑒𝓃𝓈

200 Wilmot Road
Deerfield, IL 60015
847-914-2500

Chairman and CEO: Charles R. Walgreen III
President: L. Daniel Jorndt

Earnings Growth	★ ★	Dividend Growth	★ ★ ★
Stock Growth	★ ★ ★	Consistency	★ ★ ★ ★
Dividend Yield	★ ★	Shareholder Perks	★ ★
NYSE—WAG		**Total**	**16 points**

Convenience has always been a focus of Walgreen—in its store locations, its broad product selection, and, more recently, its nationwide computer database that allows customers to refill their prescriptions at any of the more than 2,000 Walgreen stores across the country.

Now the Chicago-based retailer has taken convenience one step further. More than 500 of its stores offer drive-through windows that allow customers to pick up prescriptions without leaving their cars.

The company has also been pulling its stores out of the big shopping malls—where parking and access can be difficult—and relocating them at freestanding locations that provide quicker, easier access for busy consumers. Walgreen continues to work toward a goal of operating 3,000 stores by the year 2000. In the past five years, the company has opened 872 new stores, acquired 15 stores, remodeled 481 stores, and closed 341 stores. It plans to open about 300 stores per year through the end of this decade. At the end of fiscal 1996, Walgreen operated 2,193 stores in 34 states.

Walgreen, which was founded in 1901 by Charles Walgreen, is the nation's largest and best-managed drugstore chain. The company has posted 21 consecutive years of record sales and earnings.

Walgreen stores average about 10,000 square feet per store and carry a wide range of merchandise, including clocks, calculators, jewelry, artwork, lunch buckets, waste baskets, coffeemakers, mixers, telephones, tape decks, and TV sets, along with the usual lines of cosmetics, toiletries, and tobacco. Many Walgreens also carry dairy products, frozen foods, and a large selection of other grocery items.

The company's newest stores are 13,500 square feet and often include pharmacy waiting areas, consultation windows, fragrance bars, and one-hour photo-finishing services.

Prescription drugs account for 45 percent of the company's $11.8 billion in annual revenue. Nonprescription drugs account for 13 percent; liquor and beverages, 7 percent; cosmetics and toiletries, 8 percent; tobacco products, 3 percent; and general merchandise, 24 percent.

Walgreen's greatest concentration of stores is around its Chicago home base, with 318 stores in Illinois, 114 in Wisconsin, and 103 in Indiana. Other leading areas are Florida, with 370 stores; Arizona, 128; California, 139; Texas, 213; Massachusetts, 71; Minnesota, 61; Missouri, 71; and Tennessee, 76.

All of the company's stores are linked by satellite dish to Walgreen's home office, enabling the company to track inventory, monitor sales levels, and provide prescription histories for Walgreen customers.

Walgreen has 77,000 employees and 38,000 shareholders.

EARNINGS-PER-SHARE GROWTH ★ ★

Past 5 years: 90 percent (14 percent per year)
Past 10 years: 257 percent (14 percent per year)

STOCK GROWTH ★ ★ ★

Past 10 years: 403 percent (17.5 percent per year)
Dollar growth: $10,000 over 10 years (including reinvested dividends) would have grown to $57,000
Average annual compounded rate of return (including reinvested dividends): 19 percent

DIVIDEND YIELD

Average dividend yield in the past 3 years: 1.6 percent

DIVIDEND GROWTH

Increased dividend: 10 consecutive years
Past 5-year increase: 91 percent (14 percent per year)

CONSISTENCY ★ ★ ★ ★

Increased earnings per share: 10 consecutive years
Increased sales: 10 consecutive years

SHAREHOLDER PERKS ★ ★

Good dividend reinvestment and stock purchase plan: voluntary stock purchase plan allows contributions of $10 to $5,000 per quarter.

Shareholders who attend the Walgreen annual meeting usually receive one or two Walgreen products, such as vitamins or other personal care products.

WALGREEN AT A GLANCE

Fiscal year ended: Aug. 31
Revenue and net income in $ millions

	1991	1992	1993	1994	1995	1996	5-Year Growth Avg. Annual (%)	Total (%)
Revenue ($)	6,733	7,475	8,294.8	9,235	10,395	11,778	12	75
Net income ($)	195	220.6	221.7	281.9	320.8	371.7	14	91
Earnings/share ($)	0.79	0.89	0.99	1.14	1.30	1.50	14	90
Div. per share ($)	.23	.26	.30	.34	.39	.44	14	91
Dividend yield (%)	1.6	1.5	1.5	1.7	1.7	1.4	—	—
Avg. PE ratio	19	20	20	17	18	21	—	—

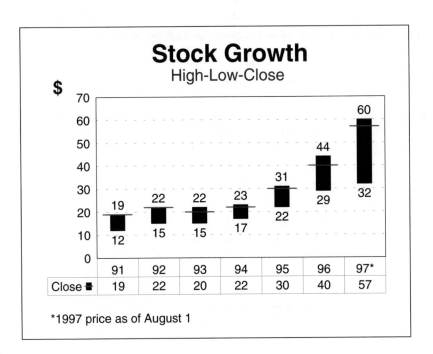

Stock Growth
High-Low-Close

	91	92	93	94	95	96	97*
Close	19	22	20	22	30	40	57

*1997 price as of August 1

26

SunTrust Banks, Inc.

SUNTRUST

303 Peachtree Street, N.E.
Atlanta, GA 30308
404-588-7711

Chairman and CEO: James B. Williams
President: L. Phillip Humann

Earnings Growth	★ ★	Dividend Growth	★ ★ ★
Stock Growth	★ ★	Consistency	★ ★ ★ ★
Dividend Yield	★ ★ ★	Shareholder Perks	★ ★
NYSE—STI		**Total**	**16 points**

SunTrust Banks continues to grow by adding innovative new services for its customers. The Atlanta-based institution was one of the first banks to offer "PC Banking," a home-banking service using personal computers, and it recently launched an in-store banking program to offer customers convenient banking services in Publix Super Markets in Georgia and Winn-Dixie stores in Tennessee.

SunTrust operates more than 650 banking offices in Florida, Georgia, Tennessee, and Alabama.

The company offers traditional banking services such as savings, consumer loans, trust and investment management, as well as such additional services as corporate finance, mortgage banking, credit cards, discount brokerage, data processing, and information services.

SunTrust is the third largest bank holding company in the Southeast.

The company's Florida operations account for 49 percent of its $616 million in net income generated by the firm's banking segment, while its

Georgia banks account for 37 percent of its net income, and its combined Tennessee and Alabama operations account for 14 percent.

The company took on its present identity as SunTrust Banks in 1985 with the merger of Sun Banks of Florida and Trust Company of Georgia. It has grown rapidly through a series of acquisitions throughout its four-state operating area.

The Atlanta-based institution must credit part of its strong recent growth to an investment it picked up in 1919 as the Trust Company of Georgia.

When the Coca-Cola Company went public in 1919, it gave 5,000 shares (worth $110,000) of its stock as part of the underwriting fee to the two underwriters, JP Morgan Bank and the Trust Company of Georgia (now SunTrust Banks). JP Morgan sold its stock, but Trust Company held on to its original shares.

After years of stock splits, that original $110,000 investment is now worth about $3 billion. Over the past ten years, Coca-Cola has been one of the fastest-growing stocks on the New York Stock Exchange. Even when the banking business is in a funk, SunTrust continues to ride high on the strength of its Coca-Cola stock.

SunTrust has about 19,400 employees.

EARNINGS-PER-SHARE GROWTH ★ ★

Past 5 years: 90 percent (14 percent per year)
Past 10 years: 197 percent (11.5 percent per year)

STOCK GROWTH ★ ★

Past 10 years: 334 percent (16 percent per year)
Dollar growth: $10,000 over 10 years (including reinvested dividends) would have grown to $57,000
Average annual compounded rate of return (including reinvested dividends): 19 percent

DIVIDEND YIELD ★ ★ ★

Average dividend yield in the past 3 years: 2.5 percent

DIVIDEND GROWTH

Increased dividend: More than 19 consecutive years
Past 5-year increase: 77 percent (12 percent per year)

CONSISTENCY ★ ★ ★ ★

Increased earnings per share: 17 consecutive years

SHAREHOLDER PERKS

Good dividend reinvestment and stock purchase plan: voluntary stock purchase plan allows contributions of $10 to $60,000 per year.

SUNTRUST BANKS AT A GLANCE

Fiscal year ended: Dec. 31
Total assets and net income in $ millions

	1991	1992	1993	1994	1995	1996	5-Year Growth Avg. Annual (%)	5-Year Growth Total (%)
Total assets ($)	34.554	36,649	40,728	42,709	46,471	52,468	9	52
Net income ($)	377.3	404.4	473.7	522.7	565.5	616.6	10	63
Earnings/share ($)	1.45	1.64	1.89	2.19	2.47	2.76	14	90
Div. per share ($)	.47	.52	.58	.66	.74	.83	12	77
Dividend yield (%)	3.0	2.6	2.6	2.8	2.5	2.1	—	—
Avg. PE ratio	11	12	12	11	12	14	—	—

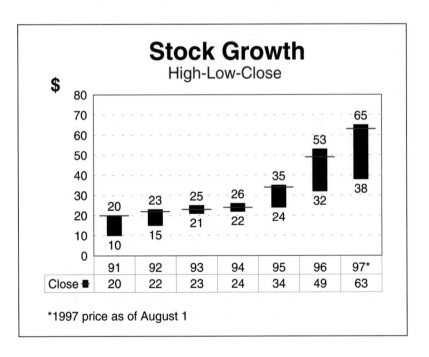

Stock Growth
High-Low-Close

	91	92	93	94	95	96	97*
Close	20	22	23	24	34	49	63

*1997 price as of August 1

ConAgra, Inc.

One ConAgra Drive
Omaha, NE 68102-5001
402-595-4000

Chairman and CEO: Philip B. Fletcher

Earnings Growth	★	Dividend Growth	★ ★ ★ ★
Stock Growth	★ ★	Consistency	★ ★ ★ ★
Dividend Yield	★ ★ ★	Shareholder Perks	★ ★
NYSE—CAG		**Total**	**16 points**

ConAgra operates across the broad food chain, providing farmers with feed grains and fertilizer, and consumers with a wide spread of meats, seafood, and brand-name frozen and prepared foods.

Among the company's most recognized brands are Hunt's, Peter Pan, Orville Redenbacher's, Wesson, Morton, Chun King, Banquet, Armour, Country Pride, Eckrich, and Healthy Choice. Other well-known brands include Swiss Miss, Manwich, La Choy, Patio, Decker, Butterball turkey, and Country Skillet. Grocery and diversified products account for about 21 percent of the company's $24.8 billion in annual revenue, while refrigerated foods account for about 52 percent of its revenue. In addition to its popular name-brand foods, the company also produces frozen potato products, delicatessen and food-service products, pet accessories, and Singer sewing accessories.

The company's other leading business segment is its food inputs and ingredients division, which accounts for 26.5 percent of the company's revenue. The company is involved in a wide range of agricultural-related ventures, including grain merchandising, crop inputs (fertilizers, seeds, insecticides, and other crop protection chemicals), commodity services, specialty food ingredients, and dry edible bean production. Based in Omaha, Nebraska, the 77-year-old operation has been one of the nation's most consistent food companies. It has posted record earnings and revenue for 16 consecutive years. It is the nation's second-largest food processor.

ConAgra owns 120 retail stores under the names Country General, Wheelers, S & S, Sanvig's, and Peavy Ranch, Home, and Security Feed & Seed. ConAgra Flour Milling Company is a leader in the U.S. flour milling industry with 24 mills in 13 states. ConAgra's commodity trading business has offices in 15 nations, trading agricultural commodities and foodstuffs on the world market.

The company has 83,000 employees and 144,000 shareholders of record. In all, ConAgra has operations in 27 countries.

EARNINGS-PER-SHARE GROWTH   ★

Past 5 years: 65 percent (11 percent per year)
Past 10 years: 244 percent (13 percent per year)

STOCK GROWTH   ★ ★

Past 10 years: 334 percent (16 percent per year)
Dollar growth: $10,000 over 10 years (including reinvested dividends) would have grown to $53,000
Average annual compounded rate of return (including reinvested dividends): 18 percent

DIVIDEND YIELD   ★ ★ ★

Average dividend yield in the past 3 years: 2.6 percent

DIVIDEND GROWTH   ★ ★ ★ ★

Increased dividend: 21 consecutive years
Past 5-year increase: 111 percent (16 percent per year)

CONSISTENCY   ★ ★ ★ ★

Increased earnings per share: 16 consecutive years
Increased sales: 16 consecutive years

SHAREHOLDER PERKS   ★ ★

Good dividend reinvestment and stock purchase plan: voluntary stock purchase plan allows contributions of $50 to $50,000 per year. Nearly 40 percent of stockholders participate.

At its annual meetings, the company passes out gift packs of some of its foods to its shareholders, and it sometimes sends out discount offers along with its quarterly earnings reports.

CONAGRA AT A GLANCE

Fiscal year ended: May 31
Revenue and net income in $ millions

	1991	1992	1993	1994	1995	1996	5-Year Growth Avg. Annual (%)	5-Year Growth Total (%)
Revenue ($)	19,528	21,236	21,544	23,517	24,112	24,821	5	27
Net income ($)	311.2	372.4	391.5	437.1	495.6	545.2	12	75
Earnings/share ($)	1.42	1.50	1.58	1.81	2.06	2.34	11	65
Div. per share ($)	.45	.52	.60	.70	.80	.95	16	111
Dividend yield (%)	1.8	1.7	2.3	2.7	2.6	2.4	—	—
Avg. PE ratio	18	20	18	15	16	17	—	—

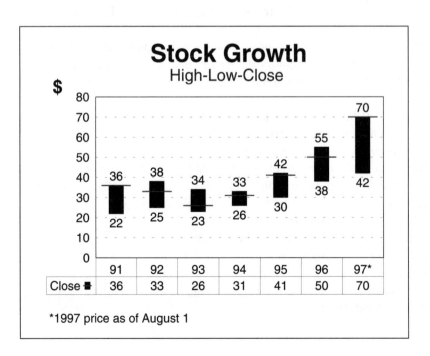

Stock Growth
High-Low-Close

	91	92	93	94	95	96	97*
Close	36	33	26	31	41	50	70

*1997 price as of August 1

28
Intel Corp.

2200 Mission College Blvd.
Santa Clara, CA 95052-8119
408-765-8080

Chairman: Gordon E. Moore
President and CEO: Andrew S. Grove

Earnings Growth	★ ★ ★ ★	Dividend Growth	★ ★
Stock Growth	★ ★ ★ ★	Consistency	★ ★ ★
Dividend Yield		Shareholder Perks	★ ★
Nasdaq—INTC		**Total**	**15 points**

The speed and power of personal computers continue to grow at a dizzying pace, thanks to the continuing development of the Intel microprocessors.

Intel's computer microchips process system data and control input, output, and peripheral and memory devices in the PC. With its Pentium chips, Intel is the dominant player in the worldwide microprocessor market.

Founded in 1968, the Santa Clara, California, company has been the world leader in the microchip market since the mid-1980s, after designing the original microprocessor for the IBM PC. It has maintained its lead by first turning out its popular 286 chip, followed by the 386, then the 486, and finally the Pentium generation of chips. Worldwide, well over 100 million PCs are based on Intel architecture. Intel's primary customers are manufacturers of microcomputers.

The U.S. market accounts for about 49 percent of Intel's $20.8 billion in annual revenue. Its other leading markets are Europe (28 percent of revenue), Asia-Pacific (12 percent), and Japan (11 percent).

In addition to its standard microprocessing chips, Intel produces a line of related products including:

- **Microcontrollers.** Intel produces a wide range of single-chip computers (also called "embedded controllers") used to control the operation of communications systems, automobile control applications, robotics, electronic instrumentation, keyboards, home video machines, and other high-tech products.
- **Computer modules and boards.** These are sold to manufacturers who integrate them into their products.
- **Network and communications products.** Intel's products help computers communicate with each other and provide access to online services.
- **Personal conferencing products.** PC users can install Intel software and cards that allow two users to view and manipulate the same documents simultaneously.
- **Parallel supercomputers.** The company's high-performance computer systems use multiple microprocessors to speed up the processing function and solve complex computational problems.
- **Semiconductor products.** Intel's flash memory products provide easily reprogrammable memory for cellular phones, computers, and other systems.

Intel has about 46,000 employees and 70,000 shareholders.

EARNINGS-PER-SHARE GROWTH ★ ★ ★ ★

Past 5 years: 492 percent (42 percent per year)
Past 10 years: 2,224 percent (37 percent per year)

STOCK GROWTH ★ ★ ★ ★

Past 10 years: 3,133 percent (45 percent per year)
Dollar growth: $10,000 over 10 years (including reinvested dividends) would have grown to $320,000
Average annual compounded rate of return (including reinvested dividends): 45 percent

DIVIDEND YIELD   (no points)

Average dividend yield in the past 3 years: 0.3 percent

DIVIDEND GROWTH

Increased dividend: 5 consecutive years
Past 4-year increase (Intel has only offered a dividend for 5 years): 280 percent (31 percent per year)

CONSISTENCY   ★ ★ ★

Increased earnings per share: 9 of the past 10 years
Increased sales: 10 consecutive years

SHAREHOLDER PERKS

The company offers an excellent dividend reinvestment and stock purchase plan. Shareholders of record may have their dividends automatically reinvested, and purchase $25 to $15,000 per month in additional shares through the voluntary stock purchase plan.

INTEL AT A GLANCE

Fiscal year ended: Dec. 31
Revenue and net income in $ millions

	1991	1992	1993	1994	1995	1996	5-Year Growth Avg. Annual (%)	Total (%)
Revenue ($)	4,779	5,844	8,782	11,521	16,202	20,807	34	335
Net income ($)	819	1,067	2,295	2,288	3,566	5,147	44	528
Earnings/share ($)	.098	1.24	2.60	2.62	4.03	5.80	42	492
Div. per share ($)	—	.05	.10	.12	.15	.19	31	280 4-Yr.
Dividend yield (%)	—	.2	.3	.4	.3	.2	—	—
Avg. PE ratio	12	12	11	11	14	14	—	—

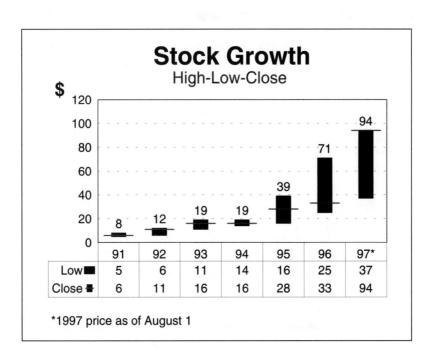

Stock Growth
High-Low-Close

	91	92	93	94	95	96	97*
Low ■	5	6	11	14	16	25	37
Close ✹	6	11	16	16	28	33	94

*1997 price as of August 1

29

Newell Company

29 East Stephenson Street
Freeport, IL 61032-0943
815-235-4171

Chairman: Daniel C. Ferguson
CEO: William P. Scovey
President: Thomas A. Ferguson, Jr.

Earnings Growth	★ ★	Dividend Growth	★ ★
Stock Growth	★ ★ ★ ★	Consistency	★ ★ ★
Dividend Yield	★ ★	Shareholder Perks	★ ★
NYSE—NWL		**Total**	**15 points**

Newellization—a term the Newell Company has coined to describe its phenomenal success in acquiring other companies, streamlining them, and assimilating them into the Newel system. Newell has been one of the nation's fastest-growing companies primarily by acquiring smaller related operations and increasing their profitability.

Newell, which is one of the nation's largest manufacturers of housewares, home furnishings, hardware, and office products, has added more than $2 billion in annual revenue through the acquisitions it has made in the past decade. The Freeport, Illinois, manufacturer is a leading supplier for Wal-Mart, Kmart, Home Depot, Target, Office Depot, JC Penney, and other leading discount and department stores.

Newell's success has come with little consumer awareness. Although its goods are sold in hundreds of stores from coast to coast, you may never see the Newell brand name on the shelves. Many of its goods are custom-labeled for its clients (such as True Value paintbrushes or Target cookware). The company also markets a wide range of products under other labels. Among its leading brands are Anchor Hocking glassware, Amerock hardware, Mirro cookware, and EZ Paintr paint applicators.

Newell's leading product segment is housewares, which accounts for about 33 percent of its $2.9 billion in annual sales. Its other segments are home furnishings (29 percent), office products (23 percent), and hardware (15 percent). Newell has 23,000 employees and 12,500 stockholders.

EARNINGS-PER-SHARE GROWTH

Past 5 years: 82 percent (13 percent per year)
Past 10 years: 500 percent (20 percent per year)

STOCK GROWTH ★ ★ ★ ★

Past 10 years: 775 percent (24 percent per year)
Dollar growth: $10,000 over 10 years (including reinvested dividends) would have grown to $100,000
Average annual compounded rate of return (including reinvested dividends): 26 percent

DIVIDEND YIELD ★ ★

Average dividend yield in the past 3 years: 1.9 percent

DIVIDEND GROWTH ★ ★

Increased dividend: 9 of the past 10 years
Past 5-year increase: 87 percent (13 percent per year)

CONSISTENCY ★ ★ ★

Increased earnings per share: 9 of the past 10 years
Increased sales: 9 of the past 10 years

SHAREHOLDER PERKS

Good dividend reinvestment and stock purchase plan: voluntary stock purchase plan allows contributions of $10 to $30,000 per year.

The company often hands out product samples or special gifts to shareholders at the annual meeting.

NEWELL AT A GLANCE

Fiscal year ended: Dec. 31
Revenue and net income in $ millions

	1991	1992	1993	1994	1995	1996	5-Year Growth Avg. Annual (%)	Total (%)
Revenue ($)	1,259	1,452	1,645	2,075	2,498	2,873	18	128
Net income ($)	135.6	163.3	165.3	195.6	222.5	256.5	14	89
Earnings/share ($)	0.89	1.05	1.05	1.24	1.41	1.62	13	82
Div. per share ($)	.30	.30	.35	.39	.46	.56	13	87
Dividend yield (%)	1.7	1.4	1.8	1.8	1.9	1.9	—	—
Avg. PE ratio	20	20	18	17	17	19	—	—

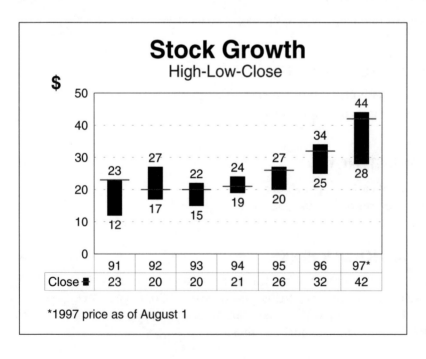

Stock Growth
High-Low-Close

	91	92	93	94	95	96	97*
Close	23	20	20	21	26	32	42

*1997 price as of August 1

The Procter & Gamble Company

One Procter & Gamble Plaza
Cincinnati, OH 45202
513-983-1100

Chairman and CEO: John E. Pepper
President: Durk I. Jager

Earnings Growth	★	Dividend Growth	★ ★ ★
Stock Growth	★ ★ ★	Consistency	★ ★ ★ ★
Dividend Yield	★ ★	Shareholder Perks	★ ★
NYSE—PG		**Total**	**15 points**

For half a century, Tide detergent has been sudsing its way through America's dirty laundry. Since shortly after it was introduced in 1946, Tide has been the nation's number one laundry detergent. It is the sixth largest of all brands sold in U.S. grocery stores, and the single-largest-selling product of the Procter & Gamble Company.

But several other P&G products are close behind. The Cincinnati-based operation makes many of America's favorite consumer products, including Cheer, Crest, Pampers, Pringles, Bounty, and Joy.

Founded in 1837 by William Procter and James Gamble, the company is the world's leading producer of soaps and cosmetics. It also churns out a wide range of other consumer staples. In fact, in all, the company puts more than 300 brands on the market in more than 140 countries around the world. Sales outside of North America account for just over 50 percent of the company's $35.3 billion in annual revenue.

Procter & Gamble has managed to maintain its strong market position through a relentless advertising approach. For many years, the company has been TV's biggest advertiser.

The firm divides its product offerings into several key categories:

- **Laundry and cleaning products** (30 percent of total revenue). Leading brands include Tide, Cheer, Spic and Span, Prell, Comet, Lestoil, Mr. Clean, Bold, Dash, Dreft, Era, Gain, Ivory, Oxydol, Top Job, Cascade, Dawn, Bounce, Downy, and Joy.
- **Paper** (29 percent of revenue). Leading brands include Bounty, Pampers, Always, Charmin, Whisper, and Attends.
- **Beauty care** (20 percent). The company makes a wide range of beauty care products, including Vidal Sassoon, Secret, Clearasil, Noxzema, Coast, Lava, Oil of Olay, Safeguard, Zest, Cover Girl, Max Factor, Sure, Head & Shoulders, and Old Spice.
- **Food and beverages** (12 percent). Leading products include Crisco, Duncan Hines, Pringles, Fisher Nuts, Folgers Coffee, Hawaiian Punch, Jif, Pringles, and Sunny Delight Florida Citrus Punch.
- **Health care** (9 percent). The company makes Crest, Gleem, Scope, Metamucil, Vicks, Pepto-Bismol, and a number of prescription and over-the-counter medications.

P&G has 103,000 employees and about 215,000 shareholders.

EARNINGS-PER-SHARE GROWTH ★

Past 5 years: 74 percent (12 percent per year)
Past 10 years: 309 percent (15 percent per year)

STOCK GROWTH

Past 10 years: 490 percent (19 percent per year)
Dollar growth: $10,000 over 10 years (including reinvested dividends) would have grown to $67,000
Average annual compounded rate of return (including reinvested dividends): 22 percent

DIVIDEND YIELD

Average dividend yield in the past 3 years: 2.2 percent

DIVIDEND GROWTH ★ ★ ★

Increased dividend: 40 consecutive years
Past 5-year increase: 63 percent (10 percent per year)

CONSISTENCY ★ ★ ★ ★

Increased earnings per share: 10 consecutive years
Increased sales: 9 of the past 10 years

SHAREHOLDER PERKS ★ ★

Good dividend reinvestment and stock purchase plan: initial minimum of
$250, then payments of a minimum of $100 to a maximum of $120,000
annually.

PROCTER & GAMBLE AT A GLANCE

Fiscal year ended: Dec. 31
Revenue and net income in $ millions

	1991	1992	1993	1994	1995	1996	5-Year Growth Avg. Annual (%)	Total (%)
Revenue ($)	27.0	29.4	30.5	30.4	33.5	35.3	6	31
Net income ($)	1.8	1.9	2.2	2.2	2.6	3.0	11	67
Earnings/share ($)	2.46	2.62	2.82	3.09	3.71	4.29	12	74
Div. per share ($)	0.98	1.03	1.10	1.24	1.40	1.60	10	63
Dividend yield (%)	2.4	2.3	2.2	2.3	2.2	2.0	—	—
Avg. PE ratio	17	17	18	18	17	19	—	—

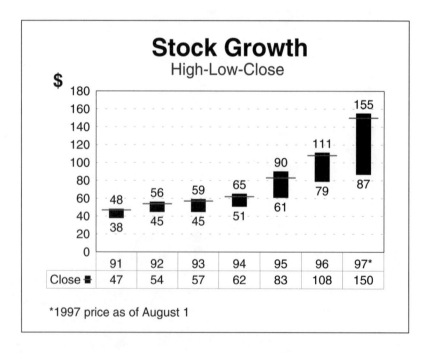

Stock Growth
High-Low-Close

	91	92	93	94	95	96	97*
Close ■	47	54	57	62	83	108	150

*1997 price as of August 1

31

Cintas Corp.

6800 Cintas Blvd.
P. O. Box 625737
Cincinnati, OH 45262-5737
513-459-1200

Chairman: Richard T. Farmer
President and CEO: Robert J. Kohlhepp

Earnings Growth	★ ★ ★	Dividend Growth	★ ★ ★ ★
Stock Growth	★ ★ ★	Consistency	★ ★ ★ ★
Dividend Yield	★	Shareholder Perks	
Nasdaq—CTAS		**Total**	**15 points**

Cintas puts more than a million men and women in uniform every working day. The Cincinnati-based operation supplies uniforms for a wide range of businesses—from airlines and delivery services to service stations and retail chains. For Cintas, the uniform business has produced uniform financial returns for many years. The company has posted 27 consecutive years of record sales and earnings.

Cintas operates 126 uniform rental centers in 118 cities in 35 states and the province of Ontario, Canada. It also has four garment manufacturing plants and three distribution centers. The company's customer base extends from coast to coast. It is the largest public company in the uniform business. The company rents or sells the uniforms to customer companies, and typically provides the laundry services as well.

Much of the company's growth has come through acquisitions. Since going public in 1983, Cintas has acquired more than 80 smaller regional uniform companies. And with more than 700 mostly family-owned uniform rental companies still operating in the United States, Cintas plans to continue its aggressive acquisition policy.

Most of the company's revenue comes from uniform rentals, which accounted for 67 percent of its $730 million in total revenue. Uniform sales accounted for 11 percent of revenue, and nonuniform rentals

113

(towels, mops, mats, fender covers, and linen products) accounted for about 21 percent. Founded in 1929, Cintas has about 11,000 employees and 1,700 shareholders.

EARNINGS-PER-SHARE GROWTH   ★ ★ ★

Past 5 years: 132 percent (19 percent per year)
Past 10 years: 452 percent (16 percent per year)

STOCK GROWTH   ★ ★ ★

Past 10 years: 587 percent (21 percent per year)
Dollar growth: $10,000 over 10 years (including reinvested dividends) would have grown to $71,000
Average annual compounded rate of return (including reinvested dividends): 21.5 percent

DIVIDEND YIELD   ★

Average dividend yield in the past 3 years: 0.6 percent

DIVIDEND GROWTH   ★ ★ ★ ★

Increased dividend: 12 consecutive years
Past 5-year increase: 150 percent (20 percent per year)

CONSISTENCY   ★ ★ ★ ★

Increased earnings per share: 27 consecutive years
Increased sales: 27 consecutive years

SHAREHOLDER PERKS   (no points)

The company offers no dividend reinvestment and stock purchase plan, nor does it provide any other shareholder perks.

CINTAS AT A GLANCE

Fiscal year ended: May 31
Revenue and net income in $ millions

	1991	1992	1993	1994	1995	1996	5-Year Growth Avg. Annual (%)	Total (%)
Revenue ($)	352.5	401.6	452.7	523.2	615.1	730.1	16	107
Net income ($)	31.3	36.5	44.9	52.2	62.7	75.2	20	142
Earnings/share ($)	0.69	0.79	0.97	1.13	1.34	1.60	19	132
Div. per share ($)	.10	.11	.14	.17	.20	.25	20	150
Dividend yield (%)	.5	.4	.5	.6	.6	.6	—	—
Avg. PE ratio	23	33	28	26	26	28	—	—

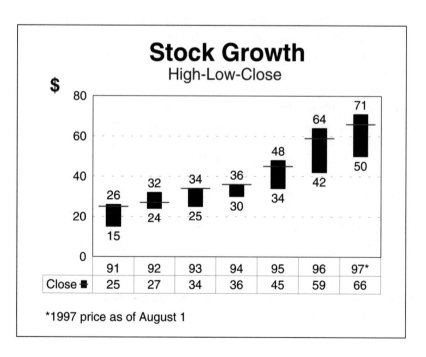

Stock Growth
High-Low-Close

Close	91	92	93	94	95	96	97*
	25	27	34	36	45	59	66

*1997 price as of August 1

32

Valspar Corp.

The Valspar Corporation

1101 Third Street South
Minneapolis, MN 55415
612-332-7371

Chairman: C. Angus Wurtele
Vice Chairman: Robert E. Pajor
President and CEO: Richard M. Rompala

Earnings Growth	★ ★	Dividend Growth	★ ★ ★ ★
Stock Growth	★ ★ ★	Consistency	★ ★ ★ ★
Dividend Yield	★ ★	Shareholder Perks	
NYSE—VAL		**Total**	**15 points**

Valspar is taking aim at the global market. The Minneapolis-based paints and coatings manufacturer has been pressing into the European and Asian markets, and recently began production at its new can-coatings plant in Shenzhen, China.

Valspar's biggest step yet in the international market has been its recent acquisition of Coates Coatings, a can-coatings and metal-decorating inks company with global sales of about $125 million per year. Under the agreement, Valspar acquired Coates divisions in France, the United Kingdom, Norway, Germany, Spain, Australia, Hong Kong, and China in 1996, and will acquire other divisions in South Africa, India, and several other Southeast Asian countries over the next four years.

Valspar is the sixth largest manufacturer of paints and coatings in the United States, with 20 plants throughout North America.

The company's largest and fastest-growing division is the consumer paints group, which accounts for 34 percent of Valspar's $860 million in annual sales. The company sells a line of latex and oil-based paints, stains, and varnishes primarily to the do-it-yourself market. Brand names include Colony, Valspar, Enterprise, Magicolor, BPS, McCloskey, and Masury.

Valspar's other divisions include:

- **Packaging coatings** (27 percent of revenue). Valspar is North America's largest supplier of coatings for the rigid packaging industry. Its leading segment is the production of coatings for food and beverage cans.
- **Industrial coatings** (24 percent). The firm produces decorative and protective coatings for wood, metal, and plastics, and is a major supplier to the furniture and wood-paneling industry.
- **Special products** (15 percent). Valspar manufactures coatings and resins for marine applications, heavy-duty maintenance, and high-performance floor finishing.

Valspar traces its origins to a Boston paint shop called Color and Paint, which opened in 1806. That business eventually became Valentine & Company, which introduced a line of Valspar quick-drying varnishes and stains in 1906. Valspar was touted as "the varnish that won't turn white." Its claim to fame was a boiling-water test that Valspar-varnished woods could endure with no apparent ill effects.

The company has 2,800 employees and about 1,900 shareholders.

EARNINGS-PER-SHARE GROWTH ★ ★

Past 5 years: 98 percent (14 percent per year)
Past 10 years: 313 percent (15 percent per year)

STOCK GROWTH ★ ★ ★

Past 10 years: 487 percent (19 percent per year)
Dollar growth: $10,000 over 10 years (including reinvested dividends) would have grown to $67,000
Average annual compounded rate of return (including reinvested dividends): 21 percent

DIVIDEND YIELD ★ ★

Average dividend yield in the past 3 years: 1.5 percent

DIVIDEND GROWTH   ★ ★ ★ ★

Increased dividend: 19 consecutive years
Past 5-year increase: 120 percent (17 percent per year)

CONSISTENCY   ★ ★ ★ ★

Increased earnings per share: 22 consecutive years
Increased sales: 10 consecutive years

SHAREHOLDER PERKS   (no points)

Valspar provides no dividend reinvestment plan, nor does it offer any other special perks for its shareholders.

VALSPAR AT A GLANCE

Fiscal year ended: Sept. 30
Revenue and net income in $ millions

	1991	1992	1993	1994	1995	1996	5-Year Growth Avg. Annual (%)	Total (%)
Revenue ($)	632.6	683.5	700.9	795.3	790.2	859.8	6	36
Net income ($)	27.7	34.4	40.2	45.8	47.5	55.9	15	102
Earnings/share ($)	1.27	1.57	1.85	2.07	2.15	2.52	14	98
Div. per share ($)	.30	.36	.44	.52	.60	.66	17	120
Dividend yield (%)	1.5	1.2	1.2	1.5	1.6	1.5	—	—
Avg. PE ratio	16	20	19	18	17	18	—	—

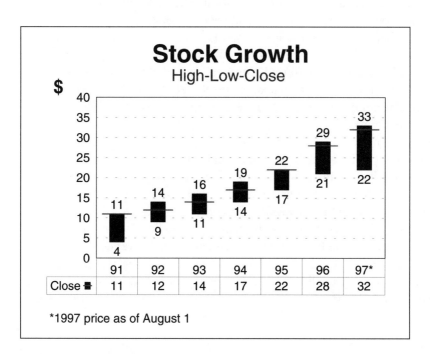

Stock Growth
High-Low-Close

	91	92	93	94	95	96	97*
Close	11	12	14	17	22	28	32

*1997 price as of August 1

33

Sara Lee Corp.

Three First National Plaza
Chicago, IL 60602-4260
312-726-2600

Chairman and CEO: John H. Bryan

Earnings Growth	★	Dividend Growth	★ ★ ★
Stock Growth	★ ★	Consistency	★ ★ ★ ★
Dividend Yield	★ ★ ★	Shareholder Perks	★ ★
NYSE—SLE		**Total**	**15 points**

Sara Lee's tasty baked goods get all the attention, but behind the scenes, slowly, steadily, through a series of acquisitions, the Chicago-based operation has also become the world leader in packaged meats.

The maker of Ball Park Franks, Best's Kosher, Hillshire Farms, Mr. Turkey, State Fair, Argal, Hygrade, Imperial, and Jimmy Dean packaged meats, Sara Lee recently acquired European-based Aoste meats. The acquisition tripled its European packaged meats sales to well over $1 billion a year. The company already had the number one position in the U.S. packaged meat market.

Sara Lee's packaged meats and bakery goods divisions account for about 35 percent of its $18.6 billion in annual sales.

But despite its dominant position in packaged meats and frozen desserts, Sara Lee's leading product segment is personal products. With its Hanes, Playtex, L'eggs, Isotoner, Sheer Energy, Wonderbra, Champion, and other lines of hosiery, knits, and intimate apparel, Sara Lee's personal products segment accounts for about 40 percent of total revenue.

Sara Lee is the leading manufacturer of women's hosiery and brassieres, and the second leading manufacturer of men's and boys' underwear and printed T-shirts.

Sara Lee's other segments include:

- **Household and body care products** (10 percent of revenue). Sara Lee's household goods and personal care products divisions generate 90 percent of its sales revenue outside the United States. The company makes shoe care products (Kiwi, Esquire, and Meltonian shoe polish), toiletries, over-the-counter medications, specialty detergents, and insecticides.
- **Coffee and grocery products** (15 percent of sales). Sara Lee holds leading positions in coffee sales in several Scandinavian countries. Its brands include Chat Noir, Douwe Egbert, Maison du Cafe, Merrild, and several other lines. It also owns Duyvis nuts. More than 80 percent of the company's coffee and grocery products revenue is generated outside the United States.

Sara Lee has operations in more than 40 countries and sales in about 140 countries. Foreign sales account for about 39 percent of total revenue.

Sara Lee was founded in 1939 when Nathan Cummings acquired the C. D. Kenny Company, a small Baltimore sugar, tea, and coffee distributor. The company changed its named to Consolidated Grocers Corporation in 1945—a name that stuck until 1985 when the firm changed names again, this time to Sara Lee.

The company has about 135,000 employees and 91,000 shareholders.

EARNINGS-PER-SHARE GROWTH ★

Past 5 years: 69 percent (11 percent per year)
Past 10 years: 259 percent (13 percent per year)

STOCK GROWTH ★ ★

Past 10 years: 393 percent (17 percent per year)
Dollar growth: $10,000 over 10 years (including reinvested dividends) would have grown to $61,000
Average annual compounded rate of return (including reinvested dividends): 20 percent

DIVIDEND YIELD   ★ ★ ★

Average dividend yield in the past 3 years: 2.6 percent

DIVIDEND GROWTH   ★ ★ ★

Increased dividend: 19 consecutive years
Past 5-year increase: 61 percent (10 percent per year)

CONSISTENCY   ★ ★ ★ ★

Increased earnings per share: 21 consecutive years
Increased sales: 9 of the past 10 years

SHAREHOLDER PERKS   ★ ★

Good dividend reinvestment and stock purchase plan: voluntary stock purchase plan allows contributions of $10 to $5,000 per quarter.

Each year at the annual meeting, Sara Lee shareholders receive gift boxes of Sara Lee products, including such items as coupons, bath soaps, and coffee samples. At a recent meeting, shareholders also received Chicago Bulls T-shirts and key chains.

SARA LEE AT A GLANCE

Fiscal year ended: Dec. 31
Revenue and net income in $ millions

	1991	1992	1993	1994	1995	1996	5-Year Growth Avg. Annual (%)	Total (%)
Revenue ($)	12,381	13,243	14,580	15,536	17,719	18,624	9	50
Net income ($)	535	761	704	729	804	916	12	71
Earnings/share ($)	1.08	1.54	1.40	1.47	1.62	1.83	11	69
Div. per share ($)	.46	.61	.56	.63	.67	.74	10	61
Dividend yield (%)	2.8	2.5	2.0	2.6	2.7	2.4	—	—
Avg. PE ratio	15	19	20	16	15	17	—	—

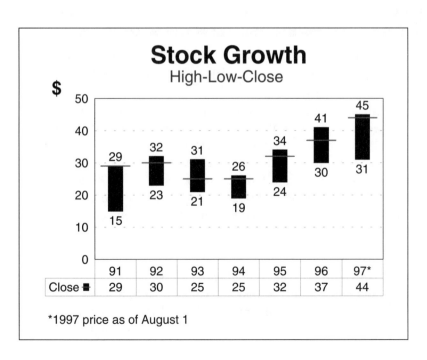

Stock Growth
High-Low-Close

	91	92	93	94	95	96	97*
Close	29	30	25	25	32	37	44

*1997 price as of August 1

Colgate-Palmolive Company

300 Park Avenue
New York, NY 10022
212-310-2000

Chairman and CEO: Reuben Mark
President: William S. Shanahan

Earnings Growth	★ ★	Dividend Growth	★ ★ ★
Stock Growth	★ ★	Consistency	★ ★ ★
Dividend Yield	★ ★ ★	Shareholder Perks	★ ★
NYSE—CL		**Total**	**15 points**

Founded in 1806, Colgate-Palmolive does a lot more these days than brighten your teeth. It feeds the dog, mops the floor, washes the laundry, lathers the baby, and softens the whiskers.

Colgate commands half of the world's market share of toothpaste and about one quarter of the soap and all-purpose cleaner markets. Its products are sold in 194 countries. Foreign sales account for about 68 percent of the company's $8.75 billion in annual revenue.

In addition to its Colgate and Ultra Brite toothpastes, the company makes a line of toothbrushes, dental floss, mouthwash, and professional dental products. Oral care products account for about 30 percent of total sales.

Colgate has four other leading product segments, including:

1. **Personal care products** (22 percent of revenue). The company makes a variety of soaps and related products such as Irish Spring and Palmolive bar soap, Softsoap liquid soap, Wash 'n Dri disposable towelettes, Speedstick and Irish Spring deodorants, Baby Magic baby

care products, and Colgate and Palmolive shave cream, Skin Bracer and Afta Aftershave.

2. **Household and surface care** (16 percent). Its leading brands include Ajax cleaners, Palmolive cleaners and detergents, and Murphy Oil Soap Cleaner.
3. **Fabric care** (18 percent). The company makes Fab and Dynamo, Ajax Ultra and Fresh Strt laundry detergents.
4. **Pet nutrition** (9 percent). Its Science Diet line of pet foods is one of the fastest-growing brands in the business.

One of the keys to Colgate's international success has been the development of new products that can work in multiple markets. The company has been generating more than half its sales in foreign markets since 1960, and has been selling toothpaste in Latin America since 1925.

The company's new product development process begins with its Global Technology and Business Development Groups that analyze consumer insights from targeted countries to create universal products. To improve the odds of their success, potential new products are test-marketed in leading countries that represent both developing and mature economies. For example, its Protex antibacterial soap was first introduced as bar soap nine years ago. Protex is now sold in 30 countries throughout Africa, Asia, and Latin America and is available in many countries as a talcum powder and a shower gel.

Colgate has about 33,000 employees and 44,000 shareholders.

EARNINGS-PER-SHARE GROWTH ★ ★

Past 5 years: 61 percent (10 percent per year)
Past 10 years: 233 percent (13 percent per year)

STOCK GROWTH ★ ★

Past 10 years: 376 percent (17 percent per year)
Dollar growth: $10,000 over 10 years (including reinvested dividends) would have grown to $61,000
Average annual compounded rate of return (including reinvested dividends): 20 percent

DIVIDEND YIELD   ★ ★ ★

Average dividend yield in the past 3 years: 2.5 percent

DIVIDEND GROWTH   ★ ★ ★

Increased dividend: More than 19 consecutive years
Past 5-year increase: 84 percent (13 percent per year)

CONSISTENCY   ★ ★ ★

Increased earnings per share: 9 of the past 10 years
Increased sales: 9 of the past 10 years

SHAREHOLDER PERKS   ★ ★

Good dividend reinvestment and stock purchase plan: voluntary stock
purchase plan allows contributions of $20 per month up to $60,000 per
year. (Nominal cash-in fee of $10 plus 12 cents per share.)

COLGATE-PALMOLIVE AT A GLANCE

Fiscal year ended: Dec. 31
Revenue and net income in $ millions

	1991	1992	1993	1994	1995	1996	5-Year Growth Avg. Annual (%)	Total (%)
Revenue ($)	6,060.3	7,007.2	7,141.3	7,587.9	8,358.2	8,749	8	44
Net income ($)	368	477	548.1	580.2	541.2	635	12	72
Earnings/share ($)	2.57	2.92	3.38	3.82	3.58	4.15	10	61
Div. per share ($)	1.02	1.15	1.34	1.54	1.76	1.88	13	84
Dividend yield (%)	2.5	2.1	2.2	2.5	2.5	2.3	—	—
Avg. PE ratio	15	18	17	15	19	20	—	—

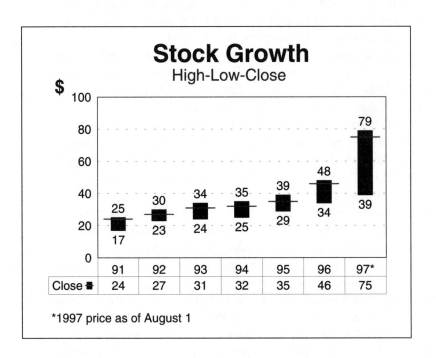

Stock Growth
High-Low-Close

	91	92	93	94	95	96	97*
Close	24	27	31	32	35	46	75

*1997 price as of August 1

35

Kimberly-Clark Corp.

P.O. Box 619100
Dallas, TX 75261-9100
972-281-1200

Chairman and CEO: Wayne R. Sanders

Earnings Growth	★ ★ ★ ★	Dividend Growth	★
Stock Growth	★ ★	Consistency	★ ★ ★
Dividend Yield	★ ★ ★	Shareholder Perks	★ ★
NYSE—KMB		**Total**	**15 points**

When Kimberly-Clark merged with Scott Paper in 1995, the combined operation suddenly became one of the world's largest personal care products companies. In fact, the Dallas-based manufacturer produces more tissue products than any other company in the world.

Of course, Kimberly-Clark had already been a major player in the tissue market even before the merger. Its Kleenex brand, which the company introduced in 1924, holds a 48 percent share of the U.S. facial tissue market. Kleenex tissues are sold in about 150 countries.

One of the company's biggest profit centers over the past several years has been disposable diapers. Its Huggies brand diaper is the top selling diaper in the United States, with about a 32 percent share. Huggies baby wipes hold a 23 percent share of the U.S. market. Huggies are sold in more than 100 countries.

Other familiar Kimberly-Clark products include Hi-Dri paper towels, Delsey toilet paper, Depend adult shields and undergarments, Scott napkins and paper products, and New Freedom feminine pads.

Kimberly-Clark's personal care products account for about 31 percent of its $13.1 billion in annual revenue.

The company's tissue-based products (paper towels, toilet paper, facial tissues, etc.) account for about 58 percent of its revenue.

Kimberly-Clark's other leading business segment is its newsprint and paper division, which accounts for 11 percent of the company's revenue.

Kimberly-Clark has operations worldwide, with manufacturing plants in 33 countries and sales in 150 countries. About 29 percent of its revenue is generated outside of North America. Founded in 1872, Kimberly-Clark has about 55,000 employees and 58,000 shareholders.

EARNINGS-PER-SHARE GROWTH ★ ★ ★ ★

Past 5 years: 190 percent (24 percent per year)
Past 10 years: 239 percent (13 percent per year)

STOCK GROWTH ★ ★

Past 10 years: 388 percent (17 percent per year)
Dollar growth: $10,000 over 10 years (including reinvested dividends) would have grown to $62,000
Average annual compounded rate of return (including reinvested dividends): 20 percent

DIVIDEND YIELD ★ ★ ★

Average dividend yield in the past 3 years: 2.8 percent

DIVIDEND GROWTH ★

Increased dividend: 24 consecutive years
Past 5-year increase: 26 percent (5 percent per year)

CONSISTENCY ★ ★ ★

Increased earnings per share: 9 of the past 10 years
Increased sales: 9 of the past 10 years

SHAREHOLDER PERKS

Dividend reinvestment and stock purchase plan: voluntary stock purchase plan allows contributions of up to $3,000 per quarter.

Kimberly-Clark also gives away a sample package of its products to shareholders who attend the annual meeting.

KIMBERLY-CLARK AT A GLANCE

Fiscal year ended: Dec. 31
Revenue and net income in $ millions

	1991	1992	1993	1994	1995	1996	5-Year Growth Avg. Annual (%)	Total (%)
Revenue ($)	11,627	12,024	11,646	11,979	13,788	13,149	3	13
Net income ($)	435.2	150.1	231	753.8	33.2	1,328.1	25	205
Earnings/share ($)	1.72	1.77	1.03	2.76	0.12	4.98	24	190
Div. per share ($)	1.45	1.64	1.70	1.75	1.79	1.83	5	26
Dividend yield (%)	3.3	3.0	3.3	3.2	2.9	2.3	—	—
Avg. PE ratio	14	17	16	17	16	17	—	—

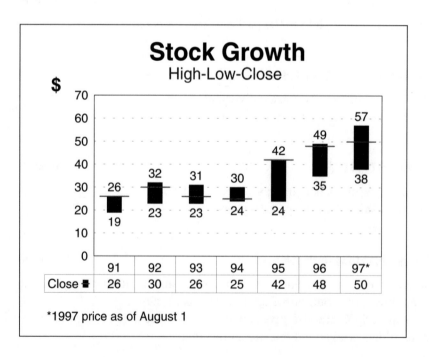

Stock Growth
High-Low-Close

	91	92	93	94	95	96	97*
Close ■	26	30	26	25	42	48	50

*1997 price as of August 1

Abbott Laboratories

One Abbot Park Road
Abbott Park, IL 60064-3500
847-937-6100

Chairman and CEO: Duane L. Burnham
President: Thomas R. Hodgson

Earnings Growth	★ ★	Dividend Growth	★ ★ ★
Stock Growth	★ ★	Consistency	★ ★ ★ ★
Dividend Yield	★ ★	Shareholder Perks	★ ★
NYSE—ABT		**Total**	**15 points**

The medical advances keep coming—and so do the profits —at Abbott Laboratories. The Chicago-based operation is one of the world's largest producers of pharmaceuticals and hospital products. The company has posted record sales, earnings, and dividends every year since 1971.

In addition to a broad range of prescription drugs and hospital supplies, the company has been expanding its line of over-the-counter nutritional products. Along with its traditional standards, Similac and Isomil infant formula, Abbott produces a variety of supplements geared to specific types of users.

Among its leading brands are Gain, a nutritional formula for children six months to three years old; Pedialyte, an oral electrolyte solution for fluid maintenance in infants and children; Ensure (and Ensure Light), an adult nutritional beverage; Glucerna, a beverage for diabetics; Advera, a nutritional beverage geared to patients with HIV and AIDS; and Pedia-Sure, a complete nutritional beverage for children one to ten years old.

Pharmaceutical and nutritional products account for about 56 percent of Abbott's $11 billion in annual sales.

Among its leading pharmaceuticals are clarithromycin (marketed under the brand names Biaxin, Klacid, and Karicid), an antibiotic originally developed to treat respiratory infections, and now also used to treat bacterial infection common in AIDS patients. The company also makes drugs for the treatment of anxiety, epilepsy, and hypertension. It is a leading producer of antibiotics, and it manufactures a broad line of cardiovascular products, cough and cold formulas, and vitamins.

The 107-year-old operation may be most widely recognized for its diagnostic products. It is the world leader in blood-screening equipment, and it was the first company to introduce an AIDS antibody test. It is also the world leader in tests for AIDS, hepatitis, sexually transmitted diseases, cancer, thyroid function, pregnancy, illicit drugs, and drug monitoring.

Hospital and laboratory products account for about 44 percent of Abbott's annual revenue. Leading products include critical care monitoring instruments, intravenous and irrigation fluids (and the equipment to administer them), drug delivery devices, and multiapplication diagnostic machines.

Abbott is the world leader in anesthesia products and a major manufacturer of urine-drug-sample-testing systems for corporations and other organizations.

While most of Abbott's products are specialized for the medical profession, the company produces a handful of consumer products such as Murine eye drops, Selsun Blue dandruff shampoo, and Tronolane hemorrhoid medication.

Abbott is also a leading producer of biological pesticides, plant growth regulators, herbicides, and related agricultural products.

The firm boasts a strong international business, which accounts for about 30 percent of its total revenue. It has sales or operations in more than 130 countries.

Abbott Laboratories was founded in 1888 when Dr. Wallace C. Abbott began a sideline venture in his small Chicago apartment making pills from the alkaloid of plants.

Abbott has about 52,000 employees and 90,000 shareholders.

EARNINGS-PER-SHARE GROWTH   ★ ★

Past 5 years: 90 percent (14 percent per year)
Past 10 years: 316 percent (15 percent per year)

STOCK GROWTH ★ ★

Past 10 years: 368 percent (17 percent per year)
Dollar growth: $10,000 over 10 years (including reinvested dividends)
would have grown to $57,000
Average annual compounded rate of return (including reinvested dividends): 19 percent

DIVIDEND YIELD ★ ★

Average dividend yield in the past 3 years: 2.3 percent

DIVIDEND GROWTH ★ ★ ★

Increased dividend: Every year since 1971
Past 5-year increase: 86 percent (13 percent per year)

CONSISTENCY ★ ★ ★ ★

Increased earnings per share: 26 consecutive years
Increased sales: 26 consecutive years

SHAREHOLDER PERKS ★ ★

Good dividend reinvestment and stock purchase plan: voluntary stock
purchase plan allows contributions of $10 to $5,000 per quarter.

Shareholders who attend the annual meeting receive a sampling of
Abbott's consumer products such as Selsun Blue, Murine, Tronolane, and
Ensure nutritional drink.

ABBOTT LABORATORIES AT A GLANCE

Fiscal year ended: Dec. 31
Revenue and net income in $ millions

	1991	1992	1993	1994	1995	1996	5-Year Growth Avg. Annual (%)	5-Year Growth Total (%)
Revenue ($)	6,876.6	7,851.9	8,407.8	9,156	10,012	11,013	10	60
Net income ($)	1,088.7	1,239.1	1,399.1	1,516.7	1,688.7	1,882.0	12	73
Earnings/share ($)	1.27	1.47	1.69	1.87	2.12	2.41	14	90
Div. per share ($)	.50	.60	.68	.76	.84	.93	13	86
Dividend yield (%)	1.5	2.0	2.3	2.3	2.0	2.0	—	—
Avg. PE ratio	21	22	16	16	18	20	—	—

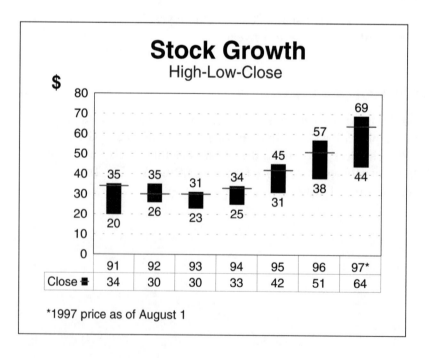

Stock Growth
High-Low-Close

	91	92	93	94	95	96	97*
Close	34	30	30	33	42	51	64

*1997 price as of August 1

37

SouthTrust Corp.

SouthTrust Corporation

420 North 20th Street
Birmingham, AL 35203
205-254-6868

Chairman and CEO: Wallace D. Malone, Jr.

Earnings Growth	★ ★	Dividend Growth	★ ★ ★
Stock Growth	★ ★	Consistency	★ ★ ★
Dividend Yield	★ ★ ★	Shareholder Perks	★ ★
Nasdaq—SOTR		**Total**	**15 points**

SouthTrust Corp. is spreading like kudzu across the South. The Birmingham-based bank operates 511 banking offices and several bank-related affiliates in Alabama, Florida, Georgia, Mississippi, North Carolina, South Carolina, and Tennessee. The company has posted increased earnings during nine of the past ten years.

SouthTrust has grown quickly through internal expansion and acquisitions. In 1996, it acquired nine financial institutions in Georgia and Florida, adding 47 offices. It also opened 17 offices in other states, including North Carolina and South Carolina.

Commercial banking is the bread and butter of SouthTrust's business. Its banks offer a broad range of standard services such as checking and savings accounts, cash management, lending and credit services, discount brokerage accounts, corporate and trust accounts, and data-processing.

The firm operates a number of bank-related subsidiaries, including SouthTrust Mortgage Corporation, SouthTrust Data Services, SouthTrust Life Insurance Company, SouthTrust Insurance Agency, SouthTrust Securities, and SouthTrust Asset Management Company.

SouthTrust has been modernizing its operations through several technological initiatives. For instance, it now offers online banking services to small businesses and retailers who can use their personal computers to handle many of their financial tasks.

SouthTrust was among the first banks to offer corporate-imaging technology for cash management customers. Using software provided by SouthTrust, customers can access check images online or on CD-ROM and electronically store those images, providing customers with permanent records of all of their canceled checks.

The company has about 9,100 employees and 15,000 shareholders of record.

EARNINGS-PER-SHARE GROWTH ★ ★

Past 5 years: 89 percent (14 percent per year)
Past 10 years: 177 percent (11 percent per year)

STOCK GROWTH ★ ★

Past 10 years: 265 percent (14 percent per year)
Dollar growth: $10,000 over 10 years (including reinvested dividends) would have grown to $52,000
Average annual compounded rate of return (including reinvested dividends): 18 percent

DIVIDEND YIELD ★ ★ ★

Average dividend yield in the past 3 years: 3.3 percent

DIVIDEND GROWTH ★ ★ ★

Increased dividend: 27 consecutive years
Past 5-year increase: 83 percent (13 percent per year)

CONSISTENCY ★ ★ ★

Increased earnings per share: 9 of the past 10 years
Increased loans: 10 consecutive years

SHAREHOLDER PERKS

Good dividend reinvestment and stock purchase plan: voluntary stock purchase plan allows contributions of $25 to $10,000 per quarter.

SOUTHTRUST AT A GLANCE

Fiscal year ended: Dec. 31
Total assets and net income in $ millions

	1991	1992	1993	1994	1995	1996	5-Year Growth Avg. Annual (%)	Total (%)
Total assets ($)	10,158	12,714	14,708	17,632	20,787	26,223	21	158
Net income ($)	90	114.2	150.5	173	199	254.7	23	183
Earnings/share ($)	1.42	1.66	1.94	2.15	2.36	2.69	14	89
Div. per share ($)	.48	.52	.60	.68	.80	.88	13	83
Dividend yield (%)	4.3	3.2	3.1	3.5	3.5	3.0	—	—
Avg. PE ratio	8	10	10	9	10	11	—	—

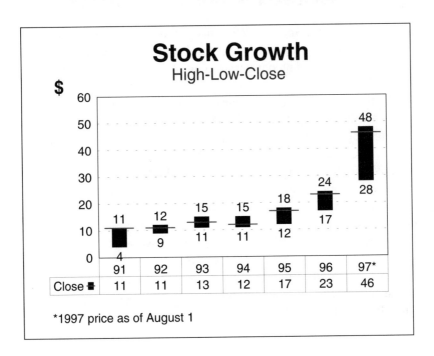

Stock Growth
High-Low-Close

Close	91	92	93	94	95	96	97*
	11	11	13	12	17	23	46

*1997 price as of August 1

38

The Sherwin-Williams Company

101 Prospect Avenue, N.W.
Cleveland, OH 44115-1075
216-566-2000

Chairman and CEO: John G. Breen
President: Thomas A. Commes

Earnings Growth	★ ★	Dividend Growth	★ ★ ★
Stock Growth	★ ★	Consistency	★ ★ ★ ★
Dividend Yield	★ ★	Shareholder Perks	★ ★
NYSE—SHW		**Total**	**15 points**

Despite its corporate motto, Sherwin-Williams still doesn't quite "cover the earth," but it's getting closer. The Cleveland-based company operates in more than 30 countries, and recently it made new business acquisitions in Mexico, Brazil, and Chile.

Sherwin-Williams is the nation's largest producer of paints and varnishes, with about 2,200 paint stores in 48 states. Among its leading brands are Dutch Boy, Kem-Tone, Sherwin-Williams, Martin-Senour, Curinol, Acme, ProMar, Perma-Clad, Western Automotive, Standox, Krylon, Color Works, Rust Tough, Rubberset, and Dupli-Color.

The company's paint stores business segment generates revenue of $2.4 billion a year, which accounts for 58 percent of its $4.13 billion in total annual revenue.

The stores offer paints, wall coverings, floor coverings, window treatments, spray equipment, brushes, scrapers, rollers, and related products. The stores are geared to the do-it-yourself customer, professional painters, industrial and commercial maintenance customers, and small to midsized manufacturers.

The greatest concentration of Sherwin-Williams stores is in the Midwest, with 150 stores in Ohio, 76 in Illinois, 105 in Pennsylvania, 77 in Michigan, 76 in Indiana, and 55 in Missouri.

Sherwin-Williams' other core business is its coatings segment, which accounts for 41 percent of the company's total revenue. The coatings segment has four key divisions (plus a separate transportation division):

1. **Coatings division.** Manufactures the company's line of paint and related products for homeowners, professional painters, and manufacturers of factory-finished products.
2. **Consumer brands division.** Markets the company's line of consumer paints and private label paints to independent dealers, mass merchandisers, independent dealers, and distributors.
3. **Automotive division.** Makes auto finishes and refinishing coatings that it markets to body shops and other refinishers. The company operates 135 branches throughout the United States and Canada.
4. **Diversified brands division.** Sherwin-Williams manufactures and markets custom and industrial aerosol paints, paint applicators, retail and wholesale consumer aerosols, and cleaning products.

Sherwin-Williams' paints first adorned homes and barns in northern Ohio shortly after the Civil War in 1866. The company has posted record earnings for 19 consecutive years.

Sherwin-Williams has 18,500 employees and 12,000 shareholders.

EARNINGS-PER-SHARE GROWTH ★ ★

Past 5 years: 83 percent (13 percent per year)
Past 10 years: 219 percent (12 percent per year)

STOCK GROWTH ★ ★

Past 10 years: 318 percent (15 percent per year)
Dollar growth: $10,000 over 10 years (including reinvested dividends) would have grown to $48,000
Average annual compounded rate of return (including reinvested dividends): 17 percent

DIVIDEND YIELD ★ ★

Average dividend yield in the past 3 years: 1.6 percent

DIVIDEND GROWTH ★ ★ ★

Increased dividend: 19 consecutive years
Past 5-year increase: 67 percent (11 percent per year)

CONSISTENCY ★ ★ ★ ★

Increased earnings per share: 19 consecutive years
Increased sales: 10 straight years

SHAREHOLDER PERKS ★ ★

Good dividend reinvestment and stock purchase plan: voluntary stock purchase plan allows contributions of $10 to $2,000 per month.

SHERWIN-WILLIAMS AT A GLANCE

Fiscal year ended: Dec. 31
Revenue and net income in $ millions

	1991	1992	1993	1994	1995	1996	5-Year Growth Avg. Annual (%)	5-Year Growth Total (%)
Revenue ($)	2,541.4	2,747.8	2,949.3	3,100.1	3,273.8	4,132.9	10	63
Net income ($)	128.2	144.6	165.3	186.6	200.6	229.1	12	79
Earnings/share ($)	1.45	1.63	1.85	2.15	2.34	2.65	13	83
Div. per share ($)	.21	.22	.25	.28	.32	.35	11	67
Dividend yield (%)	1.8	1.5	1.5	1.7	1.6	1.5	—	—
Avg. PE ratio	16	18	18	15	15	18	—	—

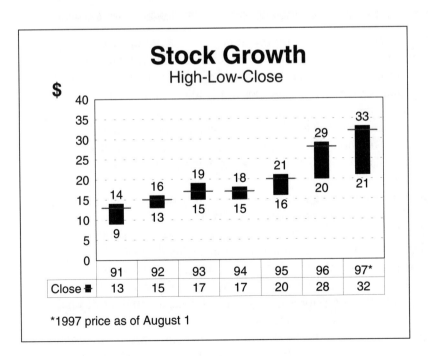

Stock Growth
High-Low-Close

	91	92	93	94	95	96	97*
Close ■	13	15	17	17	20	28	32

*1997 price as of August 1

39

Wal-Mart Stores, Inc.

WAL★MART

Bentonville, AR 72716
501-273-4000

Chairman: S. Robson Walton
President and CEO: David D. Glass

Earnings Growth	★ ★	Dividend Growth	★ ★ ★ ★
Stock Growth	★ ★	Consistency	★ ★ ★ ★
Dividend Yield	★	Shareholder Perks	★ ★
NYSE—WMT		**Total**	**15 points**

Wal-Mart is betting its future on the Supercenter. First opened in 1989, the Supercenters range in size from 170,000 to 200,000 square feet, and they offer food, general merchandise, and a wide range of services, including pharmacy, dry cleaning, portrait studios, photo finishing, hair salons, and optical shops.

The company now has about 400 Supercenters, and it is opening new stores at a rate of about 100 per year. Some analysts project that Supercenter sales will account for as much as one-third of Wal-Mart's total revenue by 1999.

Wal-Mart is the world's largest retail chain, with a total annual revenue of $105 billion. The company has nearly 3,000 Wal-Mart stores in 47 states. Wal-Mart also owns about 500 Sam's Club warehouse stores.

Wal-Mart has begun to establish a presence outside the United States. The company operates about 140 stores in Canada and about 100 in Mexico through a joint venture with CIFRA SA, Mexico's largest retailer. The company is also building stores in Argentina, China, and Indonesia under joint-venture and royalty agreements.

The company's product sales break down this way: soft goods (apparel, towels, sheets, etc.), 25 percent of sales; hard goods (hardware, housewares, auto supplies, and small appliances), 25 percent; stationery and candy, 11 percent; sporting goods and toys, 9 percent; pharmaceuticals, 9 percent; gifts, records, and electronics, 10 percent; health and beauty aids, 7 percent; shoes, 2 percent; and jewelry, 2 percent.

Although Wal-Mart's stock price flattened out from 1992 through 1996, its earnings continued to climb. The Bentonville, Arkansas, retailer has posted 27 consecutive years of record sales and earnings, dating back to 1969, the year the company went public.

Wal-Mart was founded in 1962 by Sam Walton, who ultimately became a legend of American business and the nation's richest man before his death in 1992. Walton entered the retailing business in 1945 when he opened a Ben Franklin variety store franchise in Newport, Arkansas. His first Wal-Mart store (called "Wal-Mart Discount City") was opened in Rogers, Arkansas, in 1962.

Walton achieved his early success largely by locating stores in rural locations such as Rogers where there was no competition from other discounters. The retailer's "everyday low prices" attracted throngs of shoppers wherever the new stores appeared. The company has been able to keep its prices low by buying its merchandise in large volume and turning it over quickly, incurring a minimum of overhead in the process.

Wal-Mart stores have since invaded the urban areas en masse, where they compete toe-to-toe with Target, Kmart, and the other discounters. While the competition is stiffer, the urban-based Wal-Marts have still proven very profitable.

Wal-Mart has 700,000 employees and 260,000 shareholders.

EARNINGS-PER-SHARE GROWTH ★ ★

Past 5 years: 109 percent (16 percent per year)
Past 10 years: 570 percent (21 percent per year)

STOCK GROWTH ★ ★

Past 10 years: 342 percent (16 percent per year)
Dollar growth: $10,000 over 10 years (including reinvested dividends) would have grown to $46,000
Average annual compounded rate of return (including reinvested dividends): 16.5 percent

DIVIDEND YIELD ★

Average dividend yield in the past 3 years: 0.8 percent

DIVIDEND GROWTH ★ ★ ★ ★

Increased dividend: 19 consecutive years
Past 5-year increase: 186 percent (23 percent per year)

CONSISTENCY ★ ★ ★ ★

Increased earnings per share: 27 consecutive years (every year since going public in 1969)
Increased sales: 27 consecutive years

SHAREHOLDER PERKS ★ ★

Excellent dividend reinvestment and stock purchase program: voluntary stock purchase plan allows contributions of $50 to $150,000 per year.

WAL-MART STORES AT A GLANCE

Fiscal year ended: Jan. 31
Revenue and net income in $ millions

	1991	1992	1993	1994	1995	1996	5-Year Growth Avg. Annual (%)	5-Year Growth Total (%)
Revenue ($)	32,602	43,887	55,484	67,344	82,494	93,627	23	187
Net income ($)	1,291	1,609	1,995	2,333	2,681	2,740	16	112
Earnings/share ($)	0.57	0.70	0.87	1.02	1.17	1.19	16	109
Div. per share ($)	.07	.09	.11	.13	.17	.20	23	186
Dividend yield (%)	.4	.4	.5	.7	.8	.9	—	—
Avg. PE ratio	33	33	27	21	20	19	—	—

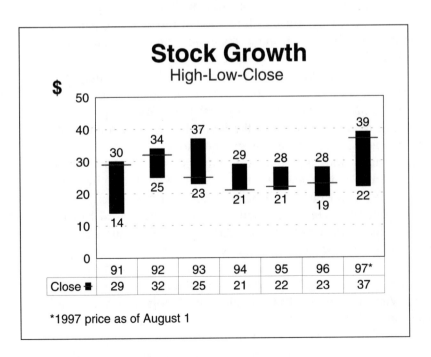

Stock Growth
High-Low-Close

	91	92	93	94	95	96	97*
Close	29	32	25	21	22	23	37

*1997 price as of August 1

Banc One Corp.

100 East Broad Street
Columbus, OH 43271
614-248-5944

Chairman and CEO: John B. McCoy
President: Richard J. Lehmann

Earnings Growth	★ ★	Dividend Growth	★ ★ ★
Stock Growth	★	Consistency	★ ★ ★
Dividend Yield	★ ★ ★ ★	Shareholder Perks	★ ★
NYSE—ONE		**Total**	**15 points**

There's no institution in the banking business with a bigger appetite for acquisitions than Banc One. Since its formation in 1968, the company has acquired more than 100 other banking institutions and has expanded its network of branch offices from 24 to more than 1,500.

Banc One now ranks tenth among publicly owned bank holding companies in terms of consolidated average total assets and seventh in consolidated net income. Over the past ten years, Banc One has posted the highest average return on assets and the fourth-highest return on equity among the nation's 25 largest banking organizations.

Already a major force in the retail banking market in several states, Banc One added two more states to its empire in 1996. It acquired Premier Bancorp of Baton Rouge, Louisiana, which operates 150 branch offices throughout the state, and it acquired Oklahoma-based Liberty Bancorp, with its 29 branch offices in Oklahoma City and Tulsa.

Thanks to a series of past acquisitions, Banc One is now the largest bank in Kentucky and Arizona (in terms of total bank deposits); second largest in Indiana, Ohio, and West Virginia; and third largest in Colorado, Texas, and Wisconsin. It also has operations in Illinois, Oklahoma, and Utah. The company has 47,000 employees and 87,600 shareholders.

Like many other banks around the country, Banc One suffered through a lean year in 1994 when the prime interest rate was hiked six times. But the company has rebounded strongly since then, with record earnings and revenue in 1995 and 1996. In fact, 1994 is the only year in Banc One's 28-year history that it did not post record earnings.

Banc One's loan portfolio breaks down this way: commercial loans, 28 percent; real estate, 32 percent; consumer loans, 29 percent; credit card and other loans, 11 percent.

EARNINGS-PER-SHARE GROWTH ★ ★

Past 5 years: 95 percent (14 percent per year)
Past 10 years: 205 percent (12 percent per year)

STOCK GROWTH ★

Past 10 years: 217 percent (12 percent per year)
Dollar growth: $10,000 over 10 years (including reinvested dividends) would have grown to $44,000
Average annual compounded rate of return (including reinvested dividends): 16 percent

DIVIDEND YIELD ★ ★ ★ ★

Average dividend yield in the past 3 years: 3.9 percent
(The company has also paid out five special 10 percent dividends in the past 10 years.)

DIVIDEND GROWTH ★ ★ ★

Increased dividend: 26 consecutive years
Past 5-year increase: 93 percent (14 percent per year)

CONSISTENCY ★ ★ ★

Increased earnings per share: 9 of the past 10 years

SHAREHOLDER PERKS ★ ★

Good dividend reinvestment and stock purchase plan: voluntary stock purchase plan allows contributions of up to $5,000 per quarter.

BANC ONE AT A GLANCE

Fiscal year ended: Dec. 31
Total assets and net income in $ millions

	1991	1992	1993	1994	1995	1996	5-Year Growth Avg. Annual (%)	Total (%)
Total assets ($)	46,293	61,417	79,919	88,923	90,454	101,848	17	120
Net income ($)	664.3	922.2	1,172.1	1,005.1	1,277.9	1,426.5	16	115
Earnings/share ($)	1.66	2.07	2.62	2.20	2.91	3.23	14	95
Div. per share ($)	0.69	0.81	0.97	1.13	1.24	1.33	14	93
Dividend yield (%)	2.9	2.6	2.8	3.9	4.2	3.6	—	—
Avg. PE ratio	13	14	13	13	10	12	—	—

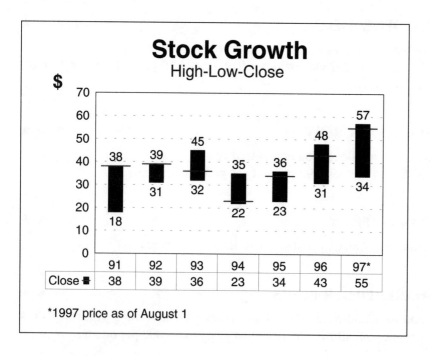

Stock Growth
High-Low-Close

$	91	92	93	94	95	96	97*
High	38	39	45	35	36	48	57
Low	18	31	32	22	23	31	34
Close ■	38	39	36	23	34	43	55

*1997 price as of August 1

Pitney Bowes, Inc.

Pitney Bowes

1 Elmcroft Road
Stamford, CT 06926-0700
203-356-5000

Chairman and CEO: Mark J. Critelli

Earnings Growth	★	Dividend Growth	★ ★ ★ ★
Stock Growth	★ ★	Consistency	★ ★ ★
Dividend Yield	★ ★ ★	Shareholder Perks	★ ★
NYSE—PBI		**Total**	**15 points**

The mechanical postage meter, which for many decades has been the backbone of the Pitney Bowes organization, is quickly heading for extinction. The company recently made a decision to stop marketing and installing the mechanical meters, opting instead to push its newer lines of electronic and digital meters.

The Stamford, Connecticut, operation is the world's largest maker of postage meters and mailing equipment. It also offers a broad range of fax machines, copiers, and other office equipment. The firm recently sold its Dictaphone and Monarch Marketing Systems divisions.

About 70 percent of Pitney's $3.86 billion in annual revenue comes from its business equipment segment, which includes mailing systems, shipping and weighing systems, fax machines, and copiers.

Pitney is the only facsimile systems supplier in the United States that markets exclusively through its own direct sales force. The company concentrates its copier sales on larger corporations with multiunit installations. It endears itself to the large companies with preventive-maintenance programs covering all elements of copier performance.

Pitney also has a financial services unit that provides equipment financing for non–Pitney Bowes equipment. Products financed include aircraft, over-the-road trucks and trailers, railcars, locomotives, commercial real estate, and high-tech equipment.

Pitney has about 28,000 employees and 31,000 shareholders.

EARNINGS-PER-SHARE GROWTH   ★

Past 5 years: 73 percent (12 percent per year)
Past 10 years: 197 percent (11 percent per year)

STOCK GROWTH   ★ ★

Past 10 years: 259 percent (14 percent per year)
Dollar growth: $10,000 over 10 years (including reinvested dividends) would have grown to $44,000
Average annual compounded rate of return (including reinvested dividends): 16 percent

DIVIDEND YIELD   ★ ★ ★

Average dividend yield in the past 3 years: 2.8 percent

DIVIDEND GROWTH   ★ ★ ★ ★

Increased dividend: 14 consecutive years
Past 5-year increase: 103 percent (15 percent per year)

CONSISTENCY   ★ ★ ★

Increased earnings per share: 9 of the past 10 years
Increased sales: 9 of the past 10 years

SHAREHOLDER PERKS   ★ ★

Good dividend reinvestment and stock purchase plan: voluntary stock purchase plan allows contributions of $100 to $3,000 per quarter.

PITNEY BOWES AT A GLANCE

Fiscal year ended: Dec. 31
Revenue and net income in $ millions

	1991	1992	1993	1994	1995	1996	5-Year Growth Avg. Annual (%)	5-Year Growth Total (%)
Revenue ($)	3,332.5	2,887.6	3,000.4	3,270.6	3,554.8	3,858.6	3	16
Net income ($)	287.8	260.7	305.7	348.4	407.7	469.4	10	63
Earnings/share ($)	1.80	1.64	1.92	2.21	2.68	3.12	12	73
Div. per share ($)	0.68	0.78	0.90	1.04	1.20	1.38	15	103
Dividend yield (%)	2.4	2.3	2.2	2.8	3.0	2.7	—	—
Avg. PE ratio	16	17	18	17	15	16	—	—

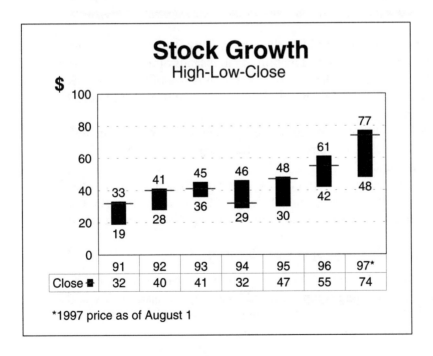

Stryker Corp.

stryker

P. O. Box 4085
Kalamazoo, MI 49003
616-385-2600

Chairman, President, and CEO: John W. Brown

Earnings Growth	★ ★ ★ ★	Dividend Growth	★ ★
Stock Growth	★ ★ ★ ★	Consistency	★ ★ ★ ★
Dividend Yield		Shareholder Perks	
Nasdaq—STRY		**Total**	**14 points**

Stryker specializes in rebuilding the human body. The company's line of artificial limbs gives renewed mobility to thousands of injured and arthritis-riddled patients. The Kalamazoo operation is one of the world's leading manufacturers of reconstructive products and powered surgical instruments.

In addition to its knee and hip replacements, Stryker also manufactures spinal implant systems used to treat degenerative spinal diseases and related ailments.

Surgical products account for 73 percent of Stryker's $910 million in annual sales. The company markets its products in more than 100 countries. Foreign operations and exports make up 37 percent of its total revenue.

Stryker's other surgical products include:

- **Powered surgical tools.** The company makes powered drills, saws, fixation and reaming equipment, and other surgical instruments. It also makes micropowered tools for more delicate operations such as spinal surgery, neurosurgery, and plastic surgery.

- **Endoscopic systems.** Stryker makes medical video cameras, light sources, laparoscopes, and related products used in less-invasive surgery such as arthroscopy. Stryker's high-definition medical video system can be inserted into a patient's joint area to give surgeons a broadcast-quality image of the interior of the joint.

About 21 percent of the company's revenue comes from medical products. Stryker makes a line of specialty stretchers and beds and other patient-handling equipment. Its critical care beds enable physicians to weigh patients, take X rays, and perform other functions without removing the patient from the bed. Its patient-handling equipment is assembled on a design-to-order basis.

The other 6 percent of the company's revenue comes from Stryker's Japanese subsidiary, Matsumoto Distributed Products, which is a distributor of medical products.

Stryker was founded in 1941 by Dr. Homer H. Stryker, a prominent orthopedic surgeon and the inventor of several leading orthopedic products.

Stryker has about 3,700 employees and 4,600 stockholders.

EARNINGS-PER-SHARE GROWTH ★ ★ ★ ★

Past 5 years: 209 percent (25 percent per year)
Past 10 years: 882 percent (26 percent per year)

STOCK GROWTH ★ ★ ★ ★

Past 10 years: 967 percent (26 percent per year)
Dollar growth: $10,000 over 10 years (including reinvested dividends) would have grown to $110,000
Average annual compounded rate of return (including reinvested dividends): 26 percent

DIVIDEND YIELD (no points)

Average dividend yield in the past 3 years: 0.2 percent

DIVIDEND GROWTH   ★ ★

Increased dividend: 5 consecutive years
Past 5-year increase: 233 percent (27 percent per year)

CONSISTENCY   ★ ★ ★ ★

Increased earnings per share: More than 19 consecutive years
Increased sales: More than 19 consecutive years

SHAREHOLDER PERKS   (no points)

Stryker does not offer a dividend reinvestment plan, nor does it provide
any other shareholder perks.

STRYKER AT A GLANCE

Fiscal year ended: Dec. 31
Revenue and net income in $ millions

	1991	1992	1993	1994	1995	1996	Avg. Annual (%)	Total (%)
							5-Year Growth	
Revenue ($)	364.8	477.1	557.3	681.9	872	910.1	20	149
Net income ($)	33.1	47.7	60.2	72.4	87	106.3	26	221
Earnings/share ($)	0.35	0.50	0.62	0.75	0.90	1.08	25	209
Div. per share ($)	.03	.03	.04	.04	.05	.10	27	233
Dividend yield (%)	.1	.2	.3	.3	.2	.2	—	—
Avg. PE ratio	39	37	22	21	25	26	—	—

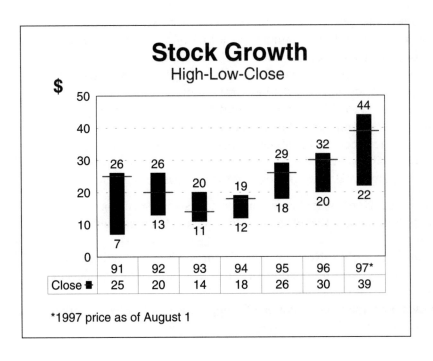

Stock Growth
High-Low-Close

	91	92	93	94	95	96	97*
Close	25	20	14	18	26	30	39

*1997 price as of August 1

43

Nordson Corp.

28601 Clemens Road
Westlake, OH 44145
216-892-1580

Chairman: Eric T. Nord
President: Edward P. Campbell
CEO: William P. Madar

Earnings Growth	★	Dividend Growth	★ ★ ★
Stock Growth	★ ★ ★ ★	Consistency	★ ★ ★
Dividend Yield	★	Shareholder Perks	★ ★
Nasdaq—NDSN		**Total**	**14 points**

Manufacturers the world over count on Nordson to seal the deal. The Westlake, Ohio, operation manufactures a line of adhesive-dispensing systems used to attach, fasten, connect, seal, or otherwise assemble furniture, books, automobile body parts, circuit boards, baby diapers, packaging for foods and cosmetics, and a vast array of other products.

Founded in 1954, Nordson has operations throughout Europe and Asia and markets its equipment in 52 countries.

Foreign sales account for about 61 percent of the company's $609 million in annual revenue.

The company breaks its operations into ten separate segments:

1. **Packaging.** Nordson makes automated adhesive-dispensing systems for applying product labels and sealing corrugated cases and paperboard cartons.
2. **Product assembly.** Nordson manufactures adhesive- and sealant-dispensing systems for bonding plastic, metal, and wood products in a wide range of industries.
3. **Nonwovens.** Includes equipment for applying adhesives and liquids in the assembly of diapers and feminine hygiene products.

4. **Converting.** The firm makes coating and laminating systems used to manufacture continuous-roll goods such as back-coated textiles, medical disposables, and automotive body cloth.
5. **Gasketing and composites.** Nordson makes custom-engineered systems to dispense foamed adhesives and sealants in gaskets for automotive components, appliances, and electrical enclosures.
6. **Power coating.** The company makes electrostatic spray systems for applying powder paints and coatings to appliances, automotive components, and other applications.
7. **Liquid finishing.** The firm makes electrostatic spray systems for applying paints and coatings to plastic, metal, and wood products.
8. **Automotive.** Nordson makes liquid- and powder-finishing systems for spray-coating automotive parts. It also makes adhesive-dispensing systems for bonding glass and sealing interior seams.
9. **Container coating.** It makes equipment for adding coatings to food and beverage metal containers.
10. **Electronics.** Nordson makes equipment for applying protective coatings and solder flux to printed circuit boards and electronic assemblies.

The company also offers automated fluid-dispensing equipment for applying adhesives and soldering pastes to assemble semiconductor packages and printed circuit-board assemblies. Nordson also makes accelerated drying and curing systems for finishing and assembly operations in electronics, flooring, packaging, and other applications.

Nordson has about 3,800 employees and 3,000 shareholders.

EARNINGS-PER-SHARE GROWTH ★

Past 5 years: 65 percent (11 percent per year)
Past 10 years: 336 percent (16 percent per year)

STOCK GROWTH ★ ★ ★ ★

Past 10 years: 682 percent (23 percent per year)
Dollar growth: $10,000 over 10 years (including reinvested dividends) would have grown to $89,000

Average annual compounded rate of return (including reinvested dividends): 24.5 percent

DIVIDEND YIELD   ★

Average dividend yield in the past 3 years: 1.1 percent

DIVIDEND GROWTH   ★ ★ ★

Increased dividend: 33 consecutive years
Past 5-year increase: 80 percent (13 percent per year)

CONSISTENCY   ★ ★ ★

Increased earnings per share: 9 of the past 10 years
Increased sales: 10 consecutive years

SHAREHOLDER PERKS   ★ ★

Good dividend reinvestment and stock purchase plan: voluntary stock purchase plan allows contributions of $10 to $4,000 per quarter.

NORDSON AT A GLANCE

Fiscal year ended: Sept. 30
Revenue and net income in $ millions

	1991	1992	1993	1994	1995	1996	5-Year Growth Avg. Annual (%)	Total (%)
Revenue ($)	388	425.6	461.6	506.7	581.4	609.4	9	57
Net income ($)	33.8	39.5	40.8	46.7	52.7	53.1	9	57
Earnings/share ($)	1.77	2.03	2.13	2.45	2.84	2.92	11	65
Div. per share ($)	.40	.44	.48	.56	.64	.72	13	80
Dividend yield (%)	1.5	.9	1.1	1.0	1.1	1.2	—	—
Avg. PE ratio	15	23	21	23	20	19	—	—

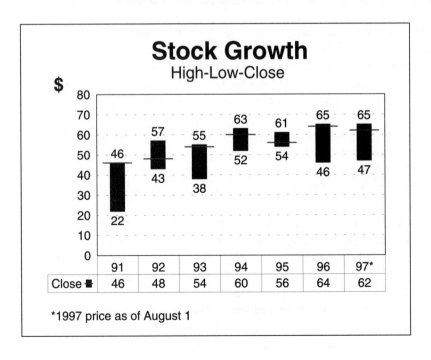

Stock Growth
High-Low-Close

	91	92	93	94	95	96	97*
Close	46	48	54	60	56	64	62

*1997 price as of August 1

44

Automatic Data Processing

One ADP Boulevard
Roseland, NJ 07068
201-994-5000

Chairman and CEO: Josh S. Weston
President: Arthur F. Weinbach

Earnings Growth	★ ★	Dividend Growth	★ ★ ★ ★
Stock Growth	★ ★ ★	Consistency	★ ★ ★ ★
Dividend Yield	★	Shareholder Perks	
NYSE—AUD		**Total**	**14 points**

Every year 22 million workers get a paycheck from Automatic Data Processing (ADP). The company provides payroll and related services to about 350,000 companies around the world. But ADP has managed to enrich more than just the wage earners for whom it cuts the checks. ADP shareholders have also enjoyed a phenomenal run of success over the past 47 years.

ADP has rung up 148 consecutive quarters (47 years) of record earnings and revenue. The Roseland, New Jersey, firm is the nation's largest payroll and tax-filing processor, and it is credited with pioneering "outsourcing," in which companies farm out tasks that don't directly relate to their core competencies.

ADP's largest and oldest business is Employer Services, which generates 18 percent of the company's $3.57 billion in annual revenue. The division provides a comprehensive range of payroll, tax deposit and reporting, benefits outsourcing, 401(k) recordkeeping, and unemployment compensation management services.

Its employer services are offered from 40 computer centers and 73 satellite sales and service centers in the United States, 14 computer centers in Western Europe, and one center in Canada.

ADP also operates in three other key segments, including:

1. **Brokerage services** (20 percent of revenue). ADP provides data services, recordkeeping, order entry, proxy processing, and other services for the financial services industry. ADP is the leading provider of third-party processing and retail equity information in the United States. It serves more than 2,600 firms around the world.
2. **Dealer services** (26 percent). The company provides some computing, data, and professional services to more than 16,000 automobile, truck, and farm equipment dealers and manufacturers in the United States, Canada, Europe, Asia, and Latin America. Auto dealers use ADP's on-site systems to manage their accounting, factory communications, inventory, sales, and service activities. To help auto dealers eliminate paperwork, ADP systems can digitize and store records that can be retrieved from workstations for viewing, faxing, or printing.
3. **Claims services** (27 percent). The company provides auto collision estimates and parts availability services to insurance companies, claims adjusters, repair shops, and salvage yards.

ADP has 29,000 employees and about 25,000 shareholders.

EARNINGS-PER-SHARE GROWTH ★ ★

Past 5 years: 94 percent (14 percent per year)
Past 10 years: 336 percent (16 percent per year)

STOCK GROWTH ★ ★ ★

Past 10 years: 597 percent (21 percent per year)
Dollar growth: $10,000 over 10 years (including reinvested dividends) would have grown to $73,000
Average annual compounded rate of return (including reinvested dividends): 22 percent

DIVIDEND YIELD ★

Average dividend yield in the past 3 years: 1.0 percent

DIVIDEND GROWTH ★ ★ ★ ★

Increased dividend: 23 consecutive years
Past 5-year increase: 105 percent (15 percent per year)

CONSISTENCY ★ ★ ★ ★

Increased earnings per share: 47 consecutive years
Increased sales: 47 consecutive years

SHAREHOLDER PERKS (no points)

The company provides no dividend reinvestment and stock purchase plan, nor does it offer any other perks for its shareholders.

AUTOMATIC DATA PROCESSING AT A GLANCE

Fiscal year ended: June 30
Revenue and net income in $ millions

	1991	1992	1993	1994	1995	1996	5-Year Growth Avg. Annual (%)	Total (%)
Revenue ($)	1,771.8	1,940.6	2,223.4	2,469	2,893.7	3,566.6	15	101
Net income ($)	222.7	256.2	294.2	329.3	394.8	454.7	15	100
Earnings/share ($)	0.81	0.92	1.04	1.19	1.39	1.57	14	94
Div. per share ($)	.19	.21	.24	.27	.31	.39	15	105
Dividend yield (%)	1.3	1.0	1.0	1.0	.8	1.1	—	—
Avg. PE ratio	18	22	24	22	21	23	—	—

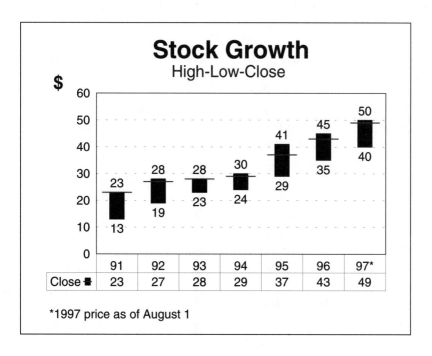

Stock Growth
High-Low-Close

Close	91	92	93	94	95	96	97*
	23	27	28	29	37	43	49

*1997 price as of August 1

45

Donaldson Company, Inc.

1400 West 94th Street
P.O. Box 1299
Minneapolis, MN 55440
612-887-3131

Chairman and CEO: William G. Van Dyke

Earnings Growth	★ ★	Dividend Growth	★ ★ ★
Stock Growth	★ ★ ★	Consistency	★ ★ ★
Dividend Yield	★	Shareholder Perks	★ ★
NYSE—DCI		**Total**	**14 points**

The issue of cleaner air and cleaner water goes well beyond the borders of the United States. In fact, Donaldson Company, which manufactures filters and purifiers for trucks, turbines, and a broad range of industrial and agricultural equipment, has seen its foreign sales grow faster than its U.S. sales.

The Minneapolis-based operation generates about 37 percent of its $758.6 million in annual sales from its foreign operations. Eleven of its 21 plants are located outside the United States, and the company has joint ventures in India, China, and Indonesia, and subsidiaries in the Netherlands, France, Italy, Japan, Hong Kong, Mexico, South Africa, and Australia.

Donaldson makes filtration systems for a wide range of applications. Its biggest market is engine filtration and exhaust products, which account for about 42 percent of its total revenue. The company makes air cleaners and accessories, liquid filters, and exhaust products such as mufflers for the construction, industrial, mining, agricultural, and transportation market.

Its other key segments include:

- **Dust collection** (16 percent of revenue). The company makes dust, fume, and mist collectors for manufacturing and assembly plants.

- **Gas turbine systems** (9 percent of revenue). Donaldson manufactures static and pulse-clean air filter systems, replacement filters, exhaust silencers, chiller coils, and anti-icing systems for turbine engines for use in the electric power generation and the oil and gas industries.
- **High-purity products** (9 percent). The firm makes specialized air filtration systems for computer disk drives, aircraft and automotive cabins, industrial and hospital clean rooms, business machines, room air cleaners, personal respirators, and air emission control.
- **Aftermarket** (25 percent). The company makes a variety of filtration products for several aftermarket distributors, including automotive jobbers, fleets, national-buying groups, specialty installers, and hydraulic distributors.

Donaldson was founded in 1915 by Frank Donaldson whose first filter was a tin can and Spanish moss air filter he made for a farmer's tractor. By the late 1920s, Donaldson had developed a spark-arresting muffler designed to cut the incidence of crop fires from engine sparks. From that beginning, the company expanded to the wide range of filter systems it offers today.

Donaldson has about 5,200 employees and 1,500 shareholders.

EARNINGS-PER-SHARE GROWTH ★ ★

Past 5 years: 99 percent (14 percent per year)
Past 10 years: 241 percent (13 percent per year)

STOCK GROWTH ★ ★ ★

Past 10 years: 532 percent (20 percent per year)
Dollar growth: $10,000 over 10 years (including reinvested dividends) would have grown to $73,000
Average annual compounded rate of return (including reinvested dividends): 22 percent

DIVIDEND YIELD ★

Average dividend yield in the past 3 years: 1.2 percent

DIVIDEND GROWTH   ★ ★ ★

Increased dividend: 9 consecutive years
Past 5-year increase: 100 percent (15 percent per year)

CONSISTENCY   ★ ★ ★

Increased earnings per share: 9 of the past 10 years
Increased sales: 11 consecutive years

SHAREHOLDER PERKS   ★ ★

Good dividend reinvestment and stock purchase plan: voluntary stock purchase plan allows contributions of $10 to $1,000 per month.

DONALDSON AT A GLANCE

Fiscal year ended: July 31
Revenue and net income in $ millions

	1991	1992	1993	1994	1995	1996	5-Year Growth Avg. Annual (%)	Total (%)
Revenue ($)	457.7	482.1	533.3	593.5	704	758.6	11	66
Net income ($)	24.0	25.8	28.2	32.0	38.5	43.4	13	81
Earnings/share ($)	0.84	0.92	1.02	1.17	1.45	1.67	14	99
Div. per share ($)	.15	.19	.21	.25	.28	.30	15	100
Dividend yield (%)	1.3	1.4	1.2	1.0	1.1	0.9	—	—
Avg. PE ratio	13	15	17	19	17	15	—	—

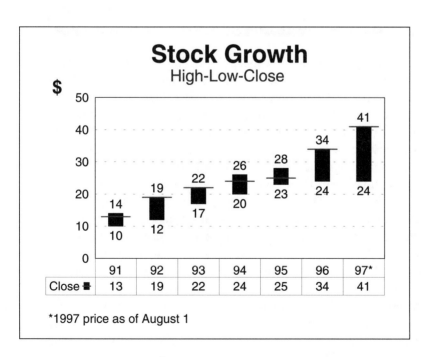

Stock Growth
High-Low-Close

Close ■	91	92	93	94	95	96	97*
	13	19	22	24	25	34	41

*1997 price as of August 1

PepsiCo, Inc.

Purchase, NY 10577-1444
914-253-2000

Chairman: D. Wayne Calloway
CEO: Roger A. Enrico
President: Craig E. Weatherup

Earnings Growth	★	Dividend Growth	★ ★ ★
Stock Growth	★ ★ ★	Consistency	★ ★ ★
Dividend Yield	★ ★	Shareholder Perks	★ ★
NYSE—PEP		**Total**	**14 points**

PepsiCo is a lot lighter on its feet these days. The soft drink company announced plans in 1997 to unload its massive chain of fast-food franchises—Taco Bell, Pizza Hut, and Kentucky Fried Chicken.

Spinning off the restaurant business in its prime (to trade as a separate stock) makes solid financial sense. Most restaurant chains enjoy their biggest growth early in their expansion, before reaching a saturation point. PepsiCo's restaurant business, which accounted for about 37 percent of its $31.6 billion in revenue in 1996, could have become a drain on the overall growth of the company. The move also gives PepsiCo an opportunity to concentrate on its two other key segments—soft drinks and snack foods.

The Purchase, New York, operation is the maker of Pepsi, Diet Pepsi, Mountain Dew, All Sport, Mug Root Beer, Oceanspray Cranberry Juice, and Slice (and the marketer of 7UP outside the United States). It sells its products in 194 countries around the world and makes up about 19 percent of the international soft drink market.

In the U.S. retail beverage market, Pepsi brands account for nearly one third of the company's total sales. Within the company, beverage sales account for about 35 percent of its total revenue.

Its other business segment is its Frito-Lay snack foods division, which accounts for about 28 percent of its total revenue. PepsiCo is the maker of Lay's potato chips, Fritos, Doritos, Chee-tos, Ruffles, Tostitos, Sun Chips, and other snack chips. In the U.S. market, Frito-Lay products account for 13 percent of all snack food sales.

The company markets its snack foods in about 40 foreign countries and continues to expand into new markets each year.

PepsiCo, which was founded in 1919, has about 480,000 employees and 170,000 shareholders.

EARNINGS-PER-SHARE GROWTH   ★

Past 5 years: 75 percent (12 percent per year)
Past 10 years: 303 percent (15 percent per year)

STOCK GROWTH   ★ ★ ★

Past 10 years: 594 percent (20 percent per year)
Dollar growth: $10,000 over 10 years (including reinvested dividends) would have grown to $70,000
Average annual compounded rate of return (including reinvested dividends): 21.5 percent

DIVIDEND YIELD   ★ ★

Average dividend yield in the past 3 years: 1.7 percent

DIVIDEND GROWTH   ★ ★ ★

Increased dividend: More than 24 consecutive years
Past 5-year increase: 96 percent (14 percent per year)

CONSISTENCY   ★ ★ ★

Increased earnings per share: 9 of the past 10 years
Increased sales: more than 21 consecutive years

SHAREHOLDER PERKS   ★ ★

Good dividend reinvestment and stock purchase plan: voluntary stock purchase plan allows contributions of $25 to $60,000 per year.

PEPSICO AT A GLANCE

Fiscal year ended: Dec. 31
Revenue and net income in $ millions

	1991	1992	1993	1994	1995	1996	5-Year Growth Avg. Annual (%)	Total (%)
Revenue ($)	19,608	21,970	25,021	28,472	30,421	31,645	10	61
Net income ($)	1,080.2	1,301.7	1,588	1,784	1,606	1,149	1	6
Earnings/share ($)	0.67	0.81	0.98	1.11	1.24	1.17	12	75
Div. per share ($)	.23	.26	.31	.35	.39	.45	14	96
Dividend yield (%)	1.5	1.4	1.6	2.0	1.7	1.5	—	—
Avg. PE ratio	20	23	20	16	19	27	—	—

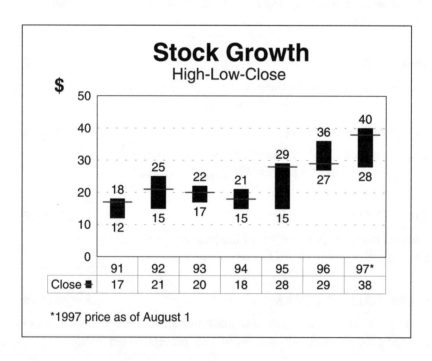

Stock Growth
High-Low-Close

	91	92	93	94	95	96	97*
Close ■	17	21	20	18	28	29	38

*1997 price as of August 1

Warner-Lambert Company

WARNER LAMBERT

201 Tabor Road
Morris Plains, NJ 07950-2693
201-540-2000

Chairman and CEO: Melvin R. Goodes
President: Lodewijk J. R. de Vink

Earnings Growth		Dividend Growth	★ ★
Stock Growth	★ ★ ★	Consistency	★ ★ ★ ★
Dividend Yield	★ ★ ★	Shareholder Perks	★ ★
NYSE—WLA		**Total**	**14 points**

With a product line that already includes Trident, Dentyne, Certs, Listerine, Schick razors, and a host of other consumer favorites, Warner-Lambert continues to add to its collection of name-brand products. In 1996, the company acquired several consumer health care brands from Glaxo Wellcome, including Sudafed and Actifed cough, cold, allergy, and sinus medications; Neosporin topical anti-infective; and Nix lice treatment.

The Morris Plains, New Jersey, manufacturer is among the world leaders in chewing gum sales, breath fresheners (such as Certs and Listerine), cough drops, and razors. It also manufactures a broad range of other over-the-counter and prescription medications.

Sales of chewing gum and other confectionery products accounts for 20 percent of the company's $7.2 billion in annual revenue. Among the company's leading brands are Trident, Dentyne, Freshen-Up, Chewels, Bubblicious, Chiclets, Clorets, Beemans, Blackjack, and Clove brands.

Other confectionery products include Junior Mints, Pom Poms, Sugar Daddy, Sugar Babies, Fazermints, and Choclairs.

Warner-Lambert acquired razormaker Wilkinson Sword Blade in 1993 to go along with its Schick subsidiary. Schick and Wilkinson are both key players in the U.S. razor market, while Schick is a market leader in Japan and Wilkinson has a strong presence in Europe.

Consumer health care products account for 47 percent of the company's revenue. In addition to razors, Warner-Lambert makes a long list of familiar consumer over-the-counter health aids, including Rolaids, Certs, Listerine, Listermint, Halls throat lozenges, Sinutab, Efferdent, Benylin, Benadryl, Lubriderm, Corn Huskers, Paramet, Listerex, Anusol, Agoral, Sterisol, and Promega.

Warner-Lambert's other key segment is pharmaceutical products, which accounts for 33 percent of its total revenue. The company produces a line of analgesics, anesthetics, anticonvulsants, anti-infectives, antihistamines, antiviral agents, bronchodilators, cardiovascular products, dermatologics, hemorrhoidal preparations, influenza vaccines, oral contraceptives, and other products.

Its Warner-Chilcott Laboratories produces more than 200 generic pharmaceutical products.

Warner-Lambert does business in more than 130 countries. Foreign sales account for about 57 percent of the company's total revenue.

The company has about 37,000 employees and 43,000 shareholders.

EARNINGS-PER-SHARE GROWTH   (no points)

Past 5 years: 39 percent (6 percent per year)
Past 10 years: 226 percent (12.5 percent per year)

STOCK GROWTH   ★ ★ ★

Past 10 years: 454 percent (18 percent per year)
Dollar growth: $10,000 over 10 years (including reinvested dividends) would have grown to $67,000
Average annual compounded rate of return (including reinvested dividends): 21 percent

DIVIDEND YIELD

Average dividend yield in the past 3 years: 3.0 percent

DIVIDEND GROWTH

Increased dividend: More than 21 consecutive years
Past 5-year increase: 57 percent (9 percent per year)

CONSISTENCY   ★ ★ ★ ★

Increased earnings per share: 10 consecutive years
Increased sales: 10 consecutive years

SHAREHOLDER PERKS   ★ ★

Good dividend reinvestment and stock purchase plan: voluntary stock purchase plan allows contributions of $10 to $60,000 per year.

The company also puts coupons for its products in some of its quarterly reports. For instance, a recent report had a coupon for Trident Val-U-Pak—buy one, get one free.

WARNER-LAMBERT AT A GLANCE

Fiscal year ended: Dec. 31
Revenue and net income in $ millions

	1991	1992	1993	1994	1995	1996	5-Year Growth Avg. Annual (%)	Total (%)
Revenue ($)	5,059	5,597.6	5,793.7	6,416.8	7,039.8	7,231.4	7	43
Net income ($)	599.1	643.7	645.4	694	739.5	855.5	7	43
Earnings/share ($)	2.08	2.39	2.45	2.59	2.74	2.90	6	39
Div. per share ($)	0.88	1.02	1.14	1.22	1.30	1.38	9	57
Dividend yield (%)	2.4	3.1	3.3	3.4	3.1	2.4	—	—
Avg. PE ratio	17	14	14	14	17	22	—	—

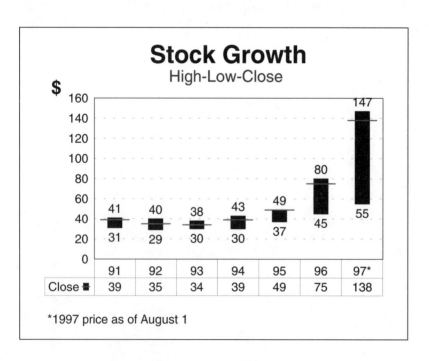

Stock Growth
High-Low-Close

	91	92	93	94	95	96	97*
Close	39	35	34	39	49	75	138

*1997 price as of August 1

Equifax, Inc.

P. O. Box 4081
1600 Peachtree Street, N.W.
Atlanta, GA 30302
404-885-8000

Chairman: C. B. Rogers, Jr.
President and CEO: Daniel W. McGlaughlin

Earnings Growth	★ ★ ★ ★	Dividend Growth	
Stock Growth	★ ★ ★	Consistency	★ ★ ★
Dividend Yield	★ ★	Shareholder Perks	★ ★
NYSE—EFX		**Total**	**14 points**

Equifax has built a billion-dollar business providing credit information on consumers for thousands of businesses around the world.

The Atlanta-based business operates the largest credit-reporting network in the United States. The company provides consumer credit reports for banks, retailers, financial institutions, utilities, oil companies, credit card companies, auto finance and leasing firms, and mortgage lenders.

The company also provides related services such as collection services, fraud detection and prevention, credit card marketing, database marketing and database management systems, mortgage loan origination information, and analytical services. Credit services account for about 32 percent of the firm's $1.8 billion in annual revenue.

Equifax also operates four other key business segments, including:

1. **Payment services** (17 percent of revenue). Equifax provides online verification of checks written at the point of sale, credit card–processing, and related services for banks and financial institutions.
2. **Insurance services** (32 percent). The company provides consumer information for insurance companies to help them determine the classification of applicants as risks for life and health insurance.

3. **International operations** (13 percent). The firm provides credit information services for customers throughout North America and South America and Europe.
4. **General information services** (6 percent). Equifax furnishes a broad range of informational and administrative services such as electronic claim processing, online eligibility verification, and claims analysis.

Equifax was founded in 1899 as a credit-reporting agency under the name Retail Credit Company. It changed its name to Equifax in 1975.

The company has about 14,000 employees and 7,000 shareholders.

EARNINGS-PER-SHARE GROWTH ★ ★ ★ ★

Past 5 years: 270 percent (30 percent per year)
Past 10 years: 307 percent (15 percent per year)

STOCK GROWTH ★ ★ ★

Past 10 years: 415 percent (18 percent per year)
Dollar growth: $10,000 over 10 years (including reinvested dividends) would have grown to $66,000
Average annual compounded rate of return (including reinvested dividends): 21 percent

DIVIDEND YIELD ★ ★

Average dividend yield in the past 3 years: 1.8 percent

DIVIDEND GROWTH (no points)

Increased dividend: 9 of the past 10 years
Past 5-year increase: 27 percent (5 percent per year)

CONSISTENCY ★ ★ ★

Increased earnings per share: 9 of the past 10 years

SHAREHOLDER PERKS ★ ★

Good dividend reinvestment and stock purchase plan: voluntary stock purchase plan allows contributions of $10 to $5,000 per quarter.

EQUIFAX AT A GLANCE

Fiscal year ended: Dec. 31
Revenue and net income in $ millions

	1991	1992	1993	1994	1995	1996	5-Year Growth Avg. Annual (%)	Total (%)
Revenue ($)	1,093.8	1,134.3	1,217.2	1,422	1,623	1,811.2	11	66
Net income ($)	54.1	85.3	63.5	120.3	147.6	177.6	27	228
Earnings/share ($)	0.33	0.52	0.42	0.81	0.98	1.22	30	270
Div. per share ($)	.26	.26	.28	.30	.32	.33	5	27
Dividend yield (%)	3.0	3.1	2.5	2.2	1.8	1.3	—	—
Avg. PE ratio	26	16	18	17	18	21	—	—

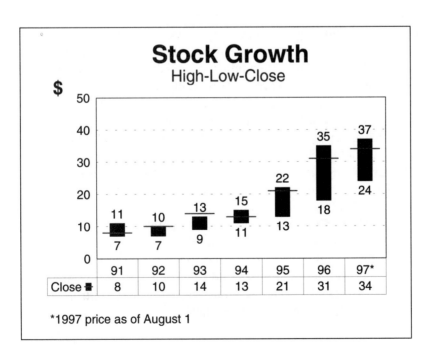

Stock Growth
High-Low-Close

$

	91	92	93	94	95	96	97*
Close	8	10	14	13	21	31	34

*1997 price as of August 1

49

Anheuser-Busch Companies, Inc.

One Busch Place
St. Louis, MO 63118-1852
800-DIAL-BUD

Chairman, CEO, and President: August A. Busch III

Earnings Growth		Dividend Growth	★ ★ ★
Stock Growth	★ ★	Consistency	★ ★ ★
Dividend Yield	★ ★ ★	Shareholder Perks	★ ★ ★
NYSE—BUD		**Total**	**14 points**

Beer has always been the driving force behind the Anheuser-Busch brewing dynasty. But the company has stepped up to the bar in several other markets as well. The St. Louis brewer is one of the nation's largest theme park operators, the second largest manufacturer of aluminum beverage containers, and the world's largest recycler of aluminum beverage cans. Not so coincidently, it also has interests in malt production, rice milling, metalized and paper label printing, and transportation services.

But Busch has given up some key parts of its business over the past couple of years. It sold the St. Louis Cardinals baseball team, spun off its Campbell Taggart baking subsidiary to shareholders, and closed its Eagle Snacks subsidiary, selling four production plants to Frito-Lay.

For Busch, the result was addition by subtraction. After a flat year in 1995, the company's earnings jumped 21 percent in 1996.

Anheuser-Busch sells about 88 million barrels of beer a year. It is the world's largest brewer and now boasts the top-selling regular beer (Budweiser), the top-selling light beer (Bud Light), and the top-selling nonalcoholic beer (O'Doul's). The St. Louis–based brewer controls a whopping 45 percent share of the U.S. beer market.

Beer sales account for about 78 percent of the company's $11.3 billion in annual revenue.

Among the company's other leading brands are Michelob, Busch, Natural Light, and King Cobra. Among its other brands are Amber Bock, Elk Mountain Amber Ale, Red Wolf Lager, and Natural Pilsner. The company also imports two European-brewed beers, Carlsberg and Elephant Malt Liquor.

Internationally, the company brews beer in eight countries and sells it in more than 70 other countries. Busch's brewing business is fully integrated. It operates 13 breweries in the United States, owns a beverage can manufacturer, a barley-processing plant, a label-printing operation, and a refrigerated railcar transportation subsidiary.

The firm also owns and operates a number of entertainment theme parks, including two Busch Gardens parks (in Tampa, Florida, and Williamsburg, Virginia); "Adventure Island" in Tampa; "Sesame Place" in Langhorne, Pennsylvania; Cypress Gardens in Winter Haven, Florida; Baseball City Sports Complex near Orlando; four Sea World parks; and "Water Country USA" in Williamsburg.

Anheuser-Busch traces its roots to a small St. Louis brewery started in 1852. After a few years of lackluster results, the original owner, George Schneider, sold out the struggling operation to an investment group headed by St. Louis soap tycoon Eberhard Anheuser. Anheuser ultimately turned the business over to his son-in-law, a portly, gregarious man by the name of Adolphus Busch.

Busch, who converted the small brewery into a national force, is generally recognized as the founder of Anheuser-Busch. Budweiser, which Busch helped develop in 1876, was one of the first beers to achieve widespread distribution. Michelob, the company's "premium" beer, was first brought to market in 1896. When Adolphus Busch died in 1913, his son, August A. Busch, assumed control of the business. The reins have since been passed through two more generations of the Busch family. August A. Busch III, 59, now directs the company as its chairman of the board, president, and CEO.

Anheuser-Busch has 24,000 employees and 64,000 shareholders.

EARNINGS-PER-SHARE GROWTH   (no points)

Past 5 years: 41 percent (7 percent per year)
Past 10 years: 171 percent (10 percent per year)

STOCK GROWTH

Past 10 years: 362 percent (16 percent per year)
Dollar growth: $10,000 over 10 years (including reinvested dividends) would have grown to $57,000
Average annual compounded rate of return (including reinvested dividends): 19 percent

DIVIDEND YIELD

Average dividend yield in the past 3 years: 2.8 percent

DIVIDEND GROWTH

Increased dividend: 24 consecutive years
Past 5-year increase: 74 percent (12 percent per year)

CONSISTENCY

Increased earnings per share: 9 of the past 10 years
Increased sales: 9 of the past 10 years

SHAREHOLDER PERKS ★ ★ ★

Good dividend reinvestment and stock purchase plan: voluntary stock purchase plan allows contributions of $25 to $5,000 per month.

New shareholders of record are sent a letter of welcome, a fact book on the company, and a pamphlet on its dividend reinvestment plan.

The company makes a point of moving its annual meetings around the country. In recent years, meetings have been staged in Tampa and Orlando, Florida; Williamsburg, Virginia; and Fort Collins, Colorado. Those who attend get a chance to sample all the company's brews.

Shareholders are also entitled to a discount on admission to the company's amusement parks.

ANHEUSER-BUSCH AT A GLANCE

Fiscal year ended: Dec. 31
Revenue and net income in $ millions

	1991	1992	1993	1994	1995	1996	5-Year Growth Avg. Annual (%)	5-Year Growth Total (%)
Revenue ($)	10,631	11,008	11,147	11,705	12,004	11,290	1	6
Net income ($)	900.9	964.1	657.2	1,014.5	886.6	1,156.1	5	28
Earnings/share ($)	1.63	1.73	1.78	1.94	1.90	2.30	7	41
Div. per share ($)	.53	.60	.68	.76	.84	.92	12	74
Dividend yield (%)	1.7	2.1	2.8	3.0	2.5	2.2	—	—
Avg. PE ratio	16	16	14	13	16	17	—	—

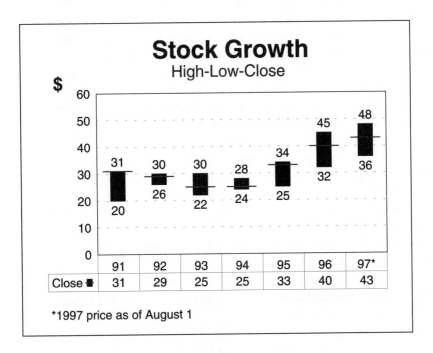

Stock Growth
High-Low-Close

	91	92	93	94	95	96	97*
Close ■	31	29	25	25	33	40	43

*1997 price as of August 1

50

Sysco Corp.

1390 Enclave Parkway
Houston, TX 77077-2027
713-584-1390

Chairman: John F. Woodhouse
President and CEO: Bill M. Lindig

Earnings Growth	★ ★	Dividend Growth	★ ★ ★ ★
Stock Growth	★ ★	Consistency	★ ★ ★ ★
Dividend Yield	★	Shareholder Perks	★
NYSE—SYY		**Total**	**14 points**

America is the breadbasket of the world, and in America, it is Sysco that delivers the bread—and the butter, meat, potatoes, fruit, and 190,000 other food and related products to thousands of food-service operations.

The Houston-based distributor is America's largest marketer of food-service products, with operations in the nation's 150 largest cities (plus parts of Canada). In all, Sysco distributes nearly 200,000 cases of food a day. Operating from 70 distribution centers, Sysco delivers food and related products to 260,000 restaurants, hotels, schools, hospitals, retirement homes, and other food-service operations.

Sysco does not produce its own products but rather procures goods from several thousand independent sources, including both large brand-name food producers and independent private-label processors.

Sysco's leading product segment is canned and dry products, which account for about 24 percent of the company's $13.4 billion in annual revenue. Other significant contributors are fresh and frozen meats, 15 percent; frozen fruits, vegetables, and bakery goods, 14 percent; dairy products, 9 percent; paper and disposables, 8 percent; and poultry, 10 percent. The company also handles beverages, fresh produce, janitorial products, seafood, and medical supplies.

Restaurant sales account for 61 percent of Sysco's annual revenue, while hospitals and nursing homes account for 11 percent; schools and colleges make up 7 percent; hotels and motels generate 6 percent; and other sources such as retail groceries account for 15 percent.

Founded in 1969 through the merger of nine small food distributors, Sysco has grown rapidly through a series of acquisitions. In all, the company has acquired about 50 other food-related businesses.

The company has 31,000 employees and 20,000 shareholders.

EARNINGS-PER-SHARE GROWTH ★ ★

Past 5 years: 81 percent (13 percent per year)
Past 10 years: 347 percent (16 percent per year)

STOCK GROWTH ★ ★

Past 10 years: 363 percent (17 percent per year)
Dollar growth: $10,000 over 10 years (including reinvested dividends) would have grown to $52,000
Average annual compounded rate of return (including reinvested dividends): 18 percent

DIVIDEND YIELD ★

Average dividend yield in the past 3 years: 1.4 percent

DIVIDEND GROWTH ★ ★ ★ ★

Increased dividend: 26 consecutive years
Past 5-year increase: 300 percent (32 percent per year)

CONSISTENCY ★ ★ ★ ★

Increased earnings per share: 20 consecutive years
Increased sales: 20 consecutive years

SHAREHOLDER PERKS ★

The company offers a dividend reinvestment plan, but no stock purchase plan.

SYSCO CORP. AT A GLANCE

Fiscal year ended: June 30
Revenue and net income in $ millions

	1991	1992	1993	1994	1995	1996	5-Year Growth Avg. Annual (%)	Total (%)
Revenue ($)	8,150	8,893	10,022	10,943	12,118	13,395	10	64
Net income ($)	153.8	172.2	201.8	216.8	251.8	277	13	80
Earnings/share ($)	0.84	0.93	1.08	1.18	1.38	1.52	13	81
Div. per share ($)	.12	.17	.26	.32	.40	.48	32	300
Dividend yield (%)	.7	.7	.9	1.2	1.5	1.5	—	—
Avg. PE ratio	21	24	24	23	19	21	—	—

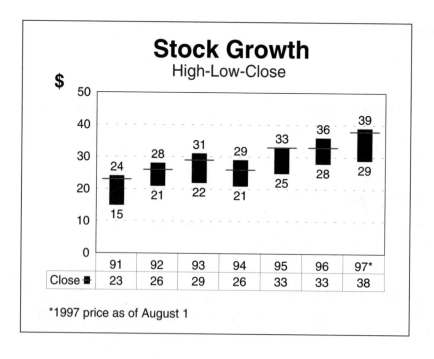

Stock Growth
High-Low-Close

$	91	92	93	94	95	96	97*
Close	23	26	29	26	33	33	38

*1997 price as of August 1

Electronic Data Systems

7171 Forest Lane
Dallas, TX 75320
214-604-6000

Chairman and CEO: Lester M. Alberthal, Jr.

Earnings Growth	★ ★	Dividend Growth	★ ★ ★
Stock Growth	★ ★	Consistency	★ ★ ★ ★
Dividend Yield	★	Shareholder Perks	★ ★
NYSE—EDS		**Total**	**14 points**

Electronic Data Systems may always be known as the company that turned Ross Perot into a billionaire. The one-time presidential hopeful founded EDS in 1962 for $1,000 and sold it to General Motors 22 years later for $2.5 billion.

The company no longer is owned by GM, but EDS still relies on the automaker for 31 percent of its $14.4 billion in annual revenue. EDS provides data-processing and telecommunications services for GM under a long-term master service agreement. It handles such tasks as benefits administration, dealer networks, engineering technologies, and business information systems for GM. The automaker spun off EDS in 1996, although EDS had already been publicly traded on the New York Stock Exchange for several years under the symbol GME. It now trades under the symbol EDS.

EDS's forte is running the computer networks of its corporate clients more efficiently than they can do it themselves.

For example, EDS has a ten-year, $3.2 billion contract with Xerox Corporation to run its telecommunications systems and computer networks. And in Taiwan, nine out of ten health claims are processed by systems supported by EDS as part of the country's national health insurance program.

With most of its clients, EDS not only assumes the customers' equipment but hires the customers' information services employees as well.

EDS has a worldwide customer base of about 9,000 customers. About one-third of its revenue is generated overseas. Its aggressive overseas marketing has resulted in much faster growth abroad than in the domestic market.

The Dallas-based operation has about 71,000 employees and about 393,000 shareholders.

EARNINGS-PER-SHARE GROWTH   ★ ★

Past 5 years: 82 percent (13 percent per year)
Past 10 years: 291 percent (14 percent per year)

STOCK GROWTH   ★ ★

Past 10 years: 365 percent (17 percent per year)
Dollar growth: $10,000 over 10 years (including reinvested dividends) would have grown to $52,000
Average annual compounded rate of return (including reinvested dividends): 18 percent

DIVIDEND YIELD   ★

Average dividend yield in the past 3 years: 1.2 percent

DIVIDEND GROWTH   ★ ★ ★

Increased dividend: 11 consecutive years
Past 5-year increase: 88 percent (14 percent per year)

CONSISTENCY   ★ ★ ★ ★

Increased earnings per share: 14 consecutive years
Increased sales: 14 consecutive years

SHAREHOLDER PERKS   ★ ★

Good dividend reinvestment and stock purchase plan: voluntary stock purchase plan allows shareholders of 50 or more shares to contribute $100 to $15,000 per quarter.

ELECTRONIC DATA SYSTEMS AT A GLANCE

Fiscal year ended: Dec. 31
Revenue and net income in $ millions

	1991	1992	1993	1994	1995	1996	5-Year Growth Avg. Annual (%)	Total (%)
Revenue ($)	7,028.5	8,155.2	8,507.3	9,960.1	12,422	14,441	15	105
Net income ($)	547.5	635.5	724	821.9	938.9	1,000	13	83
Earnings/share ($)	1.14	1.33	1.51	1.71	1.96	2.07	13	82
Div. per share ($)	.32	.36	.40	.48	.52	.60	14	88
Dividend yield (%)	1.3	1.1	1.3	1.4	1.2	1.1	—	—
Avg. PE ratio	21	22	20	20	22	26	—	—

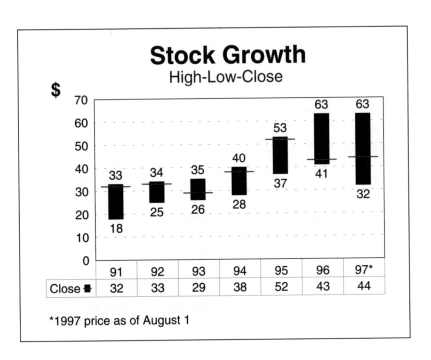

Stock Growth
High-Low-Close

	91	92	93	94	95	96	97*
Close	32	33	29	38	52	43	44

*1997 price as of August 1

52

Jefferson-Pilot Corp.

1100 North Greene Street
Greensboro, NC 27401
910-691-3000

President and CEO: David A. Stonecipher

Earnings Growth	★	Dividend Growth	★ ★ ★
Stock Growth	★ ★	Consistency	★ ★ ★
Dividend Yield	★ ★ ★	Shareholder Perks	★ ★
NYSE—JP		**Total**	**14 points**

Founded in 1890, Jefferson-Pilot offers a broad range of life insurance, group health insurance, and other types of insurance policies and investment products. The firm also owns several television and radio stations.

Through its Jefferson-Pilot and Alexander Hamilton life insurance companies, the Greensboro, North Carolina, operation offers continuous and limited-pay life and endowment policies, universal life policies and annuity contracts, retirement income plans, and level and decreasing term insurance. About 54 percent of its operating income comes from its life insurance segment.

Jefferson-Pilot also offers a range of investment products and services, including several types of annuities and two mutual funds, the Jefferson-Pilot Capital Appreciation Fund and the Jefferson-Pilot Investment Grade Bond Fund.

The company's life insurance and investment products are marketed by a staff of more than 400 full-time agents and thousands of independent agents. They are also sold by 60 financial institutions and 36 brokerage companies.

Jefferson-Pilot's accident and health insurance segment accounts for 51 percent of its premiums and 17 percent of its operating income.

About 10 percent of the company's operating income is generated by its communications division. The company owns television stations in

Charlotte, Charleston, and Richmond (Virginia), and radio stations in Atlanta, Charlotte, Denver, Miami, and San Diego. The company also produces television sports programs covering college basketball and football and professional motor sports.

The company has about 1,000 employees and 10,000 stockholders.

EARNINGS-PER-SHARE GROWTH ★

Past 5 years: 79 percent (12 percent per year)
Past 10 years: 220 percent (12 percent per year)

STOCK GROWTH ★ ★

Past 10 years: 258 percent (14 percent per year)
Dollar growth: $10,000 over 10 years (including reinvested dividends) would have grown to $48,000
Average annual compounded rate of return (including reinvested dividends): 17 percent

DIVIDEND YIELD ★ ★ ★

Average dividend yield in the past 3 years: 3.0 percent

DIVIDEND GROWTH ★ ★ ★

Increased dividend: 15 consecutive years
Past 5-year increase: 97 percent (15 percent per year)

CONSISTENCY ★ ★ ★

Increased earnings per share: 9 consecutive years

SHAREHOLDER PERKS ★ ★

Good dividend reinvestment and stock purchase plan: voluntary stock purchase plan allows contributions of $20 to $2,000 per month.

JEFFERSON-PILOT AT A GLANCE

Fiscal year ended: Dec. 31
Revenue and net income in $ millions

	1991	1992	1993	1994	1995	1996	5-Year Growth Avg. Annual (%)	Total (%)
Revenue ($)	1,173.5	1,202.3	1,246.6	1,333.7	1,605.5	2,125.2	13	81
Net income ($)	175.7	203.2	195.2	239.2	273	292.9	11	67
Earnings/share ($)	2.29	2.66	2.59	3.28	3.81	4.09	12	79
Div. per share ($)	0.73	0.87	1.04	1.12	1.25	1.44	15	97
Dividend yield (%)	3.4	3.2	3.1	3.3	3.1	2.7	—	—
Avg. PE ratio	9	10	12	11	11	12	—	—

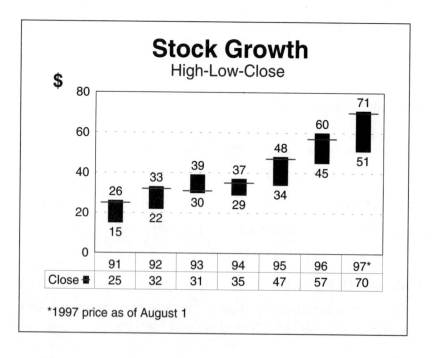

Stock Growth
High-Low-Close

$	91	92	93	94	95	96	97*
Close	25	32	31	35	47	57	70

*1997 price as of August 1

Carlisle Companies, Inc.

250 South Clinton Street, Suite 201
Syracuse, NY 13202
315-474-2500

Chairman and CEO: Stephen P. Munn
President: Dennis J. Hall

Earnings Growth	★ ★ ★ ★	Dividend Growth	★ ★
Stock Growth	★ ★	Consistency	★ ★
Dividend Yield	★ ★	Shareholder Perks	★ ★
NYSE—CSI		**Total**	**14 points**

Since Carlisle first opened shop in 1917 as a manufacturer of inner tubes for bicycle and automobile tires, the company has gradually expanded its product offerings. Now the Syracuse-based operation manufactures a broad and diverse range of products, from truck brakes and roofing materials to food-service and catering equipment.

The company's leading product segment continues to be its transportation products, which account for about 37 percent of its $1.02 billion in annual revenue.

Carlisle's primary transportation-related products include heavy-duty friction and braking systems for truck and off-highway equipment, rubber and plastic automotive components (such as precision-molded engine components and blow-molded bumper beams), high-grade aerospace wire, specialty trailers, self-contained perishable cargo shipping containers, and high-payload truck trailers and dump bodies.

Construction materials account for about 32 percent of Carlisle's total revenue. The company makes rubber, plastic, and fleece-back sheeting used on nonresidential flat roofs. It also makes related roofing accessories, such as flashings, fasteners, ceiling tapes, coatings, and waterproofing products.

Carlisle's general construction segment accounts for about 31 percent of its revenue, and includes small rubber ties, stamped and roll-formed wheels, commercial and institutional plastic food-service and catering equipment, and related products.

   Much of the company's growth in recent years has come through acquisitions of other manufacturers. Carlisle has about 6,900 employees and 2,500 shareholders.

EARNINGS-PER-SHARE GROWTH ★ ★ ★ ★

Past 5 years: 200 percent (25 percent per year)
Past 10 years: 233 percent (13 percent per year)

STOCK GROWTH ★ ★

Past 10 years: 278 percent (14 percent per year)
Dollar growth: $10,000 over 10 years (including reinvested dividends) would have grown to $48,000
Average annual compounded rate of return (including reinvested dividends): 17 percent

DIVIDEND YIELD ★ ★

Average dividend yield in the past 3 years: 2.0 percent

DIVIDEND GROWTH ★ ★

Increased dividend: 11 consecutive years
Past 5-year increase: 47 percent (8 percent per year)

CONSISTENCY ★ ★

Increased earnings per share: 8 of the past 10 years
Increased sales: 9 of the past 10 years

SHAREHOLDER PERKS ★ ★

Good dividend reinvestment and stock purchase plan: voluntary cash contributions of $10 to $3,000 per quarter.

CARLISLE COMPANIES AT A GLANCE

Fiscal year ended: Dec. 31
Revenue and net income in $ millions

	1991	1992	1993	1994	1995	1996	5-Year Growth Avg. Annual (%)	Total (%)
Revenue ($)	500.8	528.1	611.3	692.7	822.5	1,017.5	15	103
Net income ($)	6.6	24.2	28.4	35.6	44.1	55.7	54	744
Earnings/share ($)	0.60	0.79	0.92	1.15	1.41	1.80	25	200
Div. per share ($)	.32	.33	.35	.38	.42	.47	8	47
Dividend yield (%)	3.5	3.1	2.3	2.2	2.1	1.7	—	—
Avg. PE ratio	14	13	16	14	14	14	—	—

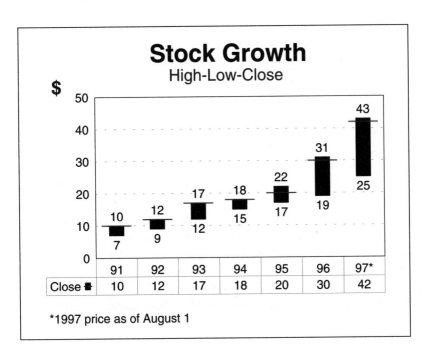

Stock Growth
High-Low-Close

	91	92	93	94	95	96	97*
Close ■	10	12	17	18	20	30	42

*1997 price as of August 1

54

Hershey Foods Corp.

100 Crystal A Drive
P. O. Box 810
Hershey, PA 17033
717-534-6799

Chairman and CEO: Kenneth L. Wolfe
President: Joseph P. Viviano

Earnings Growth	★	Dividend Growth	★ ★ ★
Stock Growth	★ ★	Consistency	★ ★ ★
Dividend Yield	★ ★	Shareholder Perks	★ ★ ★
NYSE—HSY		**Total**	**14 points**

The health food trend has never taken the starch out of Hershey Foods' growth. Even many health-conscious Americans still have a weakness for chocolate and Hershey's other confectionery delights—a weakness that has manifested itself in a steady stream of record sales and earnings for the Hershey, Pennsylvania, operation. The company has posted record earnings during 17 of the past 18 years.

Hershey is the nation's leading confectionery producer, with about a 35 percent share of the $10 billion U.S. candy market. The company claims five of the top ten chocolate brands in the United States, including Reese's, Kit Kat, Hershey's chocolate bar, Hershey's Kisses, and Hershey's chocolate bar with almonds.

Through brand extension and a series of acquisitions, Hershey has assembled a long line of other confectionery favorites as well, including Peter Paul Almond Joy, Mounds Bars, Caramello, Cadbury's Creme Eggs, Hershey's Big Block, Special Dark, Golden Almond, Golden Almond Nuggets, Krackel, and Rolo caramels.

Other well-known brands include Skor, Mr. Goodbar, Reese's Pieces, Fifth Avenue, Twizzlers, Bar None, York peppermint pattie, and Symphony. The company also produces Luden's cough drops and Mellomints.

Hershey recently acquired Henry Heide, Inc., which produces two candy brands, Jujyfruits and Wunderbeans.

In addition to its candies, Hershey offers a line of chocolate mixes, including Hershey's cocoa, chocolate milk mix, baking chocolate, chocolate syrup, fudge topping, chocolate chips and premium chunks, and chocolate flavor puddings.

The company also operates a burgeoning pasta division. Leading brands are Ronzoni, American Beauty, San Giorgio, Light 'n Fluffy, and Skinner.

Hershey's products are sold in 60 countries worldwide. Its international operations account for 13 percent of its $4 billion in annual revenue.

Founded in 1893 by Milton Hershey, the company has about 13,300 employees and 38,500 shareholders.

EARNINGS-PER-SHARE GROWTH ★

Past 5 years: 64 percent (10 percent per year)
Past 10 years: 182 percent (11 percent per year)

STOCK GROWTH ★ ★

Past 10 years: 284 percent (14 percent per year)
Dollar growth: $10,000 over 10 years (including reinvested dividends) would have grown to $46,000
Average annual compounded rate of return (including reinvested dividends): 16.5 percent

DIVIDEND YIELD ★ ★

Average dividend yield in the past 3 years: 2.3 percent

DIVIDEND GROWTH ★ ★ ★

Increased dividend: 22 consecutive years
Past 5-year increase: 62 percent (10 percent per year)

CONSISTENCY

Increased earnings per share: 9 of the past 10 years
Increased sales: 9 of the past 10 years

SHAREHOLDER PERKS ★ ★ ★

Good dividend reinvestment and stock purchase plan: voluntary stock purchase plan allows contributions of $50 to $20,000 per year.

Hershey makes Christmas shopping a lot easier for shareholders with chocolate-loving friends. Hershey's Chocolate World visitors center mails its Christmas gift catalog to any shareholder requesting it, and maintains a mailing list for annual receipt of the catalog. Shareholders may purchase special gift packages from the catalog and have them wrapped and mailed directly to their friends.

Shareholders who attend the annual meeting are treated to a free packet of Hershey's new products samples as well as a gift certificate offering 30 percent to 50 percent discounts on a variety of food and gift items.

HERSHEY AT A GLANCE

Fiscal year ended: Dec. 31
Revenue and net income in $ millions

	1991	1992	1993	1994	1995	1996	5-Year Growth Avg. Annual (%)	Total (%)
Revenue ($)	2,899.2	3,219.8	3,488.2	3,606.3	3,690.7	3,989.3	7	38
Net income ($)	219.5	242.6	297.2	184.2	281.9	273.2	5	25
Earnings/share ($)	1.22	1.35	1.66	1.06	1.70	2.00	10	64
Div. per share ($)	.47	.52	.57	.63	.69	.76	10	62
Dividend yield (%)	2.2	2.2	2.3	2.7	2.4	1.9	—	—
Avg. PE ratio	17	16	18	15	17	21	—	—

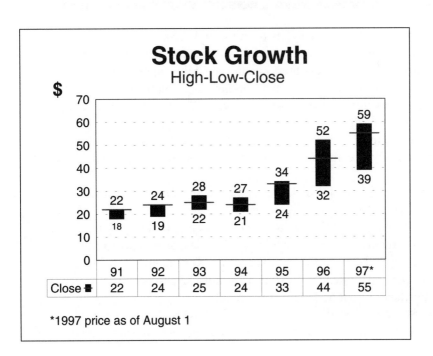

Stock Growth
High-Low-Close

	91	92	93	94	95	96	97*
Close	22	24	25	24	33	44	55

*1997 price as of August 1

55

The May Department Stores Company

611 Olive Street
St. Louis, MO 63101-1799
314-342-6300

Chairman and CEO: David C. Farrell
President: Jerome T. Loeb

Earnings Growth	★ ★	Dividend Growth	★ ★
Stock Growth	★	Consistency	★ ★ ★ ★
Dividend Yield	★ ★ ★	Shareholder Perks	★ ★
NYSE—MAY		**Total**	**14 points**

The department store business has been through a lot during the past two decades, including several economic downturns and a rapid rise in competition from the giant discounters and the specialty superstores. But May Department Stores, the largest department store chain in America, has still managed to survive the rocky times with 22 consecutive years of record sales and earnings per share.

May operates 364 stores in 30 states and the District of Columbia. Over the next five years, the company plans to open 115 new department stores.

May operates several different department store chains, including: Lord & Taylor, New York, 60 stores (15 percent of its total revenue); Hecht's, Washington D.C., 65 stores (16 percent); Foley's, Houston, 51 stores (16 percent); Robinsons-May, Los Angeles, 53 stores (15 percent); Famous-Barr, St. Louis, 30 stores (9 percent); Kaufmann's, Pittsburgh, 46 stores (13 percent); Filene's, Boston, 40 stores (12 percent); and Meier & Frank, Portland, Oregon, 8 stores (3 percent).

The St. Louis–based retailer spun off its Payless Shoe Stores subsidiary in 1996 to concentrate more on its department store business. Payless, which operates about 4,000 shoe stores, accounted for about 20 percent of May's total revenue.

The company was founded by David May, who opened his first store in Leadville, Colorado, in 1877. May has grown to include about 105,000 employees and 46,000 shareholders.

EARNINGS-PER-SHARE GROWTH ★★

Past 5 years: 86 percent (13 percent per year)
Past 10 years: 131 percent (9 percent per year)

STOCK GROWTH ★

Past 10 years: 152 percent (10 percent per year)
Dollar growth: $10,000 over 10 years (including reinvested dividends) would have grown to $34,000
Average annual compounded rate of return (including reinvested dividends): 13 percent

DIVIDEND YIELD ★★★

Average dividend yield in the past 3 years: 2.6 percent

DIVIDEND GROWTH ★★

Increased dividend: 22 consecutive years
Past 5-year increase: 43 percent (7 percent per year)

CONSISTENCY ★★★★

Increased earnings per share: 22 consecutive years
Increased sales: 22 consecutive years

SHAREHOLDER PERKS ★★

Outstanding dividend reinvestment and stock purchase plan: voluntary stock purchase plan allows contributions of $25 and up (with no upper limit) per month.

MAY AT A GLANCE

Fiscal year ended: Jan. 31
Revenue and net income in $ millions

	1991	1992	1993	1994	1995	1996	5-Year Growth Avg. Annual (%)	5-Year Growth Total (%)
Revenue ($)	9,068	9,362	9,562	10,107	10,952	12,000	6	32
Net income ($)	515	603	711	782	752	749	8	45
Earnings/share ($)	1.52	1.76	2.15	2.43	2.61	2.82	13	86
Div. per share ($)	0.81	0.83	0.90	1.01	1.12	1.16	7	43
Dividend yield (%)	3.0	2.7	2.3	2.6	2.7	2.5	—	—
Avg. PE ratio	13	13	14	13	16	17	—	—

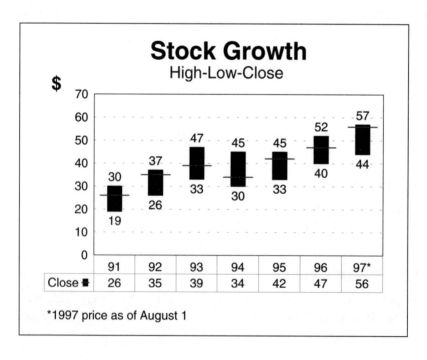

Stock Growth
High-Low-Close

	91	92	93	94	95	96	97*
Close	26	35	39	34	42	47	56

*1997 price as of August 1

Pall Corp.

2200 Northern Blvd.
East Hills, NY 11548
516-484-5400

Chairman and CEO: Eric Krasnoff
President: Jeremy Hayward-Surry

Earnings Growth	★	Dividend Growth	★ ★ ★ ★
Stock Growth	★	Consistency	★ ★ ★ ★
Dividend Yield	★ ★	Shareholder Perks	★ ★
NYSE—PLL		**Total**	**14 points**

Pall battles dust, dirt, lint, germs, and a host of other harmful microscopic particles. The company supplies filters for everything from aircraft engines and power plants to disk drives and blood filtration systems.

Nearly half of Pall's $960 million in annual revenue comes from sales to the health care industry. Pall patient protection filters, which account for 25 percent of its revenue, are used in blood centers and hospitals for patients receiving blood transfusions and undergoing open-heart surgery, organ transplants, intravenous feeding, and breathing therapy. Pall is a leader in the supply of filtration systems, validation services, and proprietary membranes used in the manufacture of pharmaceuticals, biopharmaceuticals, blood fractions, therapeutic biologicals, and food and beverages (24 percent of total revenue). Pall filters are also used for diagnostic tests and laboratory-scale filtration devices.

Pall also serves two other important industry segments:

1. **Aeropower** (24.5 percent of sales). Pall is a leading supplier of filtration products for the commercial and military aircraft market for use on aircraft, ships, and land-based vehicles. The firm also makes filters for power generation plants and manufacturers of aluminum and steel, paper, automobiles, injection molded parts, trucks, and earthmoving machinery.

2. **Fluid processing** (26.5 percent of sales). Pall's products are used in oil refining, electric generation, and computer circuitry production, as well as in the production of chemicals, plastics, photographic film, magnetic storage devices, ink-jet printers, computer terminals, and a broad range of other products.

The company has about 6,500 employees and 5,300 shareholders.

EARNINGS-PER-SHARE GROWTH ★

Past 5 years: 75 percent (12 percent per year)
Past 10 years: 218 percent (12 percent per year)

STOCK GROWTH ★

Past 10 years: 179 percent (11 percent per year)
Dollar growth: $10,000 over 10 years (including reinvested dividends) would have grown to $32,000
Average annual compounded rate of return (including reinvested dividends): 12 percent

DIVIDEND YIELD ★ ★

Average dividend yield in the past 3 years: 2.0 percent

DIVIDEND GROWTH ★ ★ ★ ★

Increased dividend: 22 consecutive years.
Past 5-year increase: 124 percent (18 percent per year)

CONSISTENCY ★ ★ ★ ★

Increased earnings per share: 25 consecutive years
Increased sales: 25 consecutive years

SHAREHOLDER PERKS ★ ★

Good dividend reinvestment and stock purchase plan: voluntary stock purchase plan allows contributions of $100 up to $60,000 per year.

PALL CORP. AT A GLANCE

Fiscal year ended: July 31
Revenue and net income in $ millions

	1991	1992	1993	1994	1995	1996	5-Year Growth Avg. Annual (%)	5-Year Growth Total (%)
Revenue ($)	657	685.1	687.2	700.8	822.8	960.4	8	46
Net income ($)	79.9	92.7	78.3	98.9	118.4	138.5	12	73
Earnings/share ($)	0.69	0.79	0.68	0.86	1.03	1.21	12	75
Div. per share ($)	.21	.26	.31	.36	.41	.47	18	124
Dividend yield (%)	1.5	1.3	1.6	2.0	2.1	1.9	—	—
Avg. PE ratio	20	25	24	20	19	21	—	—

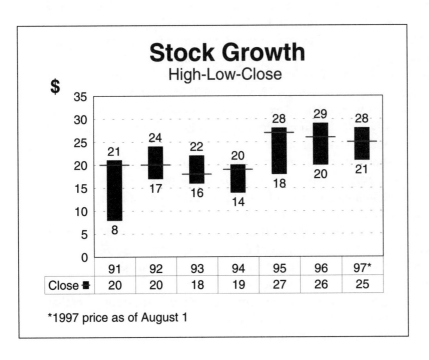

*1997 price as of August 1

57
Nike, Inc.

One Bowerman Drive
Beaverton, Oregon 97005-6453
503-671-6453

Chairman and CEO: Philip H. Knight
President: Thomas E. Clarke

Earnings Growth	★ ★	Dividend Growth	★ ★ ★ ★
Stock Growth	★ ★ ★ ★	Consistency	★ ★
Dividend Yield	★	Shareholder Perks	
NYSE—NKE		**Total**	**13 points**

Chicago Bulls fans weren't the only ones excited to see Michael Jordan give up on baseball and return to the hardwood in 1995. It was probably no coincidence that Nike had one of its worst years ever in 1994, the year Jordan was whiffing baseballs instead of swishing basketballs.

Nike's Air Jordan shoe line is probably the most famous brand of shoes in the history of footwear. In March, 1997, on the day the new models of Air Jordans were released, school administrators grumbled that parents had actually pulled their children out of school to buy them the new Air Jordan models at $140 a pop.

Athletic shoes have become one of this culture's biggest status symbols, thanks largely to Nike and its remarkably persuasive marketing ingenuity. With annual revenues of $6.5 billion, this is a company that has taken the footwear business to a new level.

Nike shoes are sold in about 110 countries around the world. Foreign sales account for about 36 percent of the company's total revenue. Based in Beaverton, Oregon, Nike manufactures nearly all of its shoes through independent contractors outside the United States.

In addition to shoes, the company markets a line of sports apparel that has become increasingly successful in recent years. Nike doubled its apparel sales in the United States in 1996, and it reported even bigger growth for the first six months of 1997. But that success did not come without considerable effort and persistence. As Nike founder and Chairman Philip Knight put it, "Our apparel business reminds me of something Shirley MacLaine said of her stardom, 'After 18 years of hard work, I'm an overnight sensation.'"

Apparel sales account for about 23 percent of Nike's total revenue.

Nike products are sold in about 18,000 U.S stores, including department stores, shoe stores, and sporting goods and related sports shops. The company makes specialty shoes for a variety of sports, including basketball, baseball, golf, tennis, soccer, track and field, volleyball, bicycling, and wrestling. The company even makes shoes specially designed for cheerleading.

First incorporated in 1968, Nike has about 17,200 employees and 77,000 shareholders.

EARNINGS-PER-SHARE GROWTH ★ ★

Past 5 years: 101 percent (15 percent per year)
Past 10 years: 895 percent (19 percent per year)

STOCK GROWTH ★ ★ ★ ★

Past 10 years: 2,977 percent (41 percent per year)
Dollar growth: $10,000 over 10 years (including reinvested dividends) would have grown to $340,000
Average annual compounded rate of return (including reinvested dividends): 42.5 percent

DIVIDEND YIELD ★

Average dividend yield in the past 3 years: 1.2

DIVIDEND GROWTH ★ ★ ★ ★

Increased dividend: 8 consecutive years
Past 5-year increase: 154 percent (21 percent per year)

CONSISTENCY   ★ ★

Increased earnings per share: 8 of the past 10 years
Increased sales: 8 of the past 10 years

SHAREHOLDER PERKS   (no points)

The company offers no stock purchase plan, nor does it provide any other
shareholder perks.

NIKE AT A GLANCE

Fiscal year ended: May 31
Revenue and net income in $ millions

	1991	1992	1993	1994	1995	1996	5-Year Growth Avg. Annual (%)	Total (%)
Revenue ($)	3,003.6	3,405.2	3,931	3,789.7	4,760.8	6,470.6	16	115
Net income ($)	287.1	329.2	365	298.8	399.7	553.2	14	93
Earnings/share ($)	0.94	1.07	1.19	1.01	1.39	1.89	15	101
Div. per share ($)	.13	.15	.19	.20	.24	.33	21	154
Dividend yield (%)	1.3	1.0	1.0	1.4	1.2	0.9	—	—
Avg. PE ratio	11	14	16	13	12	17	—	—

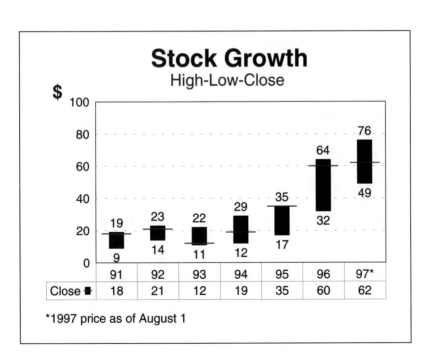

Stock Growth
High-Low-Close

$	91	92	93	94	95	96	97*
Close ▪	18	21	12	19	35	60	62

*1997 price as of August 1

58

Cardinal Health, Inc.

5555 Glendon Court
Dublin, OH 43016
614-717-5000

Chairman and CEO: Robert D. Walter
President: John C. Kane

Earnings Growth	★ ★ ★ ★	Dividend Growth	★ ★
Stock Growth	★ ★ ★ ★	Consistency	★ ★ ★
Dividend Yield		Shareholder Perks	
NYSE—CAH		**Total**	**13 points**

Founded originally as a food wholesaler in 1971, Cardinal Health long ago shed its food business to focus solely on the health care business. Over the past decade, the company has grown rapidly to a $9-billion-a-year operation through a series of acquisitions.

The Dublin, Ohio, operation made three significant acquisitions recently that provided it with an entree into three new areas of growth. The company acquired Pyxis Corporation, the nation's largest manufacturer of point-of-use systems that automate the distribution, management, and control of medications and supplies in hospitals and alternate care facilities.

Cardinal also acquired Medicine Shoppe International, the largest franchisor of independent retail pharmacies in the United States, and Allied Pharmacy Service, one of the nation's largest providers of hospital pharmacy management services.

The company's leading business segment continues to be pharmaceutical distribution. Cardinal is one of the nation's leading wholesale distributors of pharmaceutical and related health care products to independent and chain drugstores, hospitals, alternate care centers, and the pharmacy departments of supermarkets and mass merchandisers throughout the United States.

Cardinal also offers a broad range of value-added services such as computerized order entry and order confirmation systems, customized invoicing, generic sourcing programs, product movement and management reports, consultation on store operation and merchandising, and customer training.

About half the company's $8.8 billion in sales were to hospitals and managed care facilities, and the other half went to independent retail and chain pharmacies.

Cardinal's full-service national coverage, its integrated inventory management and marketing systems, coupled with guaranteed next-day delivery has helped strengthen its relationship with customers. Cardinal's innovations have also caught the attention of drug manufacturers who increasingly prefer to work with technologically sophisticated distributors that can take larger, more diversified product lines to market.

For its retail customers, Cardinal has created Healthtouch, an interactive touch-screen computer that provides health information to consumers. The kiosks, installed in more than 1,400 stores, are designed to assist the retail pharmacist's customer counseling efforts and give the pharmaceutical manufacturer an interactive medium at the point of sale.

The company has about 5,000 employees.

EARNINGS-PER-SHARE GROWTH ★ ★ ★ ★

Past 5 years: 195 percent (24 percent per year)
Past 10 years: 725 percent (23 percent per year)

STOCK GROWTH ★ ★ ★ ★

Past 10 years: 1,194 percent (29 percent per year)
Dollar growth: $10,000 over 10 years (including reinvested dividends) would have grown to $132,000
Average annual compounded rate of return (including reinvested dividends): 29 percent

DIVIDEND YIELD (no points)

Average dividend yield in the past 3 years: 0.3 percent

DIVIDEND GROWTH   ★ ★

Increased dividend: 9 of the past 10 years
Past 5-year increase: 167 percent (22 percent per year)

CONSISTENCY   ★ ★ ★

Increased earnings per share: 9 of the past 10 years
Increased sales: 9 of the past 10 years

SHAREHOLDER PERKS   (no points)

Cardinal offers no dividend reinvestment plan, nor does it offer any other perks for its shareholders.

CARDINAL HEALTH AT A GLANCE

Fiscal year ended: June 30
Revenue and net income in $ millions

	1991	1992	1993	1994	1995	1996	5-Year Growth Avg. Annual (%)	5-Year Growth Total (%)
Revenue ($)	1,647.6	3,680.7	4,633.4	5,963.3	8,022.1	8,862.4	40	438
Net income ($)	17.4	28.4	40.5	108.9	137.5	159.7	57	818
Earnings/share ($)	0.56	0.50	0.82	1.07	1.34	1.65	24	195
Div. per share ($)	.03	.04	.05	.07	.08	.08	22	167
Dividend yield (%)	.2	.2	.2	.3	.3	.2	—	—
Avg. PE ratio	29	25	18	21	22	23	—	—

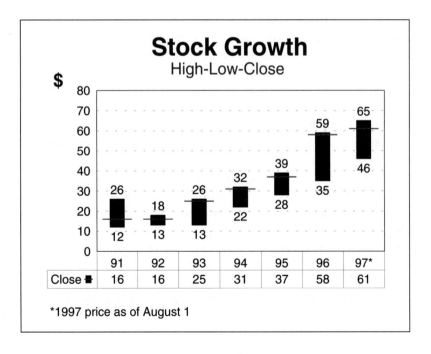

Stock Growth
High-Low-Close

Close ■	91	92	93	94	95	96	97*
	16	16	25	31	37	58	61

*1997 price as of August 1

CPC International, Inc.

International Plaza
P.O. Box 8000
Englewood Cliffs, NJ 07632-9976
201-894-4000

Chairman, President, and CEO:
Charles R. Shoemate

Earnings Growth	★	Dividend Growth	★ ★
Stock Growth	★ ★	Consistency	★ ★ ★ ★
Dividend Yield	★ ★	Shareholder Perks	★ ★
NYSE—CPC		**Total**	**13 points**

When you think of soup in the United States, the first brand that comes to mind is Campbell's. But elsewhere around the world, CPC International's Knorr brand soups and boullions hold the dominant market position in more than 30 countries.

CPC truly is international in scope. The maker of Skippy peanut butter, Hellmann's mayonnaise, and Mazola oil markets its products in more than 60 countries around the world. About 75 percent of its $9.8 billion in annual revenue is generated outside of North America. The company recently introduced Knorr soups in India, Bulgaria, and Romania, and opened two Knorr bouillon production plants in China.

CPC has been one of the most consistent U.S. foods companies, with 11 consecutive years of record earnings. CPC's largest division is its consumer foods group, which accounts for 77 percent of its total revenue. Along with Hellmann's, which is the world's top-selling mayonnaise, and Knorr foods, the company's leading brands include Skippy peanut butter, Mazola corn oil, ARGO corn starch, Henri's salad dressings, Mueller's macaroni, and Karo corn syrup. The company recently acquired the $100 million Pot Noodles business in the United Kingdom.

The company also counts its Caterplan food-services group as part of its consumer foods group. Caterplan generates more than $1 billion a year serving restaurants, cafeterias, and other dining establishments in 58 countries.

CPC's other key businesses include:

- **Corn refining** (14 percent of its revenue). Most of the company's corn-refining business relates to the production of corn sweeteners such as high-fructose and high-maltose corn syrups, dextrose, and glucose. Other leading products include starches, protein feed grains, and corn oil. The company has processing and distribution operations in about 20 countries.
- **Baking business** (8 percent). The company produces a broad range of premium baked goods such as breads, rolls, cookies, cakes, and pastries.

CPC International has about 53,000 employees and 29,000 shareholders.

EARNINGS-PER-SHARE GROWTH ★

Past 5 years: 51 percent (9 percent per year)
Past 10 years: 242 percent (13 percent per year)

STOCK GROWTH ★ ★

Past 10 years: 360 percent (16.5 percent per year)
Dollar growth: $10,000 over 10 years (including reinvested dividends) would have grown to $57,000
Average annual compounded rate of return (including reinvested dividends): 19 percent

DIVIDEND YIELD ★ ★

Average dividend yield in the past 3 years: 2.4 percent

DIVIDEND GROWTH

Increased dividend: 11 consecutive years
Past 5-year increase: 44 percent (8 percent per year)

CONSISTENCY ★ ★ ★ ★

Increased earnings per share: 11 consecutive years
Increased sales: 9 of the past 10 years

SHAREHOLDER PERKS

Good dividend reinvestment and stock purchase plan: voluntary stock purchase plan allows contributions of a minimum of $25 per month and a maximum of $25,000 per year.

CPC INTERNATIONAL AT A GLANCE

Fiscal year ended: Dec. 31
Revenue and net income in $ millions

	1991	1992	1993	1994	1995	1996	5-Year Growth Avg. Annual (%)	Total (%)
Revenue ($)	6,189	6,599	6,738	7,425	8,432	9,834	10	59
Net income ($)	404	431	455	482	548	598	8	48
Earnings/share ($)	2.61	2.78	2.95	3.15	3.67	3.93	9	51
Div. per share ($)	1.10	1.20	1.28	1.38	1.48	1.58	8	44
Dividend yield (%)	2.5	2.5	2.8	2.7	2.3	2.2	—	—
Avg. PE ratio	16	16	15	16	17	18	—	—

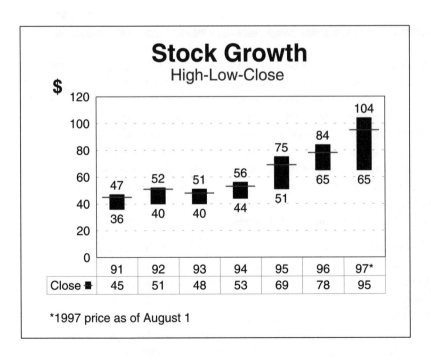

Stock Growth
High-Low-Close

Close ■	45	51	48	53	69	78	95
	91	92	93	94	95	96	97*

*1997 price as of August 1

DOVER CORPORATION

280 Park Avenue
New York, NY 10017
212-922-1640

Chairman: Gary L. Roubos
President and CEO: Thomas L. Reece

Earnings Growth	★ ★ ★ ★	Dividend Growth	★ ★
Stock Growth	★ ★	Consistency	★ ★ ★
Dividend Yield	★ ★	Shareholder Perks	
NYSE—DOV		**Total**	**13 points**

Dover Corporation operates more than 50 separate operating units that manufacture a broad range of specialized industrial equipment, from elevators, tank trucks, and garbage haulers to circuit-board soldering machines, gas-pump nozzles, and industrial cleaning equipment.

Dover Elevator is one of the nation's largest manufacturers and installers of elevators. The company specializes in elevators for low- and midrise buildings, and also makes elevators for the high-rise market. Dover's elevator business accounts for about 21 percent of its $4.1 billion in annual sales.

The company has four other business segments, including:

1. **Technologies** (24 percent of its total sales). The company sells screen printers and soldering machines for the printed circuit-board industry and components for communications equipment and military applications.
2. **Industries** (21 percent). Dover manufactures a diverse mix of equipment for the waste-handling, bulk transport, automotive service, commercial food-service, machine tool, and other industries. Its Heil

subsidiary, acquired in 1993, makes tank trailers and refuse-collecting vehicles; its Tipper Tie subsidiary makes clip closures for food packaging; its Marathon subsidiary makes solid-waste compaction, transporting, and recycling equipment; its Rotary Lift division makes automotive lifts; and its Groen division makes food-service equipment.

3. **Diversified** (18 percent). The company makes can-making machinery, process industry compressors, and refrigeration cases for supermarkets.
4. **Resources** (16 percent). Dover manufactures compressor valves, gas compressors and gasoline nozzles, and related service station equipment.

Dover has operations worldwide. Foreign sales account for about 20 percent of the company's total revenue.

Founded in 1947, Dover has about 25,000 employees and 16,000 shareholders.

EARNINGS-PER-SHARE GROWTH ★ ★ ★ ★

Past 5 years: 187 percent (23 percent per year)
Past 10 years: 393 percent (17 percent per year)

STOCK GROWTH ★ ★

Past 10 years: 372 percent (17 percent per year)
Dollar growth: $10,000 over 10 years (including reinvested dividends) would have grown to $56,000
Average annual compounded rate of return (including reinvested dividends): 19 percent

DIVIDEND YIELD ★ ★

Average dividend yield in the past 3 years: 1.6 percent

DIVIDEND GROWTH   ★ ★

Increased dividend: 16 consecutive years
Past 5-year increase: 56 percent (9 percent per year)

CONSISTENCY   ★ ★ ★

Increased earnings per share: 9 of the past 10 years
Increased sales: 9 of the past 10 years

SHAREHOLDER PERKS   (no points)

The company offers no dividend reinvestment and stock purchase plan,
nor does it provide any other shareholder perks.

DOVER AT A GLANCE

Fiscal year ended: Dec. 31
Revenue and net income in $ millions

	1991	1992	1993	1994	1995	1996	5-Year Growth Avg. Annual (%)	Total (%)
Revenue ($)	2,195.8	2,271.6	2,483.9	3,085.3	3,745.9	4,076.3	13	86
Net income ($)	128.2	129.7	158.3	202.4	278.3	340.4	21	166
Earnings/share ($)	1.05	1.12	1.39	1.77	2.45	3.01	23	187
Div. per share ($)	.41	.43	.45	.49	.56	.64	9	56
Dividend yield (%)	2.1	2.0	1.8	1.8	1.6	1.4	—	—
Avg. PE ratio	19	19	18	16	14	16	—	—

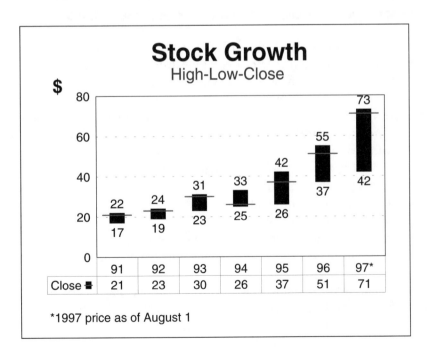

Stock Growth
High-Low-Close

	91	92	93	94	95	96	97*
Close ■	21	23	30	26	37	51	71

*1997 price as of August 1

Hewlett-Packard Company

3000 Hanover Street
Palo Alto, CA 94304
415-857-1501

Chairman, President, and CEO: Lewis E. Platt

Earnings Growth	★ ★ ★ ★	Dividend Growth	★ ★ ★ ★
Stock Growth	★ ★	Consistency	★ ★
Dividend Yield	★	Shareholder Perks	
NYSE—HWP		**Total**	**13 points**

Fresh from Stanford University, William Hewlett and David Packard set up shop in Packard's garage in 1939 to build electronic test equipment. The two worked together for the next half century building one of America's leading electronics companies.

Today, Hewlett-Packard Company makes thousands of electronics and computer products as well as equipment for measurement, computation, and communications.

Among its vast product line are computer systems, personal computers, printers and peripheral products, calculators, electronic test equipment, medical electronic equipment, and solid-state components and instrumentation for chemical analysis.

The company also offers such services as system integration, selective outsourcing management, consulting, education, and product financing and rentals.

Hewlett-Packard has operations worldwide. Foreign sales account for about 54 percent of the company's $38.4 billion in annual revenue.

The company's dominant segment is its computer products and services division, which accounts for about 82 percent of its total revenue. Among its leading products are the PA-RISC architecture for systems and workstations, the HP 9000 computer systems, the HP NetServer PC servers, the HP Pavilion multimedia home PC, and the HP Vectra series of IBM-compatible PCs. The company also makes one of the most extensive lines of printers in the business, including the HP DeskJet family and the HP LaserJet 5 Si, which combines printing and copying capabilities, enabling users to create multiple original prints.

Hewlett-Packard's electronic test measurement instrumentation systems account for 10 percent of the company's total revenue. The systems are used to test, synchronize, and extract data from communications networks, and to test and produce electronics.

Medical electronic equipment accounts for about 4 percent of its revenues, and the devices are used for patient monitoring, diagnostic cardiology, and ultrasound imaging.

Chemical analysis services and electronic components each account for about 2 percent of its revenue.

The Palo Alto, California, operation has about 102,000 employees and 73,000 shareholders.

EARNINGS-PER-SHARE GROWTH ★ ★ ★ ★

Past 5 years: 224 percent (26 percent per year)
Past 10 years: 382 percent (17 percent per year)

STOCK GROWTH ★ ★

Past 10 years: 372 percent (17 percent per year)
Dollar growth: $10,000 over 10 years (including reinvested dividends) would have grown to $52,000
Average annual compounded rate of return (including reinvested dividends): 18 percent

DIVIDEND YIELD ★

Average dividend yield in the past 3 years: 1.1 percent

DIVIDEND GROWTH

Increased dividend: 10 consecutive years
Past 5-year increase: 267 percent (29 percent per year)

CONSISTENCY

Increased earnings per share: 8 of the past 10 years
Increased sales: at least 10 consecutive years

SHAREHOLDER PERKS   (no points)

Hewlett-Packard does not offer a dividend reinvestment and stock purchase plan, nor does it offer any other perks for its shareholders.

HEWLETT-PACKARD AT A GLANCE

Fiscal year ended: Oct. 31
Revenue and net income in $ millions

	1991	1992	1993	1994	1995	1996	5-Year Growth Avg. Annual (%)	Total (%)
Revenue ($)	14,494	16,410	20,317	24,991	31,519	38,420	22	165
Net income ($)	755	881	1,177	1,599	2,433	2,586	28	242
Earnings/share ($)	0.76	0.87	1.16	1.54	2.31	2.46	26	242
Div. per share ($)	.12	.18	.23	.28	.35	.44	29	267
Dividend yield (%)	1.1	1.1	1.2	1.3	1.1	0.9	—	—
Avg. PE ratio	15	19	16	13	14	18	—	—

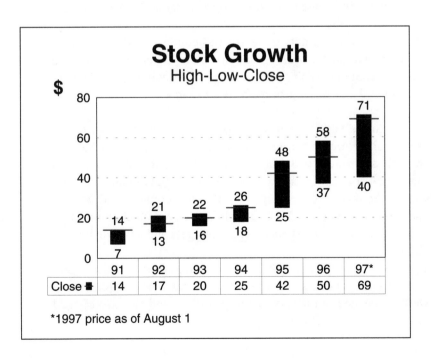

Stock Growth
High-Low-Close

Close ■	14	17	20	25	42	50	69
	91	92	93	94	95	96	97*

*1997 price as of August 1

McDonald's Corp.

McDonald's Plaza
Oak Brook, IL 60521-2278
630-623-3000

Chairman and CEO: Michael R. Quinlan

Earnings Growth	★ ★	Dividend Growth	★ ★
Stock Growth	★ ★	Consistency	★ ★ ★ ★
Dividend Yield	★	Shareholder Perks	★ ★
NYSE—MCD		**Total**	**13 points**

Expansion into the global market has helped keep McDonald's rolling through 30 consecutive years of record earnings, dating back to the year the company went public.

McDonald's has restaurants in nearly 100 countries. Of its approximately 20,000 restaurants now in operation, about 40 percent are located outside the United States. With same-store sales flattening out in the U.S. market, McDonald's is relying more heavily than ever on its overseas franchises.

The company is very careful to shape its foreign offerings to the tastes of the local culture. In Norway, McDonald's serves a grilled salmon sandwich with dill sauce; in Japan, it serves Chicken Tatsuta, a fried chicken sandwich spiced with soy sauce and ginger; in Germany, the restaurants serve frankfurters, beer, and a cold four-course meal; and in India, where the cow is sacred, McDonald's features chicken and fish sandwiches, along with some special veggie nuggets and a veggie burger. No beef is served.

In recent years, McDonald's has been opening about twice as many restaurants in foreign markets as in the United States. The fast-food chain is now well entrenched in the former Eastern Bloc, and has also opened restaurants in Russia and China.

The company has been adding new restaurants at a rate of about 2,000 per year, of which about two-thirds are outside the United States.

McDonald's biggest foreign markets are Japan (about 1,500 outlets), Canada (900 outlets), England (600 units), Germany (650 units), France (450 units), and Australia (530 units). McDonald's is the most advertised brand name in the world.

In addition to its foreign expansion, McDonald's has also tried to keep its earnings growing by introducing a continuing line of new selections, such as ice cream, pizza, submarine sandwiches, salads, breakfast products, and other specialties. McDonald's also maintains its marketing edge by keeping prices as low as any restaurant in the fast-food business.

Most McDonald's restaurants are owned by independent businesspeople who operate them through franchise agreements. Typically, the company tries to recruit investors who will be active, on-premises owners rather than outside investors. The conventional franchise arrangement is for a term of 20 years and requires an investment of about $600,000, 60 percent of which may be financed. Each outlet is also subject to franchise fees based on a percentage of sales. With few exceptions, McDonald's does not supply food, paper, or equipment to any restaurants, but approves suppliers from which those items can be purchased.

Restaurant managers receive training at the company's Hamburger University at McDonald's corporate headquarters in Oak Brook, Illinois.

Since Ray Kroc founded McDonald's in 1955, the company has served more than 100 billion burgers under the golden arches. The system serves about 30 million diners a day.

McDonald's has 183,000 employees and 530,000 shareholders.

EARNINGS-PER-SHARE GROWTH ★ ★

Past 5 years: 89 percent (14 percent per year)
Past 10 years: 256 percent (14 percent per year)

STOCK GROWTH ★ ★

Past 10 years: 334 percent (16 percent per year)
Dollar growth: $10,000 over 10 years (including reinvested dividends) would have grown to $48,000

Average annual compounded rate of return (including reinvested dividends): 17 percent

DIVIDEND YIELD

Average dividend yield in the past 3 years: 0.7 percent

DIVIDEND GROWTH

Increased dividend: Every year since the company went public in 1966
Past 5-year increase: 53 percent (9 percent per year)

CONSISTENCY ★ ★ ★ ★

Increased earnings per share: 30 consecutive years (dating back to the year the company went public)
Increased sales: 30 consecutive years

SHAREHOLDER PERKS

Outstanding dividend reinvestment and stock purchase plan: voluntary stock purchase plan allows contributions of $50 to $75,000 per year.

A wealth of literature on McDonald's and its locations and product ingredients is available to shareholders (or anyone else requesting it). The company also provides an investor hotline (not toll-free) that gives company news.

McDONALD'S AT A GLANCE

Fiscal year ended: Dec. 31
Revenue and net income in $ millions

	1991	1992	1993	1994	1995	1996	5-Year Growth Avg. Annual (%)	Total (%)
Revenue ($)	6,695	7,133	7,408	8,321	9,795	10,687	10	60
Net income ($)	860	959	1,083	1,224	1,427	1,573	13	83
Earnings/share ($)	1.17	1.30	1.45	1.68	1.97	2.21	14	89
Div. per share ($)	.19	.20	.21	.23	.26	.29	9	53
Dividend yield (%)	.9	.8	.8	.8	.7	.7	—	—
Avg. PE ratio	14	17	18	17	19	22	—	—

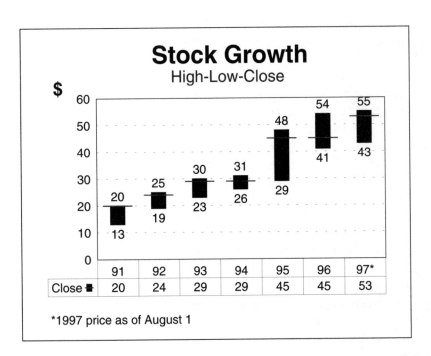

Stock Growth
High-Low-Close

Close ■	91	92	93	94	95	96	97*
	20	24	29	29	45	45	53

*1997 price as of August 1

63

The Clorox Company

1221 Broadway
Oakland, CA 94612
510-271-7000

Chairman, President, and CEO:
G. Craig Sullivan

Earnings Growth	★	Dividend Growth	★ ★
Stock Growth	★ ★	Consistency	★ ★ ★
Dividend Yield	★ ★ ★	Shareholder Perks	★ ★
NYSE—CLX		**Total**	**13 points**

Clorox bleach has been a laundry-room fixture in homes across America for most of this century. The firm was founded in 1913 as the Electro-Alkaline Company, then it changed its name to the Clorox Chemical Corporation in 1922.

In 1957, the Oakland-based bleach maker was acquired by Procter & Gamble, which held on to it for a dozen years before divesting it in 1969.

Clorox has been a very steady performer, posting increased earnings during 14 of the past 15 years.

Although its liquid bleach has long been the standard-bearer of the Clorox Company, the firm also produces an impressive array of other cleansers and consumer products. Many of its leading brands have come through acquisitions, although the firm has also become more aggressive recently in its new product launches. In 1996 Clorox went on a serious buying binge, acquiring Black Flag insecticides, Lestoil household cleaning products, and the Armor All line of automotive cleaning products. The company also introduced 14 new products during the year, including a new Floral Fresh–scented Clorox bleach. (Clorox liquid bleach now comes in four styles: original, Fresh Scent, Lemon, and Floral.)

Other leading Clorox products include Clorox Toilet Bowl cleanser, Clorox Clean-Up household spray cleaner, Formula 409 cleaning spray, Liquid Plumr, Pine-Sol spray cleaner, S.O.S. soap pads, Tackle cleaner, Tilex tile cleaner, and Tuffy mesh scrubber.

Clorox has been expanding its marketing worldwide. It sells its products in 70 countries throughout Europe, Asia, and North and South America. Foreign sales account for about 13 percent of the company's $2.22 billion in total revenue.

Clorox has 35 manufacturing plants throughout the United States and abroad. The company has 5,300 employees and 13,000 shareholders.

EARNINGS-PER-SHARE GROWTH

Past 5 years: 76 percent (12 percent per year)
Past 10 years: 138 percent (9 percent per year)

STOCK GROWTH

Past 10 years: 285 percent (14 percent per year)
Dollar growth: $10,000 over 10 years (including reinvested dividends) would have grown to $49,000
Average annual compounded rate of return (including reinvested dividends): 17 percent

DIVIDEND YIELD

Average dividend yield in the past 3 years: 3.3 percent

DIVIDEND GROWTH

Increased dividend: 16 consecutive years
Past 5-year increase: 44 percent (8 percent per year)

CONSISTENCY

Increased earnings per share: 9 of the past 10 years

SHAREHOLDER PERKS

Outstanding dividend reinvestment and stock purchase plan: voluntary stock purchase plan allows contributions of a minimum of $10 to a maximum of $60,000 a year (with no fees or commissions).

CLOROX AT A GLANCE

Fiscal year ended: June 30
Revenue and net income in $ millions

	1991	1992	1993	1994	1995	1996	5-Year Growth Avg. Annual (%)	5-Year Growth Total (%)
Revenue ($)	1,468.4	1,547.1	1,634.2	1,836.9	1,984.2	2,217.8	9	51
Net income ($)	52,746	98,704	167,051	212,057	200,832	222,092	33	321
Earnings/share ($)	2.43	2.60	3.07	3.35	3.78	4.28	12	76
Div. per share ($)	1.47	1.59	1.71	1.80	1.92	2.12	8	44
Dividend yield (%)	3.9	3.7	3.7	3.6	3.4	2.8	—	—
Avg. PE ratio	16	16	15	16	15	18	—	—

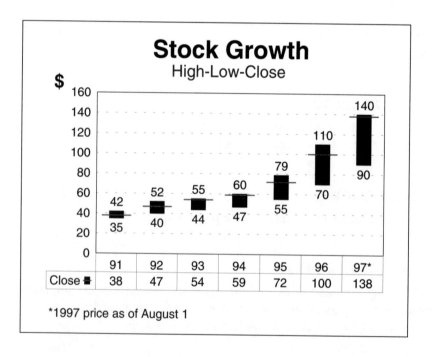

Stock Growth
High-Low-Close

	91	92	93	94	95	96	97*
Close	38	47	54	59	72	100	138

*1997 price as of August 1

64

Hubbell, Inc.

584 Derby Milford Road
Orange, CT 06477-4024
203-799-4100

Chairman, President, and CEO:
G. Jackson Ratcliffe

Earnings Growth	★	Dividend Growth	★ ★
Stock Growth	★ ★	Consistency	★ ★ ★
Dividend Yield	★ ★ ★	Shareholder Perks	★ ★
NYSE—HUB "B"		**Total**	**13 points**

Hubbell's growth the past few years has been far from dazzling, but the company has been one of the most consistent performers in American industry. The electrical products manufacturer has posted record earnings during 14 of the past 15 years and has raised its dividend 36 times in the past 36 years.

The Orange, Connecticut, operation produces thousands of electrical products, including outlets, adapters, lighting fixtures, industrial controls, measurement equipment, and electrical transmission and distribution products.

Hubbell's leading product line is low-voltage devices such as fuses, switches, wall plates, cables, plugs, surge suppressor units, connectors, adaptors, and wall outlets. The company's lighting division sells lights for athletic fields, service stations, outdoor display signs, parking lots, shopping centers, and roadways. It manufactures indoor lights for gymnasiums, industrial plants, and commercial buildings.

Other low-voltage products include industrial controls such as motor speed controls, power and grounding resistors, and overhead crane controls.

Hubbell's low-voltage segment accounts for about 43 percent of its $1.285 billion in annual revenue.

Hubbell's other two segments include:

1. **High-voltage products** (20 percent of its sales). Hubbell makes insulated wire and cable, electrical transmission and distribution products, and high-voltage test and measurement equipment. Its Ohio Brass Company subsidiary manufactures polymer insulators and high-voltage surge arresters used in the construction of electrical transmission and distribution lines and substations.
2. **Other electronics products** (36 percent). Hubbell manufactures steel and plastic boxes used at outlets, switch locations, junction points, fittings, tubing, and enclosures through its Raco subsidiary. The company's Pulse Communications division manufactures voice and data signal–processing equipment used primarily by the telephone and telecommunications industry.

Hubbell has operations in Canada, Mexico, England, Singapore, and Puerto Rico, and sales in several other countries. Foreign operations account for about 6 percent of the company's total revenue.

Founded in 1888, Hubbell has about 6,000 employees and 5,700 class B shareholders.

EARNINGS-PER-SHARE GROWTH ★

Past 5 years: 53 percent (9 percent per year)
Past 10 years: 153 percent (10 percent per year)

STOCK GROWTH ★ ★

Past 10 years: 254 percent (13.5 percent per year)
Dollar growth: $10,000 over 10 years (including reinvested dividends) would have grown to $46,000
Average annual compounded rate of return (including reinvested dividends): 16.5 percent

DIVIDEND YIELD ★ ★ ★

Average dividend yield in the past 3 years: 3.0 percent

DIVIDEND GROWTH

Increased dividend: 36 consecutive years
Past 5-year increase: 48 percent (8 percent per year)

CONSISTENCY

Increased earnings per share: 9 of the past 10 years
Increased sales: 14 consecutive years

SHAREHOLDER PERKS

Dividend reinvestment and stock purchase plan: voluntary stock purchase plan allows contributions of $100 to $1,000 per month.

HUBBELL-B AT A GLANCE

Fiscal year ended: Dec. 31
Revenue and net income in $ millions

	1991	1992	1993	1994	1995	1996	5-Year Growth Avg. Annual (%)	5-Year Growth Total (%)
Revenue ($)	756.1	786.1	832.4	1,013.7	1,143.1	1,285	11	70
Net income ($)	90.6	77.6	66.3	106.5	121.9	195	17	115
Earnings/share ($)	1.37	1.41	1.00	1.60	1.83	2.10	9	53
Div. per share ($)	0.69	0.76	0.78	0.81	0.92	1.02	8	48
Dividend yield (%)	3.0	3.0	3.0	3.0	3.2	2.8	—	—
Avg. PE ratio	17	18	26	17	16	17	—	—

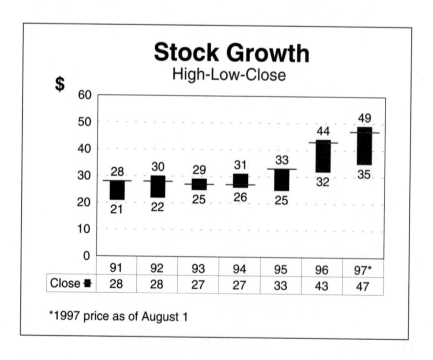

*1997 price as of August 1

65

Emerson Electric Company

8000 West Florissant Avenue
P. O. Box 4100
St. Louis, MO 63136-8506
314-553-2000

Chairman and CEO: Charles F. Knight

Earnings Growth	★	Dividend Growth	★ ★
Stock Growth	★	Consistency	★ ★ ★ ★
Dividend Yield	★ ★ ★	Shareholder Perks	★ ★
NYSE—EMR		**Total**	**13 points**

It's hard to find the glamour in fans and motors, valves and bearings, timers, switches, and compressors. But what Emerson Electric lacks in panache, it makes up for in performance. The St. Louis operation has posted 39 consecutive years of record earnings.

Much of the company's success can be traced to its ability to continue to fill the product pipeline with innovative new offerings. The company introduces about 500 new products each year. In fact, about one quarter of its annual revenue ($11.2 billion in 1996) is generated from the sale of products that were introduced over the past five years.

Emerson manufactures a wide range of electrical equipment, including motors for industrial and heavy commercial applications, industrial automation equipment, gear drives, power distribution equipment, and temperature and environmental control systems.

Emerson divides its operations into two key segments:

1. **Commercial and industrial components and systems** (60 percent of revenue). The company manufactures process control instruments and systems, industrial motors and drives, industrial machinery, and computer support products.

2. **Appliance and construction-related components** (40 percent of revenue). Emerson manufactures a wide range of small motors, appliance components, heating, ventilating, and air conditioning components, refrigeration and comfort control components, timers, switches, humidifiers, exhaust fans, wrenches, pipe cutters, and related equipment. Among its consumer products are portable and stationary power tools, hobby tools, hand tools, garbage disposers, hot-water dispensers, dishwashers, ladders, and shop vacuums.

Among the company's most recognized brand names are Skil power saws and tools, Dremeil handheld power tools, and Louisville ladders.

Emerson sells its products worldwide. Foreign sales account for 44 percent of the company's total revenue.

Emerson Electric was founded by John Wesley Emerson in 1890, shortly after Thomas A. Edison installed his first electrical generator. In his small St. Louis shop, Emerson manufactured room fans, ceiling fans, and electrical motors.

Today, Emerson Electric has about 86,000 employees and 30,000 shareholders.

EARNINGS-PER-SHARE GROWTH ★

Past 5 years: 61 percent (10 percent per year)
Past 10 years: 144 percent (9 percent per year)

STOCK GROWTH ★

Past 10 years: 241 percent (13 percent per year)
Dollar growth: $10,000 over 10 years (including reinvested dividends) would have grown to $44,000
Average annual compounded rate of return (including reinvested dividends): 16 percent

DIVIDEND YIELD ★ ★ ★

Average dividend yield in the past 3 years: 2.6 percent

DIVIDEND GROWTH

Increased dividend: 40 consecutive years
Past 5-year increase: 48 percent (8 percent per year)

CONSISTENCY ★ ★ ★ ★

Increased earnings per share: 39 consecutive years
Increased sales: 9 of the past 10 years

SHAREHOLDER PERKS

Good dividend reinvestment and stock purchase plan: voluntary stock purchase plan allows contributions of $50 to $120,000 per year.

EMERSON ELECTRIC AT A GLANCE

Fiscal year ended: Sept. 30
Revenue and net income in $ millions

	1991	1992	1993	1994	1995	1996	5-Year Growth Avg. Annual (%)	Total (%)
Revenue ($)	7,427	7,706	8,174	8,607	10,013	11,150	9	50
Net income ($)	632	663	708	789	908	1,019	10	61
Earnings/share ($)	2.83	2.96	3.15	3.52	4.06	4.55	10	61
Div. per share ($)	1.32	1.38	1.44	1.56	1.78	1.96	8	48
Dividend yield (%)	3.1	2.7	2.5	2.6	2.7	2.4	—	—
Avg. PE ratio	15	17	18	17	16	18	—	—

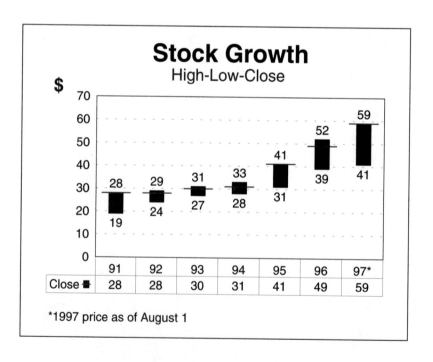

Stock Growth
High-Low-Close

$	91	92	93	94	95	96	97*
Close	28	28	30	31	41	49	59

*1997 price as of August 1

66

Becton Dickinson and Company

1 Becton Drive
Franklin Lakes, NJ 07417-1880
201-847-6800

Chairman, President, and CEO:
Clateo Castellini

Earnings Growth	★	Dividend Growth	★ ★
Stock Growth	★ ★	Consistency	★ ★ ★ ★
Dividend Yield	★ ★	Shareholder Perks	★ ★
NYSE—BDX		**Total**	**13 points**

A century ago, in 1897, Maxwell W. Becton and Fairleigh S. Dickinson opened a small medical supply business, and sold their first product, a Luer all-glass syringe, for $2.50. Now Becton Dickinson and Company is one of the world's leading manufacturers of hypodermic needles, drug infusion systems, diabetes care products, and a broad range of other medical supplies and devices.

The New Jersey–based operation is the leading maker of insulin injection systems, and holds strong positions in a number of other drug delivery and infusion therapy-related products. The company is also a leading manufacturer of thermometers, disposable scrubs, surgical blades, and other surgical products. Medical supplies and devices account for about 55 percent of Becton Dickinson's $2.77 billion in annual revenue.

Diagnostic products account for about 45 percent of the company's revenue. Becton Dickinson makes a line of blood-testing and diagnostic devices, sample collection products, tissue culture labware, hematology instruments, and immunodiagnostic test kits.

Most of Becton's growth in recent years has come from its international operations, where operating income has jumped 80 percent in the past three years. Foreign sales account for about 49 percent of the company's revenue.

Becton has manufacturing operations in Australia, Brazil, France, Germany, Ireland, Japan, Mexico, Singapore, Spain, and the United Kingdom. The company recently opened a new plant in China to manufacture syringes, catheters, and specialty needles.

Becton Dickinson has about 18,000 employees and 8,000 shareholders.

EARNINGS-PER-SHARE GROWTH ★

Past 5 years: 74 percent (12 percent per year)
Past 10 years: 220 percent (12 percent per year)

STOCK GROWTH ★ ★

Past 10 years: 277 percent (14 percent per year)
Dollar growth: $10,000 over 10 years (including reinvested dividends) would have grown to $43,000
Average annual compounded rate of return (including reinvested dividends): 16 percent

DIVIDEND YIELD ★ ★

Average dividend yield in the past 3 years: 1.5 percent

DIVIDEND GROWTH ★ ★

Increased dividend: 15 consecutive years
Past 5-year increase: 59 percent (10 percent per year)

CONSISTENCY ★ ★ ★ ★

Increased earnings per share: 13 consecutive years
Increased sales: 13 consecutive years

SHAREHOLDER PERKS ★ ★

Good dividend reinvestment and stock purchase plan: voluntary stock purchase plan allows contributions of $50 to $5,000 per month.

BECTON DICKINSON AT A GLANCE

Fiscal year ended: Dec. 31
Revenue and net income in $ millions

	1991	1992	1993	1994	1995	1996	5-Year Growth Avg. Annual (%)	Total (%)
Revenue ($)	2,172.2	2,365.3	2,465.4	2,559.5	2,712.5	2,769.8	5	28
Net income ($)	189.8	200.8	212.8	227.2	251.7	283.4	8	49
Earnings/share ($)	1.21	1.29	1.36	1.52	1.80	2.11	12	74
Div. per share ($)	.29	.30	.33	.37	.41	.46	10	59
Dividend yield (%)	1.6	1.7	1.8	1.9	1.5	1.2	—	—
Avg. PE ratio	15	14	14	13	15	19	—	—

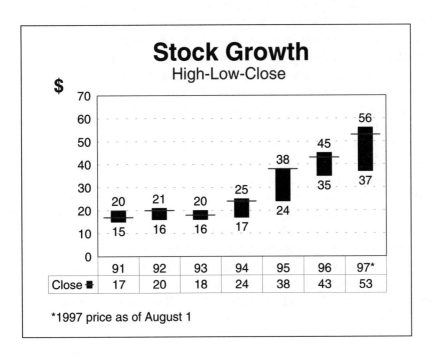

Stock Growth
High-Low-Close

Close ■	17	20	18	24	38	43	53
	91	92	93	94	95	96	97*

*1997 price as of August 1

67

Bristol-Myers Squibb

345 Park Avenue
New York, NY 10154-0037
212-546-4000

Chairman, President, and CEO:
Charles A. Heimbold, Jr.

Earnings Growth		Dividend Growth	★
Stock Growth	★	Consistency	★ ★ ★ ★
Dividend Yield	★ ★ ★ ★	Shareholder Perks	★ ★ ★
NYSE—BMY		**Total**	**13 points**

In the world of medical breakthroughs, Bristol-Myers Squibb has had more than its fair share. But the New York–based pharmaceutical giant isn't always working solo. For instance, the company is currently teaming up with SIBIA, Inc., to develop an Alzheimer's treatment, and it is helping to fund gene cancer therapy research with Somatix Therapy Corporation, and gene sequencing technology with SEQ, Ltd.

In all, Bristol-Myers invests more than $1 billion a year in research and development.

Pharmaceuticals are the leading source of revenue for Bristol-Myers, accounting for 57 percent of the company's $15.1 billion in annual revenue. The company produces a broad range of anticancer agents and diagnostic products, plus drugs for the treatment of cardiovascular ailments, high cholesterol, infections, congestion, and nervous disorders. Bristol-Myers' 1989 merger with Squibb made it the nation's second-largest pharmaceuticals manufacturer (behind Johnson & Johnson). Despite its strong presence in the pharmaceuticals market, the company is probably best known for its consumer products. Toiletries and other beauty aids (such as Clairol, Vitalis, Nice 'n Easy, Loving Care, Ban deodorant, Final Net, and Keri Lotion) account for 11 percent of its total revenue. Nonprescription medications (such as Excedrin, Bufferin, Comtrex, Nuprin, and No Doz) account for about 18 percent of the company's revenue.

The company's other major market segment is medical devices, which accounts for 14 percent of its annual sales. Among its leading medical devices are orthopedic implants such as artificial hips, knees, and shoulders; implantable hearing devices; compression garments for burn treatments; powered surgical instruments; and related devices.

Bristol-Myers does a strong international business, with sales in more than 100 countries. Foreign sales account for about 37 percent of the company's total revenue.

Bristol-Myers has 49,000 employees and 138,000 shareholders.

EARNINGS-PER-SHARE GROWTH   (no points)

Past 5 years: 43 percent (7 percent per year)
Past 10 years: 165 percent (10 percent per year)

STOCK GROWTH   ★

Past 10 years: 193 percent (11 percent per year)
Dollar growth: $10,000 over 10 years (including reinvested dividends) would have grown to $40,000
Average annual compounded rate of return (including reinvested dividends): 15 percent

DIVIDEND YIELD

Average dividend yield in the past 3 years: 4.3 percent

DIVIDEND GROWTH

Increased dividend: 24 consecutive years
Past 5-year increase: 25 percent (5 percent per year)

CONSISTENCY   ★ ★ ★ ★

Increased earnings per share: 12 consecutive years
Increased sales: 9 of the past 10 years

SHAREHOLDER PERKS   ★ ★ ★

Good dividend reinvestment and stock purchase plan: voluntary stock
purchase plan allows contributions of $100 per week up to $10,025 per
month for those holding 50 shares or more.

The company also sends all of its new shareholders of record a
welcome packet of its consumer products, including, for example, small
bottles of Excedrin, Bufferin, Nuprin, Clairol, and Ban deodorant.

BRISTOL-MYERS AT A GLANCE

Fiscal year ended: Dec. 31
Revenue and net income in $ millions

	1991	1992	1993	1994	1995	1996	5-Year Growth Avg. Annual (%)	Total (%)
Revenue ($)	10,571	11,156	11,413	11,984	13,767	15,065	7	43
Net income ($)	1,991	1,538	1,959	1,842	1,812	2,851	7	43
Earnings/share ($)	1.98	2.04	2.20	2.29	2.57	2.84	7	43
Div. per share ($)	1.20	1.38	1.44	1.46	1.48	1.50	4	25
Dividend yield (%)	3.0	3.8	4.9	5.2	4.3	3.3	—	—
Avg. PE ratio	20	18	13	12	13	16	—	—

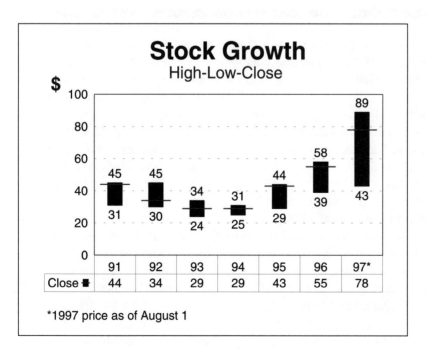

Stock Growth
High-Low-Close

Close ■	91	92	93	94	95	96	97*
	44	34	29	29	43	55	78

*1997 price as of August 1

68

RPM, Inc.

2628 Pearl Road
P.O. Box 777
Medina, OH 44258
330-273-5090
330-225-8743 (Fax)

Chairman and CEO: Thomas C. Sullivan
President: James A. Karman

Earnings Growth	★	Dividend Growth	★ ★
Stock Growth	★	Consistency	★ ★ ★ ★
Dividend Yield	★ ★ ★	Shareholder Perks	★ ★
Nasdaq—RPOW		**Total**	**13 points**

It doesn't take a degree in finance to figure out that this is a stock that belongs in the portfolio of just about anyone who invests. You don't even need to know what they make or who their customers are. All you need to know is that RPM has posted record sales and earnings for 49 consecutive years. Only one other company in the world can match that record.

RPM is a manufacturer of paints and coatings—or at least that's half the business. The other half has been finding other solid, successful companies that do the same thing and acquiring them. The Medina, Ohio, operation has made more than 40 acquisitions. And each year RPM's management scours the paints and coatings market in search of more companies to add to its stable.

RPM was founded in 1947 by Frank C. Sullivan who invented the Alumanation process for coating outdoor metal structures. While Alumanation continues to be the world's leading liquid aluminum coating solution, the process is now just a small part of RPM's total business.

The company has 42 operating companies, all of which are involved in the manufacture of coatings, sealants, and specialty chemicals (including corrosion protection, waterproofing and maintenance products, roofing materials, touch-up products for autos and furniture, and fabrics and wallcoverings).

RPM has sales in more than 100 countries. Foreign sales account for about 12 percent of the company's $1.14 billion in annual revenue.

About 60 percent of the company's sales comes from the industrial market, while the other 40 percent comes from its line of consumer products.

RPM produces products for five key markets:

1. **Corrosion control.** RPM produces a wide range of coatings and chemicals for power plants, oil rigs, rail cars, tankers, smokestacks, and other structures that are subject to harsh environments. Leading brands include Carboline, Plasite, and Bitumastic.
2. **Specialty chemicals.** The company makes fluorescent colorants and pigments; concrete additives that provide corrosion resistance and add strength to cement used in construction; additives for coatings and dyes, and coatings and cleaners for the textile trade. It produces furniture stains, fillers, and polishes; auto-refinishing products; and auto corrosion control additives. Its leading lines include Day-Glo Color, Alox, Mohawk, and American Emulsions.
3. **Waterproofing and general maintenance.** The company makes coatings for metal structures such as buildings, bridges, and industrial facilities; it also produces sheet roofing, sealants, and deck coatings. Its leading lines include RPM Alumanation coating, Mameco sealants, and Martin Mathys water-based coatings, and Stonhard polymer floors, linings, and wall systems.
4. **Consumer hobby and leisure.** RPM's Testor subsidiary is America's leading producer of models, paints, and accessory items for the model and hobby market. RPM's Craft House subsidiary markets a variety of crafts including Paint-by-Numbers sets.
5. **Consumer do-it-yourself.** The company sells a wide range of paints and coatings for the consumer market, including Zinsser shellac-based coatings, Bondax patch and repair products, Dynatron/Bondo, Talsol, and Rust-Oleum.

RPM's coatings cover the Statue of Liberty, the Eiffel Tower, and hundreds of bridges, ships, highways, factories, office towers, warehouses, and other structures around the world.

RPM has about 5,300 employees and 62,000 shareholders.

EARNINGS-PER-SHARE GROWTH ★

Past 5 years: 58 percent (10 percent per year)
Past 10 years: 200 percent (11.5 percent per year)

STOCK GROWTH

Past 10 years: 188 percent (11 percent per year)
Dollar growth: $10,000 over 10 years (including reinvested dividends) would have grown to $37,000
Average annual compounded rate of return (including reinvested dividends): 14 percent

DIVIDEND YIELD

Average dividend yield in the past 3 years: 3.0 percent

DIVIDEND GROWTH

Increased dividend: 20 consecutive years
Past 5-year increase: 47 percent (8 percent per year)

CONSISTENCY

Increased earnings per share: 49 consecutive years
Increased sales: 49 consecutive years

SHAREHOLDER PERKS ★ ★

Good dividend reinvestment and stock purchase plan: voluntary stock purchase plan allows contributions of up to $5,000 per month.

RPM AT A GLANCE

Fiscal year ended: May 31
Revenue and net income in $ millions

	1991	1992	1993	1994	1995	1996	5-Year Growth Avg. Annual (%)	5-Year Growth Total (%)
Revenue ($)	619.6	680.1	768.4	825.3	1,030.7	1,136.4	13	83
Net income ($)	37.4	38.5	39.5	53.8	62.6	68.9	13	84
Earnings/share ($)	.57	.58	.59	.74	.85	.90	10	58
Div. per share ($)	.32	.36	.38	.41	.44	.47	8	47
Dividend yield (%)	3.4	3.1	2.8	2.9	3.0	3.0	—	—
Avg. PE ratio	17	20	21	20	18	18	—	—

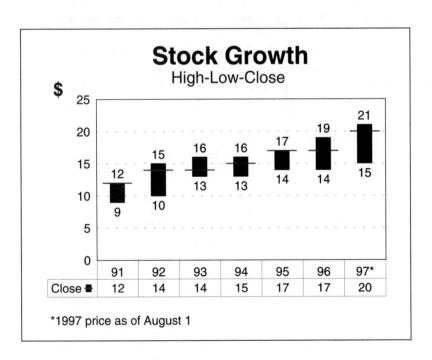

Stock Growth
High-Low-Close

Close ■	91	92	93	94	95	96	97*
	12	14	14	15	17	17	20

*1997 price as of August 1

Microsoft Corp.

Microsoft ®

One Microsoft Way
Redmond, WA 98052-6399
206-882-8080

Chairman and CEO: William Gates

Earnings Growth	★ ★ ★ ★	Dividend Growth	
Stock Growth	★ ★ ★ ★	Consistency	★ ★ ★ ★
Dividend Yield		Shareholder Perks	
NASDAQ—MSFT		**Total**	**12 points**

No one has had a more profound effect on computer technology than Microsoft founder Bill Gates. The 41-year-old Gates, who still serves as company chairman and CEO, has delivered a long line of software products that have helped make computers accessible to the common consumer.

Microsoft's Windows and DOS operating systems have been installed in more than 100 million computers worldwide. And the company has moved into other areas of computer technology as well, including Internet service and a wide range of PC software programs.

Gates' success in bringing computer technology to the average consumer has not gone unrewarded. He is the richest man in America, with a net worth somewhere in the range of $10 billion.

Founded in 1975, Microsoft is the worldwide leader in software for personal computers. Some of its leading products include Microsoft Word (word processing), Microsoft Excel (spreadsheet), Microsoft Office (business), and Microsoft PowerPoint (presentations).

Foreign sales continue to grow faster than domestic sales, and now they account for about 53 percent of the company's $8.7 billion in annual revenue (including foreign operations and exports).

Over the past decade, the Redmond, Washington, manufacturer has been the nation's fastest-growing publicly traded company. The company helps maintain its edge on the market by spending generously on product development. The company expected to spend more than $2 billion on R&D in 1997.

Microsoft divides its operations into several key segments:

- **Desktop and business systems.** Includes DOS and the whole line of Windows operating systems.
- **Internet platform and tools products.** The company makes software and desktop database products used to access the Internet.
- **Consumer platforms.** Microsoft is developing systems for a broad range of communications, entertainment, and mobile computing devices.
- **Desktop applications software.** Includes Word, Excel, PowerPoint, and Office.
- **Interactive media products.** The company develops and markets interactive entertainment and information products for a variety of media, including the Internet, Microsoft Network, and CD-ROM.
- **Microsoft Press.** Founded in 1983, Microsoft Press publishes books about software products from Microsoft and other software developers.

The company, founded in 1975, has about 21,000 employees and 38,000 shareholders.

EARNINGS-PER-SHARE GROWTH ★ ★ ★ ★

Past 5 years: 320 percent (33 percent per year)
Past 10 years: 4,200 percent (46 percent per year)

STOCK GROWTH ★ ★ ★ ★

Past 10 years: 8,163 percent (55 percent per year)
Dollar growth: $10,000 over 10 years (including reinvested dividends) would have grown to $820,000
Average annual compounded rate of return (including reinvested dividends): 55 percent

DIVIDEND YIELD   (no points)

The company pays no dividend.

DIVIDEND GROWTH   (no points)

No dividend

CONSISTENCY

Increased earnings per share: 14 consecutive years
Increased sales: 14 consecutive years

SHAREHOLDER PERKS   (no points)

The company offers no dividend reinvestment and stock purchase plan, nor does it provide any other shareholder perks.

MICROSOFT AT A GLANCE

Fiscal year ended: June 30
Revenue and net income in $ millions

	1991	1992	1993	1994	1995	1996	5-Year Growth Avg. Annual (%)	Total (%)
Revenue ($)	1,843.4	2,759	3,753	4,649	5,937	8,671	36	370
Net income ($)	462.7	708.1	953	1,146	1,453	2,195	36	374
Earnings/share ($)	0.41	0.60	0.79	0.99	1.16	1.72	33	320
Div. per share ($)	–	–	–	–	–	–	–	–
Dividend yield (%)	–	–	–	–	–	–	—	—
Avg. PE ratio	23	29	27	21	28	29	—	—

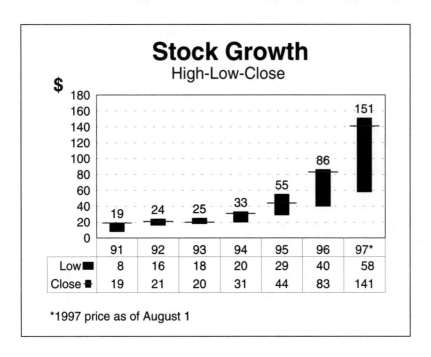

Stock Growth
High-Low-Close

	91	92	93	94	95	96	97*
Low	8	16	18	20	29	40	58
Close	19	21	20	31	44	83	141

*1997 price as of August 1

Computer Associates International, Inc.

One Computer Associates Plaza
Islandia, NY 11788-7000
516-342-5224

Chairman, President, and CEO:
Charles B. Wang

Earnings Growth	★ ★ ★	Dividend Growth	★ ★
Stock Growth	★ ★ ★ ★	Consistency	★ ★ ★
Dividend Yield		Shareholder Perks	
NYSE—CA		**Total**	**12 points**

Computer Associates continues to expand its library of computer software products both through acquisitions and internal development. Founded in 1976, the company is now the world's largest business software manufacturer with more than 500 different products. It designs software for more than 40 different desktop, midrange, and mainframe operating systems and platforms.

Much of the company's recent growth has come through acquisitions. In late 1996, it acquired Cheyenne Software, which is a leader in storage management software for the Windows NT and Novell NetWare environments. Earlier, Computer Associates acquired the ASK Group, which designs a broad range of database management systems and related products, and Legent Corporation, which designs information management software for a variety of computer operating systems.

Originally, Computer Associates developed operating software exclusively for large IBM mainframe computers. But as American industry shifted increasingly to smaller computers, Computer Associates began expanding its product base to include applications for smaller computers as well.

Most of the company's software is designed to enhance data-processing functions by providing tools to measure and improve computer hardware and software performance and programmer productivity.

The company also makes database management, business applications, and graphics software for mainframe, midrange, and desktop computers from a variety of vendors, including IBM, DEC, Hewlett-Packard, Amdahl, Data General, Sun, Sequent, Tandem, Compaq, and Apple.

Many of the company's most successful DOS-based applications have also been reintroduced for use on more powerful workstations using such operating systems as Microsoft Windows, Novell NetWare, and IBM OS/2.

The company's top-selling software product is the CA-Unicenter software, originally designed to enhance the computer "client/server environment" for Hewlett-Packard hardware. Since CA-Unicenter's introduction in 1993, the company has developed similar Unicenter software for a variety of other computer systems.

The Islandia, New York, operation has subsidiaries in 36 countries outside of North America. Foreign sales (outside North America) account for about 50 percent of its total revenue.

The company has about 9,000 employees and 8,500 shareholders.

EARNINGS-PER-SHARE GROWTH ★ ★ ★

Past 5 years: 381 percent (36 percent per year)
Past 10 years: 1,555 percent (32 percent per year)

STOCK GROWTH ★ ★ ★ ★

Past 10 years: 1,813 percent (34 percent per year)
Dollar growth: $10,000 over 10 years (including reinvested dividends) would have grown to $200,000
Average annual compounded rate of return (including reinvested dividends): 35 percent

DIVIDEND YIELD (no points)

Average dividend yield in the past 3 years: 0.4 percent

DIVIDEND GROWTH

Increased dividend: Dividends first offered in 1991 have increased twice
Past 5-year increase: 125 percent (17 percent per year)

CONSISTENCY ★ ★ ★

Increased earnings per share: 9 of the past 10 years
Increased sales: 15 consecutive years

SHAREHOLDER PERKS (no points)

The company offers no dividend reinvestment plan, nor does it provide
any other shareholder perks.

COMPUTER ASSOCIATES AT A GLANCE

Fiscal year ended: March 31
Revenue and net income in $ millions

	1991	1992	1993	1994	1995	1996	5-Year Growth Avg. Annual (%)	Total (%)
Revenue ($)	1,300.6	1,508.8	1,841	2,148.5	2,623	3,504.6	22	69
Net income ($)	130	163	246	401	432	752	41	478
Earnings/share ($)	0.31	0.41	0.64	1.04	1.16	1.49	36	381
Div. per share ($)	.04	.04	.04	.06	.09	.10	20	150
Dividend yield (%)	1.0	.6	.4	.4	.3	.2	—	—
Avg. PE ratio	11	12	14	13	18	17	—	—

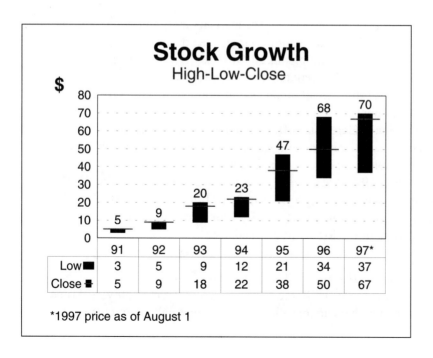

71

United HealthCare Corp.

300 Opus Center
9900 Bren Road East
Minnetonka, MN 55343
612-936-1300

Chairman, President, and CEO:
William W. McGuire, MD

Earnings Growth	★ ★ ★ ★	Dividend Growth	★
Stock Growth	★ ★ ★ ★	Consistency	★ ★ ★
Dividend Yield		Shareholder Perks	
NYSE—UNH		**Total**	**12 points**

In the growing business of health care management, United HealthCare is the king of the hill. It is the nation's largest health care management services company, with operations in all 50 states. The Minneapolis-based company owns 16 health maintenance organizations (HMOs) and manages nine other HMOs. In all, about 14 million people are enrolled in its various health plans.

United HealthCare also offers other services such as behavioral health services, utilization review services, specialized provider networks, and employee assistance programs.

Founded in 1974, the company has been aggressively adding HMOs to its stable. It is equally aggressive at controlling its own costs. Its medical-loss ratio, which measures medical costs as a percent of premium revenues, is one of the lowest in the business.

United HealthCare offers several types of services, including:

- **Commercial health plans.** The company's HMOs and related health care programs serve small, medium-sized, and large employers. Some 4.1 million members are enrolled in its commercial health care plans.

- **Commercial insurance products.** The company offers commercial insurance products for small groups and other commercial customers. Its products are used by about 9 million individuals.
- **Strategic services.** United HealthCare offers custom-designed health care management services for large national employers. In all, the company has about 185 clients with about 6 million individual members.

The company also offers indemnity products, health plans, and specialty products for 230,000 seniors enrolled in Medicare health plans. It also provides managed care products for 525,000 Medicaid beneficiaries enrolled in health plans.

United also operates a specialty business that offers various products and services designed to manage the costs of a particular health care niche or deliver unique services such as data analysis, information systems, third-party administration, and transplant network services. In all, about 48 million people receive services through the specialty business.

Utilization management is a cornerstone of United HealthCare's operations. The practice takes many forms, including programs to steer patients to the most appropriate care settings and away from expensive emergency room treatment when it's not needed. The company operates an around-the-clock "NurseLine" telephone information service that uses nurses to direct callers to proper medical attention.

United HealthCare has taken a leading role in creating programs to treat mental illness and substance abuse, and to assists its members in dealing with personal and workplace difficulties before they become serious health problems. Employers using United's mental health and substance abuse management services have reduced spending on this area from as much as 20 percent to as little as 5 percent of their overall health care costs.

The company has 28,500 employees and 4,600 shareholders.

EARNINGS-PER-SHARE GROWTH ★ ★ ★ ★

Past 5 years: 188 percent (24 percent per year)
Past 10 years: 4,300 percent (46 percent per year)

STOCK GROWTH   ★ ★ ★ ★

Past 10 years: 1,425 percent (31 percent per year)
Dollar growth: $10,000 over 10 years (including reinvested dividends) would have grown to $153,000
Average annual compounded rate of return (including reinvested dividends): 31 percent

DIVIDEND YIELD   (no points)

Average dividend yield in the past 3 years: 0.1 percent

DIVIDEND GROWTH   ★

Increased dividend: 3 of the past 6 years
Past 5-year increase: 200 percent (25 percent per year)

CONSISTENCY   ★ ★ ★

Increased earnings per share: 9 consecutive years
Increased sales: 8 of the past 10 years

SHAREHOLDER PERKS   (no points)

The company offers no dividend reinvestment and stock purchase plan, nor does it provide any other shareholder perks.

UNITED HEALTHCARE AT A GLANCE

Fiscal year ended: Dec. 31
Revenue and net income in $ millions

	1991	1992	1993	1994	1995	1996	5-Year Growth Avg. Annual (%)	Total (%)
Revenue ($)	1,065.4	2,200.6	3,115.2	3,768.9	5,670.9	10,073	57	846
Net income ($)	83.3	130.6	212.1	289.8	278.8	326.9	31	292
Earnings/share ($)	0.61	0.79	1.24	1.65	1.57	1.76	24	188
Div. per share ($)	.01	.01	.02	.03	.03	.03	25	200
Dividend yield (%)	.1	.0	.0	.1	.1	.1	—	—
Avg. PE ratio	20	27	25	26	22	26	—	—

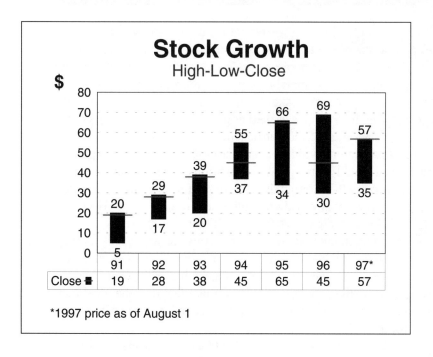

Stock Growth
High-Low-Close

	91	92	93	94	95	96	97*
Close	19	28	38	45	65	45	57

*1997 price as of August 1

72

Thermo Instrument Systems, Inc.

504 Airport Road
P. O. Box 2108
Santa Fe, NM 87504-2108
617-622-1000

President and CEO: Arvin H. Smith

Earnings Growth	★ ★ ★ ★	Dividend Growth	
Stock Growth	★ ★ ★ ★	Consistency	★ ★ ★ ★
Dividend Yield		Shareholder Perks	
AMEX—THI		**Total**	**12 points**

Laboratories, manufacturers, government agencies, and waste treatment facilities around the world use devices developed by Thermo Instrument Systems (TIS) to analyze, monitor, and measure thousands of complex chemical compounds, toxic metals, air pollutants, and other elements.

The Sante Fe operation makes a wide range of analytical, environmental-monitoring instruments as well as process-monitoring and control instruments for the oil, gas, and petrochemical industries.

Thermo Instrument, which became a publicly traded company in 1986, has grown quickly through the acquisitions of companies and product lines and through the internal development of new products and technologies. The company is worldwide in scope, drawing about 31 percent of its $1.21 billion in annual revenue from its foreign sales.

TIS is a leading manufacturer of atomic emission and atomic absorption spectrometers that identify and measure trace quantities of metals and other elements in a variety of materials, such as soil, water, wastes, foods, drugs, cosmetics, and alloys. It also manufactures chemical mass spectrometers used in analyzing foods, drugs, chemicals, petrochemicals, and waste compounds.

It also makes air-monitoring instruments used to measure pollutants in ambient air and from stationary sources such as industrial smokestacks.

The company has spun off several divisions into separate publicly traded companies, including ThermoSpectra Corp., which specializes in precision imaging, inspection, and measurement; Thermo BioAnalysis Corp. (bioinstrumentation); Thermo Quest Corp. (mass spectrometry and chromatography); and Thermo Opek Corp. (optical spectroscopy). TIS maintains majority ownership of each of its spin-off companies.

TIS has about 7,000 employees and 2,500 shareholders.

EARNINGS-PER-SHARE GROWTH ★ ★ ★ ★

Past 5 years: 324 percent (33 percent per year)
Past 10 years: 1,300 percent (31 percent per year)

STOCK GROWTH ★ ★ ★ ★

Past 10 years: 1,441 percent (31 percent per year)
Dollar growth: $10,000 over 10 years (including reinvested dividends) would have grown to $154,000
Average annual compounded rate of return (including reinvested dividends): 31 percent

DIVIDEND YIELD (no points)

The company pays no dividend.

DIVIDEND GROWTH (no points)

No dividend

CONSISTENCY ★ ★ ★ ★

Increased earnings per share: 10 consecutive years
Increased sales: 12 consecutive years

SHAREHOLDER PERKS (no points)

The company offers no stock purchase plan, nor does it offer any other shareholder perks.

THERMO INSTRUMENT AT A GLANCE

Fiscal year ended: Dec. 31
Revenue and net income in $ millions

	1991	1992	1993	1994	1995	1996	5-Year Growth Avg. Annual (%)	Total (%)
Revenue ($)	338.8	423.2	529.3	650	782.7	1,209.4	29	257
Net income ($)	24.8	33.1	44.7	60.2	79.3	138.2	42	457
Earnings/share ($)	0.33	0.41	0.51	0.66	0.88	1.40	33	324
Div. per share ($)	–	–	–	–	–	–	–	–
Dividend yield (%)	–	–	–	–	–	–	—	—
Avg. PE ratio	24	23	30	26	25	26	—	—

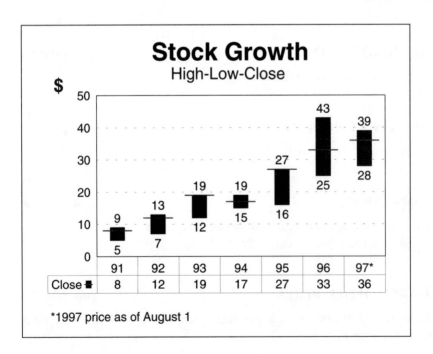

The Walt Disney Company

The
Walt Disney
Company©

500 South Buena Vista Street
Burbank, CA 91521
818-560-1000

Chairman and CEO: Michael D. Eisner

Earnings Growth	★ ★	Dividend Growth	★ ★ ★
Stock Growth	★ ★ ★	Consistency	★ ★
Dividend Yield	★	Shareholder Perks	★
NYSE—DIS		**Total**	**12 points**

The big news in the Magic Kingdom has been the recent acquisition of Capital Cities/ABC. Now Mickey has his own network.

ABC has 223 primary affiliated stations that reach 99.9 percent of the U.S. population. It also operates the ABC Radio Network, which has 2,900 affiliates, and it owns an 80 percent share of ESPN. Of course, Disney already had its own cable channel, but the Disney Channel is no ABC. It is, however, one of the more popular pay channels, with 25 million domestic and 7 million international subscribers.

As part of the ABC merger, Disney acquired a number of daily newspapers, although it quickly sold its two largest papers, *The Kansas City Star* and the *Fort Worth Star-Telegram,* to Knight-Ridder.

Disney's broadcasting business is now the largest segment of its corporate empire. Its other two primary segments are:

1. **Creative Content.** This had been Disney's largest division, with movies from Walt Disney Pictures, Touchstone Pictures, Hollywood Pictures, Miramax Film, and Caravan Pictures. Among the company's

leading movies recently have been *The English Patient, 101 Dalmations,* and *Pocahontas.*

The segment also includes the company's home-video division, which claims about 900 titles, and its network and cable television offerings. Among its top shows are *Home Improvement, Boy Meets World,* and *Ellen.*

2. **Theme parks and resorts.** The company operates a number of resorts. Its largest is Walt Disney World in Orlando, Florida, with three theme parks, The Magic Kingdom, Epcot, and the Disney–MGM Studios Theme Park. Other parks include Disneyland in Anaheim, California, and Tokyo Disneyland. The company is a 39 percent shareholder of Disneyland Paris in France. The company also sells a wide variety of Disney products, such as apparel, dolls, software games, books, and assorted merchandise. It operates about 525 Disney Stores.

Disney has about 100,000 employees and 560,000 shareholders.

EARNINGS-PER-SHARE GROWTH

Past 5 years: 86 percent (13 percent per year)
Past 10 years: 385 percent (17 percent per year)

STOCK GROWTH ★ ★ ★

Past 10 years: 574 percent (21 percent per year)
Dollar growth: $10,000 over 10 years (including reinvested dividends) would have grown to $70,000
Average annual compounded rate of return (including reinvested dividends): 21.5 percent

DIVIDEND YIELD

Average dividend yield in the past 3 years: 0.7 percent

DIVIDEND GROWTH ★ ★ ★

Increased dividend: 9 consecutive years
Past 5-year increase: 147 percent (20 percent per year)

CONSISTENCY ★ ★

Increased earnings per share: 8 of the past 10 years
Increased sales: 14 consecutive years

SHAREHOLDER PERKS ★

The company does not offer a dividend reinvestment plan, but it does offer a couple of other shareholder perks. The company offers a direct-deposit program allowing shareholders to have dividends deposited directly into their bank accounts.

The company also sometimes gives shareholders special discounts on admission to its amusement parks.

WALT DISNEY AT A GLANCE

Fiscal year ended: Sept. 30
Revenue and net income in $ millions

	1991	1992	1993	1994	1995	1996	5-Year Growth Avg. Annual (%)	5-Year Growth Total (%)
Revenue ($)	6,112	7,504	8,529.2	10,055	12,112	21,238	28	247
Net income ($)	636.6	816.7	889.1	1,110.4	1,380.1	1,533	20	141
Earnings/share ($)	1.20	1.52	1.63	2.04	2.60	2.23	13	86
Div. per share ($)	.17	.20	.24	.29	.35	.42	20	147
Dividend yield (%)	.6	.6	.6	.6	.6	.6	—	—
Avg. PE ratio	23	22	25	21	20	27	—	—

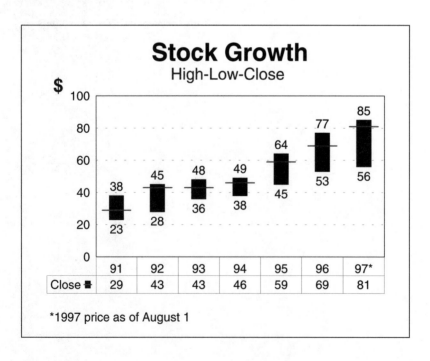

Stock Growth
High-Low-Close

	91	92	93	94	95	96	97*
Close ■	29	43	43	46	59	69	81

*1997 price as of August 1

74

American Home Products Corp.

Five Giralda Farms
Madison, NJ 07940
201-660-5000

Chairman, President, and CEO:
John R. Stafford

Earnings Growth		Dividend Growth	★
Stock Growth	★	Consistency	★ ★ ★ ★
Dividend Yield	★ ★ ★ ★	Shareholder Perks	★ ★
NYSE—AHP		**Total**	**12 points**

Spectacular growth has never been a trademark of American Home Products, but you won't find a steadier health care company in the world than the Madison, New Jersey, pharmaceutical concern. American Home has posted record earnings for 45 consecutive years.

One of the biggest reasons for the company's recent success is Premarin, a medication used to help women fight off osteoporosis after menopause. Produced by American Home Products' subsidiary Wyeth-Ayerst, Premarin is the most widely prescribed drug in the United States. It is used by 4.5 million women who take it both to combat osteoporosis and to provide relief from postmenopausal symptoms.

Premarin is also being tested for other uses, such as hormone replacement therapy in protecting against coronary heart disease.

As a result of a 1994 merger with American Cyanamid Company, American Home ranks first in the sale of nonprescription drugs, first in vitamins and vaccines in the United States, and second in the world in nonprescription drugs. The company, which has sales in 145 countries, is also a leading player in generic pharmaceuticals, biotechnology, animal health care, agricultural chemicals, and convenience food.

American Home has always had an impressive lineup of both prescription and over-the-counter drugs. Pharmaceuticals account for about 56 percent of the company's $14.1 billion in annual revenue.

Its leading nonprescription products include Anbesol, which is the leading topical analgesic for both babies and adults; Preparation H, which is the top-selling product in the hemorrhoidal relief category; and Primatene, which is the largest-selling nonprescription asthma medication. Other major over-the-counter brands include Advil, Anacin, Robitussin, and Dimetapp. Consumer health products account for about 15 percent of the company's total revenue.

American Home has three other key operating units:

1. **The food products division,** which accounts for 6 percent of its revenue, produces an array of ready-to-eat convenience foods such as Chef Boyardee pasta, Polaner All Fruit jellies, Dennison's chili, and Gulden's Mustard.
2. **The medical devices division,** which accounts for 9 percent of its revenue, manufactures such products as disposable syringes and needles, tubes, catheters, monitoring systems, and endoscopic instruments.
3. **The agricultural products group,** which accounts for 14 percent of the company's revenue, makes herbicides, insecticides, and fungicides.

American Home has about 65,000 employees and 69,000 shareholders.

EARNINGS-PER-SHARE GROWTH   (no points)

Past 5 years: 35 percent (6 percent per year)
Past 10 years: 132 percent (9 percent per year)

STOCK GROWTH   ★

Past 10 years: 201 percent (12 percent per year)
Dollar growth: $10,000 over 10 years (including reinvested dividends) would have grown to $43,000
Average annual compounded rate of return (including reinvested dividends): 16 percent

DIVIDEND YIELD

Average dividend yield in the past 3 years: 3.8 percent

DIVIDEND GROWTH

Increased dividend: 44 consecutive years
Past 5-year increase: 32 percent (6 percent per year)

CONSISTENCY   ★ ★ ★ ★

Increased earnings per share: 45 consecutive years
Increased sales: 45 consecutive years

SHAREHOLDER PERKS   ★ ★

Good dividend reinvestment and stock purchase plan: voluntary stock purchase plan allows contributions of $50 to $10,000 per month.

Occasionally, the company also sends out coupons for some of its food and health care products along with the dividend checks.

AMERICAN HOME PRODUCTS AT A GLANCE

Fiscal year ended: Dec. 31
Revenue and net income in $ millions

	1991	1992	1993	1994	1995	1996	5-Year Growth Avg. Annual (%)	Total (%)
Revenue ($)	7,079.4	7,873.7	8,304.9	8,966.2	13,375	14,088	15	99
Net income ($)	1,375.3	1,370.7	1,469.3	1,528.3	1,680.4	1,883.4	6	36
Earnings/share ($)	2.18	2.19	2.37	2.49	2.71	2.95	6	35
Div. per share ($)	1.19	1.33	1.43	1.47	1.51	1.57	6	32
Dividend yield (%)	3.8	3.6	4.5	4.9	3.8	2.8	—	—
Avg. PE ratio	15	17	14	12	18	20	—	—

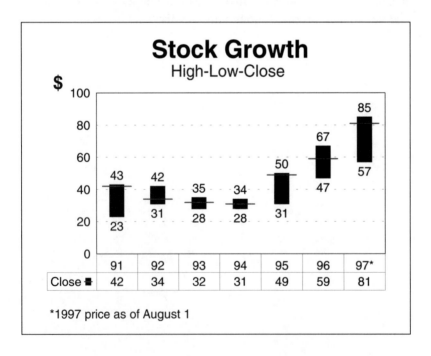

Stock Growth
High-Low-Close

Close ■	91	92	93	94	95	96	97*
	42	34	32	31	49	59	81

*1997 price as of August 1

75

Sigma-Aldrich Corp.

SIGMA-ALDRICH
CORPORATION

3050 Spruce Street
St. Louis, MO 63103
314-771-5765

Chairman: Dr. Tom Cori
President: David R. Harvey

Earnings Growth	★ ★	Dividend Growth	★ ★ ★
Stock Growth	★ ★	Consistency	★ ★ ★ ★
Dividend Yield	★	Shareholder Perks	
Nasdaq—SIAL		**Total**	**12 points**

Scientific laboratories the world over rely on Sigma-Aldrich for thousands of chemical compounds used in their research and development programs. The company supplies about 80,000 compounds in all, including biochemicals, organic and inorganic chemicals, radiolabeled chemicals, diagnostic reagents, and chromatography products.

The St. Louis–based operation also handles 81,000 rare esoteric chemicals for special research projects.

Sigma-Aldrich's chemicals are used by scientists in the fields of biochemistry, synthetic chemistry, quality control and testing, immunology, hematology, pharmacology, microbiology, neurology, endocrinology, and agriculture. The company's diagnostic products are used in the detection of heart, liver, and kidney diseases and various metabolic disorders.

In all, the company's chemical products division accounts for 81 percent of its $1.03 billion in total annual revenue.

The other 19 percent of Sigma-Aldrich's revenue comes from its B-Line Systems unit, which manufactures metal components for strut, cable tray, and pipe support systems used in routing electrical, heating, air-conditioning, and piping services in power plants, refineries, and manufacturing facilities.

Sigma-Aldrich has operations in 24 countries and sales worldwide. In all, foreign sales account for about 54 percent of the company's revenue.

Sigma-Aldrich sells its chemicals to about 138,000 customers, including scientists and technicians in hospitals, universities, clinical laboratories, and private and governmental research laboratories. The manufacturer was formed in 1975 through the merger of Sigma and Aldrich. It has posted 20 consecutive years of record earnings since the merger.

The company has 5,600 employees and 2,000 shareholders.

EARNINGS-PER-SHARE GROWTH   ★ ★

Past 5 years: 85 percent (13 percent per year)
Past 10 years: 323 percent (16 percent per year)

STOCK GROWTH   ★ ★

Past 10 years: 272 percent (14 percent per year)
Dollar growth: $10,000 over 10 years (including reinvested dividends) would have grown to $39,000
Average annual compounded rate of return (including reinvested dividends): 15 percent

DIVIDEND YIELD   ★

Average dividend yield in the past 3 years: 0.8 percent

DIVIDEND GROWTH   ★ ★ ★

Increased dividend: 22 consecutive years
Past 5-year increase: 83 percent (13 percent per year)

CONSISTENCY   ★ ★ ★ ★

Increased earnings per share: 22 consecutive years
Increased sales: 22 consecutive years

SHAREHOLDER PERKS   (no points)

Sigma-Aldrich offers no dividend reinvestment plan, nor does it offer any other shareholder perks.

SIGMA-ALDRICH AT A GLANCE

Fiscal year ended: Dec. 31
Revenue and net income in $ millions

	1991	1992	1993	1994	1995	1996	5-Year Growth Avg. Annual (%)	5-Year Growth Total (%)
Revenue ($)	589.4	654.4	739.4	851.2	959.8	1,034.6	12	76
Net income ($)	79.8	95.5	107.1	110.3	131.7	147.9	13	85
Earnings/share ($)	0.80	0.96	1.08	1.11	1.32	1.48	13	85
Div. per share ($)	.12	.13	.15	.17	.19	.22	13	83
Dividend yield (%)	.6	.5	.6	.8	.9	.8	—	—
Avg. PE ratio	25	26	23	19	17	19	—	—

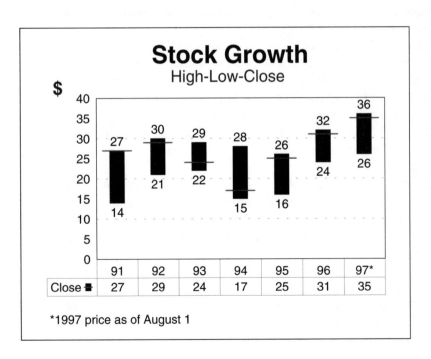

Stock Growth
High-Low-Close

$	91	92	93	94	95	96	97*
Close	27	29	24	17	25	31	35

*1997 price as of August 1

H. J. Heinz Company

600 Grant Street
P. O. Box 57
Pittsburgh, PA 15320-0057
412-456-5700

Chairman and CEO:
Anthony J. F. O'Reilly
President: William R. Johnson

Earnings Growth		Dividend Growth	★ ★ ★
Stock Growth	★	Consistency	★ ★ ★
Dividend Yield	★ ★ ★	Shareholder Perks	★ ★
NYSE—HNZ		**Total**	**12 points**

There's a lot of red on this company's balance sheet, but it has nothing to do with debt. Heinz sells about 600 million bottles of ketchup a year—roughly $1 billion in total sales. This Pittsburgh-based company accounts for more than half of all retail ketchup sales in the United States, and it sells ketchup in more than 90 other countries.

But Heinz is a lot more than ketchup. Ketchup, sauces, and other condiments account for just 19 percent of the company's $9.1 billion in annual revenue.

The firm's food-service business, which accounts for 20 percent of its total sales, is the nation's leading supplier of prepared food to the food-service market. It offers a vast range of items, including ketchup, french fries, single-serve condiments, frozen soups, sauces, baked goods, and tomato products.

Heinz is also a major player in the pet food market, which accounts for 12 percent of its total revenue. Its leading brands include Vet's Choice, 9-Lives, Reward, Cycle, Kibbles 'N Bits, Gravy Train, Ken-L Ration, Meaty Bone, Jerky Treats, and Snausages.

Infant foods account for about 10 percent of Heinz' total revenue, although nearly 90 percent of its sales are made in foreign markets. Heinz recently acquired Earth's Best, the leading organic baby food company in the United States.

Tuna and other seafood products account for about 9 percent of the company's total revenue, led by its StarKist brand. Heinz accounts for about 20 percent of all branded tuna sales in the world. It is the world's largest purchaser of tuna.

The company's other major product segment is weight control products. Its Weight Watchers brand has annual food and service revenues of nearly $1 billion a year worldwide. Weight Watchers operates in more than 20 countries and is, by far, the world's number one weight control brand.

Heinz has operations worldwide. Foreign sales account for about 43 percent of its total revenue.

The company has about 45,000 employees and 63,000 shareholders.

EARNINGS-PER-SHARE GROWTH   (no points)

Past 5 years: 23 percent (5 percent per year)
Past 10 years: 140 percent (9 percent per year)

STOCK GROWTH   ★

Past 10 years: 176 percent (11 percent per year)
Dollar growth: $10,000 over 10 years (including reinvested dividends) would have grown to $37,000
Average annual compounded rate of return (including reinvested dividends): 14 percent

DIVIDEND YIELD   ★ ★ ★

Average dividend yield in the past 3 years: 3.4 percent

DIVIDEND GROWTH

Increased dividend: Every year since 1967
Past 5-year increase: 68 percent (11 percent per year)

CONSISTENCY   ★ ★ ★

Increased earnings per share: 9 of the past 10 years
Increased sales: 8 of the past 10 years

SHAREHOLDER PERKS   ★ ★

Good dividend reinvestment and stock purchase plan: voluntary stock
purchase plan allows contributions of $25 to $5,000 per month.

Shareholders who attend the annual meeting receive gift packages of
some of the company's newer products.

H. J. HEINZ AT A GLANCE

Fiscal year ended: April 30
Revenue and net income in $ millions

	1991	1992	1993	1994	1995	1996	5-Year Growth Avg. Annual (%)	Total (%)
Revenue ($)	6,647.1	6581.9	7,103.4	7,046.7	8,086.8	9,112.3	8	37
Net income ($)	568	638.3	529.9	602.9	591	659.3	4	16
Earnings/share ($)	1.42	1.60	1.36	1.57	1.59	1.75	5	23
Div. per share ($)	0.62	0.70	0.78	0.86	0.94	1.04	11	68
Dividend yield (%)	2.7	2.8	3.5	3.8	3.3	3.2	—	—
Avg. PE ratio	21	16	17	15	18	18	—	—

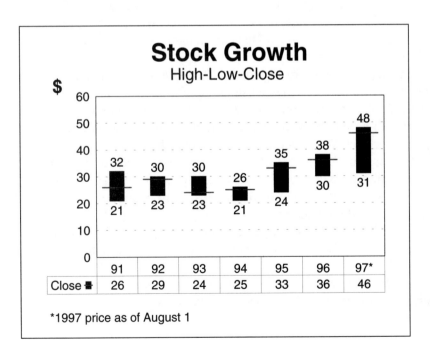

Stock Growth
High-Low-Close

Close ■	26	29	24	25	33	36	46
	91	92	93	94	95	96	97*

*1997 price as of August 1

77

Genuine Parts Company

2999 Circle 75 Parkway
Atlanta, GA 30339
707-953-1700

Chairman and CEO: Larry L. Prince
President: Thomas C. Gallagher

Earnings Growth	★	Dividend Growth	★ ★
Stock Growth		Consistency	★ ★ ★ ★
Dividend Yield	★ ★ ★	Shareholder Perks	★ ★
NYSE—GPC		**Total**	**12 points**

The Genuine Parts Company continues to purr like a finely tuned car. The company has posted increased sales for 47 consecutive years and increased net earnings for 36 consecutive years. It has raised its shareholder dividend for 40 straight years.

Genuine supplies parts to nearly 6,000 NAPA auto parts stores, including about 740 company-owned stores. In all, the company carries more than 165,000 different replacement parts and accessory items.

The Atlanta-based operation is the market leader in the auto parts industry, with an annual revenue of $5.72 billion. The firm's auto parts division accounts for 53 percent of its total revenue. In addition to its broad line of auto parts, the company handles parts for trucks, buses, motorcycles, watercraft, recreational vehicles, farm equipment, small engines, and heavy-duty equipment.

In Canada, Genuine owns a 49 percent interest in UAP/NAPA, which operates nine automotive parts distribution centers and 115 auto parts stores.

Genuine does no manufacturing itself but serves strictly as a wholesale distributor. It buys parts from about 150 suppliers.

Genuine also operates in two other segments:

1. **Industrial parts** (29 percent of revenue). Through its Motion Industries subsidiary, the company is a distributor of industrial replacement parts, including bearings and fluid transmission equipment, hydraulic and pneumatic products, and agricultural and irrigation equipment. In all, the company serves about 150,000 customers in the United States and Canada.
2. **Office products** (18 percent of revenue). Genuine's S. P. Richards Company subsidiary distributes a broad line of computer supplies, office furniture, office machines, and general office supplies. The company distributes more than 20,000 items to more than 6,000 office supply dealers in 30 states.

Founded in 1928, Genuine has 21,300 employees and about 6,700 shareholders.

EARNINGS-PER-SHARE GROWTH   ★

Past 5 years: 50 percent (9 percent per year)
Past 10 years: 168 percent (10 percent per year)

STOCK GROWTH   (no points)

Past 10 years: 139 percent (9 percent per year)
Dollar growth: $10,000 over 10 years (including reinvested dividends) would have grown to $35,000
Average annual compounded rate of return (including reinvested dividends): 12 percent

DIVIDEND YIELD   ★ ★ ★

Average dividend yield in the past 3 years: 3.2 percent

DIVIDEND GROWTH   ★ ★

Increased dividend: 40 consecutive years
Past 5-year increase: 38 percent (6 percent per year)

CONSISTENCY   ★ ★ ★ ★

Increased earnings per share: 36 consecutive years
Increased sales: 47 consecutive years

SHAREHOLDER PERKS   ★ ★

Good dividend reinvestment and stock purchase plan: voluntary stock purchase plan allows contributions of $10 to $3,000 per quarter.

GENUINE PARTS AT A GLANCE

Fiscal year ended: Dec. 31
Revenue and net income in $ millions

	1991	1992	1993	1994	1995	1996	5-Year Growth Avg. Annual (%)	Total (%)
Revenue ($)	3,763.7	4,016.8	4,384.3	4,858.4	5,261.9	5,721	9	52
Net income ($)	224	237	257.8	288.5	309.2	330.1	8	47
Earnings/share ($)	1.21	1.28	1.39	1.55	1.68	1.82	9	50
Div. per share ($)	.64	.67	.70	.77	.84	.88	6	38
Dividend yield (%)	3.3	3.1	2.9	3.2	3.1	3.0	—	—
Avg. PE ratio	15	16	17	15	16	16	—	—

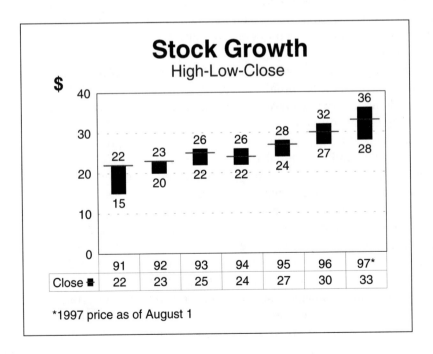

Stock Growth
High-Low-Close

	91	92	93	94	95	96	97*
Close ■	22	23	25	24	27	30	33

*1997 price as of August 1

78

Cisco Systems

CISCO SYSTEMS

170 West Tasman Drive
San Jose, CA 95134
408-526-4000

Chairman: John Morgridge
President and CEO: John Chambers

Earnings Growth	★ ★ ★ ★	Dividend Growth	
Stock Growth	★ ★ ★ ★	Consistency	★ ★ ★
Dividend Yield		Shareholder Perks	
Nasdaq—CSCO		**Total**	**11 points**

Cisco Systems has become one of the nation's fastest-growing companies by developing products that help computers communicate with each other, and tap into resources such as host computers, databases, printers, software, and the Internet.

The company produces a broad range of networking products, including routers, bridges, terminal servers, local area network (LAN) switches, wide area network (WAN) switches, dial access servers, and network management software.

Cisco is the leading global supplier of Internetworking products for corporate intranets and the global Internet. The San Jose, California, operation markets its products to four types of buyers. Its leading buyers are large organizations with complex Internetworking needs such as corporations, government agencies, and universities. It also sells to service providers such as telecommunications carriers, cable companies, and Internet service providers; volume markets such as small businesses, home offices, and residential users; and other suppliers who license features of Cisco software for inclusion in their products or services.

Nearly half of the company's $4.1 billion in annual sales is generated outside the United States. The company has a direct sales force of about 2,500 individuals, plus an international network of about 75 distributors and resellers around the world.

Cisco was formed in 1984 by a group of Stanford University scientists who were interested in developing a way to link the computer world together. The company brought its first product to market in 1986, and sales have been soaring ever since.

The company has about 6,000 employees and 5,300 shareholders.

EARNINGS-PER-SHARE GROWTH ★ ★ ★ ★

Past 5 years: 1,422 percent (73 percent per year)
Past 6 years: 4,470 percent (89 percent per year)
(Cisco was first publicly traded in 1990.)

STOCK GROWTH ★ ★ ★ ★

Past 6 years: 6,263 percent (99 percent per year)
Dollar growth: $10,000 over 6 years would have grown to $626,000
Average annual compounded rate of return: 99 percent

DIVIDEND YIELD (no points)

The company pays no dividend.

DIVIDEND GROWTH (no points)

No dividend

CONSISTENCY ★ ★ ★

Increased earnings per share: 7 consecutive years
Increased sales: 9 consecutive years

SHAREHOLDER PERKS (no points)

The company provides no dividend reinvestment and stock purchase plan, nor does it offer any other perks for its shareholders.

CISCO SYSTEMS AT A GLANCE

Fiscal year ended: July 31
Revenue and net income in $ millions

	1991	1992	1993	1994	1995	1996	5-Year Growth Avg. Annual (%)	5-Year Growth Total (%)
Revenue ($)	183.2	339.6	649	1,334.4	2,232.6	4,096	85	2,136
Net income ($)	43.2	84.4	172	323	456.5	913.3	84	2,014
Earnings/share ($)	0.09	0.17	0.33	0.54	0.72	1.37	73	1,422
Div. per share ($)	–	–	–	–	–	–	–	–
Dividend yield (%)	–	–	–	–	–	–	—	—
Avg. PE ratio	17	26	30	24	21	32	—	—

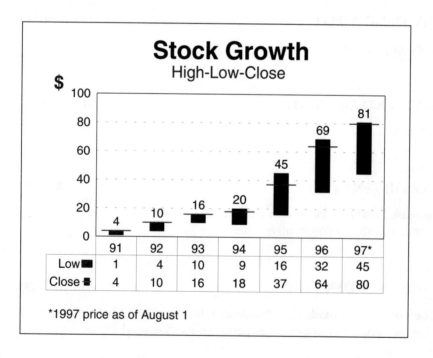

Stock Growth
High-Low-Close

$	91	92	93	94	95	96	97*
	4	10	16	20	45	69	81
Low	1	4	10	9	16	32	45
Close	4	10	16	18	37	64	80

*1997 price as of August 1

79

Oracle Corp.

500 Oracle Parkway
Redwood Shores, CA 94065
415-506-7000

Chairman and CEO: Lawrence J. Ellison
President: Raymond J. Lane

Earnings Growth	★ ★ ★ ★	Dividend Growth	
Stock Growth	★ ★ ★ ★	Consistency	★ ★ ★
Dividend Yield		Shareholder Perks	
NASDAQ—ORCL		**Total**	**11 points**

Oracle software gives computer users the ability to tap into computer resources anywhere, anytime. Its Oracle relational database management systems enable users to define, retrieve, manipulate, and control data stored on multiple computers, and to manage video, audio, text, messaging, and spatial data.

Even laptop users can tap into other computers with the Oracle Mobile Agents product, which uses digital radio networks to link up with other computers. Oracle also makes a WebSystem software program that helps companies create and manage Web applications.

Oracle is the world's leading supplier of database software and information management services. It makes software products that fit into three different categories: "server technologies," "application development and business intelligence tools," and "client server applications."

Its leading product is its relational database management system (considered a "server technology" product), which runs on a broad range of computers, including massively parallel, clustered, and symmetrical multiprocessing, plus minicomputers, workstations, personal computers, and laptop computers. It works in conjunction with more than 85 different operating systems.

Oracle makes a broad range of application development and business intelligence tools, including Oracle Power Objects, a development tool for client server and Web applications for personal computers and small work groups of two to 20 users. The company also makes similar software programs for larger groups (20 to 20,000 users), including the Designer 2000 and Developer 2000 server technology tools.

Oracle markets its products in 93 countries around the world. About 57 percent of its $4.2 billion in annual revenue comes from its foreign sales.

Founded in 1977, the company has about 23,000 employees and 5,500 shareholders.

EARNINGS-PER-SHARE GROWTH ★ ★ ★ ★

Past 5 years: 850 percent (57 percent per year)
Past 10 years: 9,500 percent (57 percent per year)

STOCK GROWTH ★ ★ ★ ★

Past 10 years: 6,858 percent (53 percent per year)
Dollar growth: $10,000 over 10 years would have grown to about $700,000
Average annual compounded rate of return: 53 percent

DIVIDEND YIELD (no points)

The company pays no dividend.

DIVIDEND GROWTH (no points)

No dividend

CONSISTENCY ★ ★ ★

Increased earnings per share: 9 of the past 10 years
Increased sales: 10 consecutive years

SHAREHOLDER PERKS (no points)

Oracle does not offer a dividend reinvestment and stock purchase plan, nor does it provide any other shareholder perks.

ORACLE AT A GLANCE

Fiscal year ended: May 31
Revenue and net income in $ millions

	1991	1992	1993	1994	1995	1996	5-Year Growth Avg. Annual (%)	Total (%)
Revenue ($)	1,027.9	1,178.5	1,502.8	2,001.1	2,966.9	4,223.3	33	311
Net income ($)	−12.4	113.7	217.0	420.0	649.7	904.9	52	694 4-yr.
Earnings/share ($)	−.02	.10	.24	.43	.67	.95	57	850 4-yr.
Div. per share ($)	–	–	–	–	–	–	–	–
Dividend yield (%)	–	–	–	–	–	–	—	—
Avg. PE ratio	–	32	24	31	29	31	—	—

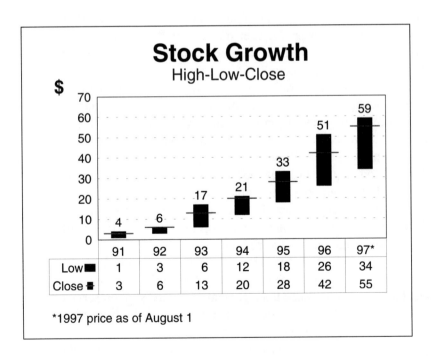

Stock Growth
High-Low-Close

	91	92	93	94	95	96	97*
Low ■	1	3	6	12	18	26	34
Close ■	3	6	13	20	28	42	55

*1997 price as of August 1

Cabletron Systems, Inc.

35 Industrial Way
P. O. Box 5005
Rochester, NH 03866-5005
603-332-9400

Chairman: Craig R. Benson
President and CEO: Donald Reed

Earnings Growth	★ ★ ★ ★	Dividend Growth	
Stock Growth	★ ★ ★ ★	Consistency	★ ★ ★
Dividend Yield		Shareholder Perks	
NYSE—CS		**Total**	**11 points**

Cabletron Systems specializes in helping computers talk among themselves. The fast-growing manufacturer makes a wide range of cables, connectors, and networking systems designed to link computers to printers, modems, and other computers.

The New Hampshire operation was founded in 1983 by Craig R. Benson and S. Robert Levine, who continue to serve as chairman and president, respectively. They began the company as a part-time venture working out of a garage. Now Cabletron has more than 6,300 employees and annual revenues of $1.1 billion.

Cabletron produces the broadest line of interconnectivity products in the industry, including network management software, computer network switches, repeaters, transceivers, bridges, diagnostic test equipment, transmission media and components, desktop network interface cards, and intelligent and nonintelligent wiring hubs.

Cabletron's approach to networking is based on its Synthesis framework of products and services. Synthesis combines infrastructure products and technologies, automated management tools, and support services designed to help users move smoothly from traditional router-based Internetworks to switch-based virtual enterprise Internetworks.

In the U.S. market, Cabletron markets its products through a 200-person sales staff backed up by a 2,500-person in-house technical sales and support staff. The company counts among its customer base 80 of the Fortune 100 companies. Its main customers include financial institutions, government agencies, industrial and manufacturing companies, health care facilities, and academic institutions.

Cabletron also has strong sales in Europe, where it generates more than 20 percent of its revenue. In all, its foreign sales account for about 29 percent of its total revenue. The company has 1,750 shareholders.

EARNINGS-PER-SHARE GROWTH ★ ★ ★ ★

Past 5 years: 252 percent (29 percent per year)
Past 9 years: 4,129 percent (51 percent per year)

STOCK GROWTH ★ ★ ★ ★

Past 7 years: 1,269 percent (44 percent per year)
(The stock has only been trading for 8 years.)
Dollar growth: $10,000 over 7 years (including reinvested dividends) would have grown to $128,000
Average annual compounded rate of return (including reinvested dividends): 44 percent

DIVIDEND YIELD (no points)

The company pays no dividend.

DIVIDEND GROWTH (no points)

No dividend

CONSISTENCY ★ ★ ★

Increased earnings per share: 9 consecutive years
Increased sales: 9 consecutive years

SHAREHOLDER PERKS (no points)

Cabletron does not offer a dividend reinvestment and stock purchase plan.

CABLETRON SYSTEMS AT A GLANCE

Fiscal year ended: Feb. 28
Revenue and net income in $ millions

	1991	1992	1993	1994	1995	1996	5-Year Growth Avg. Annual (%)	5-Year Growth Total (%)
Revenue ($)	290.5	418.2	598.1	810.7	1,069.7	1,399	37	382
Net income ($)	58	83.5	119.2	162.0	164.4	225	31	288
Earnings/share ($)	0.42	0.59	0.84	1.13	1.14	1.48	29	252
Div. per share ($)	–	–	–	–	–	–	–	–
Dividend yield (%)	–	–	–	–	–	–	—	—
Avg. PE ratio	21	25	19	21	20	23	—	—

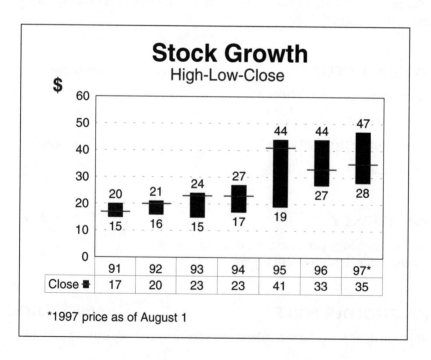

Stock Growth
High-Low-Close

Close ■	91	92	93	94	95	96	97*
	17	20	23	23	41	33	35

*1997 price as of August 1

Compaq Computer Corp.

20555 SH 249
Houston, TX 77070
713-370-0670

Chairman: Benjamin M. Rosen
President and CEO: Eckhard Pfeiffer

Earnings Growth	★ ★ ★ ★	Dividend Growth	
Stock Growth	★ ★ ★ ★	Consistency	★ ★ ★
Dividend Yield		Shareholder Perks	
NYSE—CPQ		**Total**	**11 points**

IBM may be the big name in computers—and the originator of the IBM PC (personal computer)—but Compaq sells more IBM-style PCs than any other company in the world, including IBM. Compaq holds about a 10 percent share of the total worldwide PC market.

Based on all types of computer sales, Compaq ranks as the fifth-largest manufacturer in the world. The Houston-based operation has sales in more than 100 countries worldwide. About half of the company's sales are generated outside of North America. It has manufacturing operations in Scotland, Singapore, Brazil, China, and Houston.

Compaq's primary customers are business computer users who are attracted to Compaq because of the company's strong sales and marketing force, the three-year warranties on its computers, and its reputation for reliability, competitive price, and performance.

Founded in 1982, Compaq has become one of the nation's fastest-growing company's through an aggressive program of product development and marketing. It puts out more than 100 new models of computer PCs each year, along with a vast array of related products. Compaq's major PC lines include the Deskpro computers, which are considered the high-performance business models, the ProLinea economy business models, and the Presario consumer PCs.

Sales of commercial desktop personal computers and related products account for about 45 percent of the company's $18.1 billion in annual revenue, while computer sales to the consumer and home office market account for about 16 percent of its total revenue. Sales of portable personal computers and related products account for 17 percent of the company's revenue, while sales of PC system products and related options account for 22 percent of its revenue.

Compaq has about 17,000 employees and 9,000 shareholders.

EARNINGS-PER-SHARE GROWTH ★ ★ ★ ★

Past 5 years: 443 percent (40 percent per year)
Past 10 years: 2,045 percent (36 percent per year)

STOCK GROWTH ★ ★ ★ ★

Past 10 years: 2,605 percent (38 percent per year)
Dollar growth: $10,000 over 10 years (including reinvested dividends) would have grown to $271,000
Average annual compounded rate of return (including reinvested dividends): 38 percent

DIVIDEND YIELD (no points)

The company pays no dividend.

DIVIDEND GROWTH (no points)

No dividend

CONSISTENCY ★ ★ ★

Increased earnings per share: 9 of the past 10 years

SHAREHOLDER PERKS (no points)

No dividend reinvestment and stock purchase plan is available.

COMPAQ COMPUTER AT A GLANCE

Fiscal year ended: Dec. 31
Revenue and net income in $ millions

	1991	1992	1993	1994	1995	1996	5-Year Growth Avg. Annual (%)	5-Year Growth Total (%)
Revenue ($)	3,271	4,100	7,191	10,866	14,755	18,109	41	454
Net income ($)	230	213	462	867	789	1,313	42	471
Earnings/share ($)	0.87	0.98	1.78	3.21	3.75	4.72	40	443
Div. per share ($)	–	–	–	–	–	–	–	–
Dividend yield (%)	–	–	–	–	–	–	—	—
Avg. PE ratio	16	11	10	11	12	12	—	—

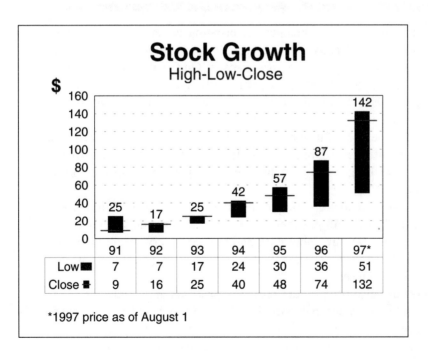

Stock Growth
High-Low-Close

	91	92	93	94	95	96	97*
Low	7	7	17	24	30	36	51
Close	9	16	25	40	48	74	132

*1997 price as of August 1

82

PacifiCare Health Systems, Inc.

5995 Plaza Drive
Cypress, CA 90630
714-952-1121

Chairman: Terry Hartshorn
President and CEO: Alan Hoops

Earnings Growth	★ ★ ★ ★	Dividend Growth	
Stock Growth	★ ★ ★ ★	Consistency	★ ★ ★
Dividend Yield		Shareholder Perks	
Nasdaq—PHSY A		**Total**	**11 points**

Managed health care—the business of bringing patients and physicians together more cost-effectively—has been one of the most profitable areas of the medical industry over the past decade. On the West Coast, PacifiCare has been adding about a quarter of a million new members a year to its network of HMOs. In all, the Cypress, California, HMO has about 2 million members.

About 70 percent of its members are California residents. PacifiCare also has operations in Oregon (which accounts for 8 percent of the members), Washington (6 percent), Texas (7 percent), and Oklahoma (7 percent).

PacifiCare provides a variety of health care services for commercial, Medicare, and Medicaid members, including primary and specialty physician care, hospital care, laboratory and radiology services, prescription drugs, dental and vision care, skilled nursing care, physical therapy, and psychological counseling.

PacifiCare also offers other specialty products and services such as life and health insurance, behavioral health, military health care management, workers' compensation, managed care, and health promotion.

The company's Secure Horizons subsidiary operates the nation's largest Medicare risk program and serves about 500,000 members.

The company recently launched a new Express Referral program that is designed to speed up a patient's access to specialty physicians. The program allows primary care physicians to send patients directly to specialists. In the past, each physician's referral recommendation had to be approved by a review committee.

PacifiCare has about 4,400 employees and 1,000 shareholders.

EARNINGS-PER-SHARE GROWTH ★ ★ ★ ★

Past 5 years: 285 percent (31 percent per year)
Past 10 years: 1,792 percent (34 percent per year)

STOCK GROWTH ★ ★ ★ ★

Past 10 years: 2,301 percent (37 percent per year)
Dollar growth: $10,000 over 10 years would have grown to $240,000
Average annual compounded rate of return: 37 percent

DIVIDEND YIELD (no points)

The company pays no dividend.

DIVIDEND GROWTH (no points)

No dividend

CONSISTENCY ★ ★ ★

Increased earnings per share: 8 consecutive years
Increased sales: 9 consecutive years

SHAREHOLDER PERKS (no points)

The company offers no stock purchase plan, nor does it provide any other shareholder perks.

PACIFICARE HEALTH AT A GLANCE

Fiscal year ended: Sept. 30
Revenue and net income in $ millions

	1991	1992	1993	1994	1995	1996	5-Year Growth Avg. Annual (%)	Total (%)
Revenue ($)	1,242.4	1,686.3	2,221.1	2,893.3	3,731	4,637.3	30	273
Net income ($)	25.7	43.6	62.7	84.6	108.1	134.1	39	422
Earnings/share ($)	1.10	1.78	2.25	3.02	3.62	4.23	31	285
Div. per share ($)	–	–	–	–	–	–	–	–
Dividend yield (%)	–	–	–	–	–	–	—	—
Avg. PE ratio	11	14	18	17	18	19	—	—

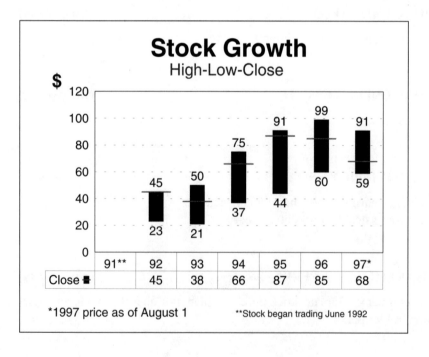

Stock Growth
High-Low-Close

Close ■	91**	92	93	94	95	96	97*
		45	38	66	87	85	68

*1997 price as of August 1   **Stock began trading June 1992

83

Danaher Corp.

1250 24th Street, N.W.
Suite 800
Washington, DC 20037
202-828-0850

Chairman: Steven M. Rales
President and CEO: George M. Sherman

Earnings Growth	★ ★ ★ ★	Dividend Growth	★
Stock Growth	★ ★ ★ ★	Consistency	★ ★
Dividend Yield		Shareholder Perks	
NYSE—DHR		**Total**	**11 points**

Toolmaker Danaher Corporation could hardly be considered a household name, but some of the tools it manufactures are fixtures in millions of homes across the country and around the world. Danaher is the maker of Sears, Roebuck's Craftsman ratchets, sockets, wrenches, and other mechanics hand tools.

Danaher is also a primary supplier of specialized automotive service tools and general-purpose mechanics' hand tools for the 6,500 NAPA auto parts stores.

The company's automotive service tools are also sold under the K-D Tools brand, and its industrial tools and products are sold under the Armstrong and Allen brand names. It also makes the Holo-Krome fastener tools and manufactures tools under a number of other brand names, including Matco Tools, Jacobs Chuck, Iseli, Delta, and Hennessy.

Danaher's tools and components division accounts for about 68 percent of the company's $1.8 million in annual sales.

The company's other product segment—process and environmental controls—accounts for the remaining 32 percent of its revenue. The company makes a broad range of monitoring, sensing, controlling, measuring, counting, and electrical power quality products, systems, and components.

Originally known as DMG, Inc., Danaher was organized in 1969 as a Massachusetts real estate investment trust. It later changed its focus and its name, reorganizing as Danaher Corporation in 1984.

Danaher has about 11,000 employees and 5,000 shareholders.

EARNINGS-PER-SHARE GROWTH   ★ ★ ★ ★

Past 5 years: 634 percent (48 percent per year)
Past 10 years: 914 percent (26 percent per year)

STOCK GROWTH   ★ ★ ★ ★

Past 10 years: 1,729 percent (34 percent per year)
Dollar growth: $10,000 over 10 years (including reinvested dividends) would have grown to $183,000
Average annual compounded rate of return (including reinvested dividends): 34 percent

DIVIDEND YIELD   (no points)

Average dividend yield in the past 3 years: 0.3 percent

DIVIDEND GROWTH   ★

Increased dividend: 2 of the past 3 years
Past 3-year increase: 50 percent (9 percent per year)

CONSISTENCY   ★ ★

Increased earnings per share: 8 of the past 10 years
Increased sales: 9 of the past 10 years

SHAREHOLDER PERKS   (no points)

The company offers no dividend reinvestment and stock purchase plan.

DANAHER AT A GLANCE

Fiscal year ended: Dec. 31
Revenue and net income in $ millions

	1991	1992	1993	1994	1995	1996	5-Year Growth Avg. Annual (%)	Total (%)
Revenue ($)	837.4	955.5	937.6	1,114	1,486.8	1,811.9	17	116
Net income ($)	13.3	31.6	17.7	81.6	108.3	128	58	862
Earnings/share ($)	0.29	0.53	0.93	1.40	1.81	2.13	48	634
Div. per share ($)	–	–	.06	.07	.08	.09	9	50 3-Yr.
Dividend yield (%)	–	–	.4	.3	.3	.2	–	–
Avg. PE ratio	31	19	17	15	17	18	–	–

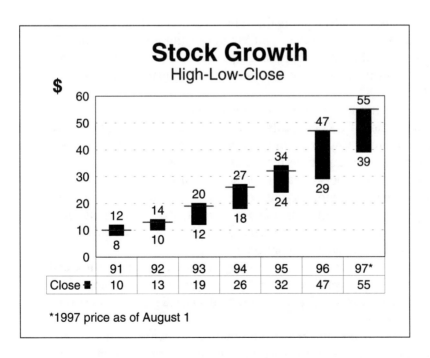

Stock Growth
High-Low-Close

Close ◼	91	92	93	94	95	96	97*
	10	13	19	26	32	47	55

*1997 price as of August 1

Fiserv, Inc.

25 Fiserv Drive
Brookfield, WI 53045
414-879-5000
800-425-FISV (investor relations)

Chairman and CEO: George D. Dalton
President: Kenneth Jensen, Sr.

Earnings Growth	★ ★ ★	Dividend Growth	
Stock Growth	★ ★ ★ ★	Consistency	★ ★ ★ ★
Dividend Yield		Shareholder Perks	
Nasdaq—FISV		**Total**	**11 points**

One thing bankers understand is the value of a dollar. That's why more than 5,000 banks, credit unions, and savings institutions have turned to Fiserv to handle their data-processing operations. Fiserv can do it more effectively and inexpensively than the financial institutions can do it themselves.

Fiserv was formed in 1984 by George Dalton (who continues to serve as chairman and CEO) and Leslie Muma, through the merger of two regional data-processing firms. Since then, the Milwaukee-area operation has made nearly 60 acquisitions that helped turn it into the nation's largest data-processing provider for banks and savings institutions.

The company provides a wide range of data-processing services, including software systems for account, item, and financial transaction processing and recordkeeping; regulatory reporting; electronic funds transfer; and related database management.

It also provides account-processing services, administration and trusteeship of self-directed retirement plans, marketing communications and graphic design services, plastic card products and services, and disaster recovery services.

Fiserv also offers backroom automation software systems, self-directed retirement plan processing, network installation and integration services, human resources outsourcing, and delivery and support of third-party software and hardware products.

The company also made a foray into the foreign market with its 1996 joint venture with Canadian Imperial Bank of Commerce (CIBC) to form a new item-processing services company comprised of all of CIBC's item-processing and currency operations centers in Canada.

Fiserv has about 9,000 employees and 20,000 shareholders.

EARNINGS-PER-SHARE GROWTH ★ ★ ★

Past 5 years: 135 percent (19 percent per year)
Past 10 years: 509 percent (20 percent per year)

STOCK GROWTH ★ ★ ★ ★

Past 10 years: 807 percent (25 percent per year)
Dollar growth: $10,000 over 10 years would have grown to $90,700
Average annual compounded rate of return (including reinvested dividends): 25 percent

DIVIDEND YIELD (no points)

The company pays no dividend.

DIVIDEND GROWTH (no points)

No dividend

CONSISTENCY ★ ★ ★ ★

Increased earnings per share: 11 consecutive years
Increased sales: 11 consecutive years

SHAREHOLDER PERKS (no points)

The company offers no dividend reinvestment and stock purchase plan, nor does it provide any other shareholder perks.

FISERV AT A GLANCE

Fiscal year ended: Dec. 31
Revenue and net income in $ millions

	1991	1992	1993	1994	1995	1996	5-Year Growth Avg. Annual (%)	Total (%)
Revenue ($)	288.4	341.4	467.8	579.8	703.4	798.3	22	177
Net income ($)	19	24.4	32.7	40.4	49.8	61.7	26	225
Earnings/share ($)	0.57	0.69	0.83	0.99	1.13	1.34	19	135
Div. per share ($)	–	–	–	–	–	–	–	–
Dividend yield (%)	–	–	–	–	–	–	—	—
Avg. PE ratio	–	–	–	–	–	–	—	—

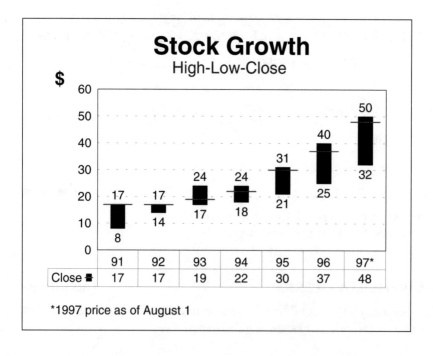

Stock Growth
High-Low-Close

	91	92	93	94	95	96	97*
Close	17	17	19	22	30	37	48

*1997 price as of August 1

Thermo Electron Corp.

⚟ Thermo Electron

81 Wyman Street
P.O. Box 9046
Waltham, MA 02254-9046
617-622-1000

Chairman and CEO: George N. Hatsopoulos
President: John N. Hatsopoulos

Earnings Growth	★ ★ ★	Dividend Growth	
Stock Growth	★ ★ ★ ★	Consistency	★ ★ ★ ★
Dividend Yield		Shareholder Perks	
NYSE—TMO		**Total**	**11 points**

When Thermo Electron Founder and Chairman George Hatsopoulos discovers a commercial need that corporate America has yet to fulfill, he sends his research teams into action to find a way to fill the void and turn a buck.

His quest has taken Thermo Electron into a vastly divergent range of pursuits. The company manufactures environmental-monitoring and analysis instruments, biomedical products (including heart-assist devices, respiratory care equipment, and mammography systems), paper-recycling and paper-making equipment, alternative energy systems, and industrial process equipment, among other things.

Hatsopoulos founded Thermo Electron in 1956 while he was still a graduate student at the Massachusetts Institute of Technology (MIT) to research commercial aspects of his doctoral thesis in energy conversion. Thermo Electron's key segments include:

- **Instruments.** The company makes a wide range of analytical and monitoring instruments used to detect and measure air pollution, nuclear radioactivity, toxic substances, chemical compounds, trace quantities of metals, and other elements.

- **Alternative energy systems.** The firm builds and operates alternative-energy power plants such as waste-to-energy electric power plants and fossil fuel cogeneration plants that generate electricity and thermal energy in the form of steam or hot or chilled water.
- **Process equipment.** Thermo Electron develops computer-controlled thermal-processing systems used to treat, mold, and strengthen metals and metal parts. The company also manufactures systems for the thermal treatment of toxic wastes such as soil contaminated by petroleum products.
- **Biomedical products.** The company makes a variety of biomedical devices and special instruments, including instruments used to detect ultratrace concentrations of nitrogen-based compounds, ventricular-assist devices, and high-voltage power conversion systems, modulators, and related equipment.
- **Services.** The company provides lab testing, engineering, and environmental science services such as the monitoring of hazardous wastes and radioactive materials, the design and construction inspection of water supply and wastewater treatment facilities, and metallurgical heat-treating services for customers in aerospace and other industries.

The company has strong international sales, particularly in Europe. Foreign exports account for about 20 percent of the company's $2.9 billion in annual revenue.

The company has about 15,000 employees and 7,000 shareholders.

EARNINGS-PER-SHARE GROWTH ★ ★ ★

Past 5 years: 133 percent (19 percent per year)
Past 10 years: 440 percent (18 percent per year)

STOCK GROWTH ★ ★ ★ ★

Past 10 years: 664 percent (22.5 percent per year)
Dollar growth: $10,000 over 10 years (including reinvested dividends) would have grown to $76,000
Average annual compounded rate of return (including reinvested dividends): 22.5 percent

DIVIDEND YIELD (no points)

The company pays no dividend.

DIVIDEND GROWTH (no points)

No dividend

CONSISTENCY ★ ★ ★ ★

Increased earnings per share: 13 consecutive years
Increased sales: 10 consecutive years

SHAREHOLDER PERKS (no points)

The company offers no stock purchase plan, nor does it provide any other
shareholder perks.

THERMO ELECTRON AT A GLANCE

Fiscal year ended: Dec. 31
Revenue and net income in $ millions

	1991	1992	1993	1994	1995	1996	5-Year Growth Avg. Annual (%)	5-Year Growth Total (%)
Revenue ($)	805.5	949	1,354.5	1,729.2	2,207.3	2,932.7	29	264
Net income ($)	54.3	74.5	76.9	104.7	140.1	263.7	35	386
Earnings/share ($)	0.58	0.67	0.78	0.93	1.11	1.35	19	133
Div. per share ($)	–	–	–	–	–	–	–	–
Dividend yield (%)	–	–	–	–	–	–	—	—
Avg. PE ratio	19	19	22	20	24	28	—	—

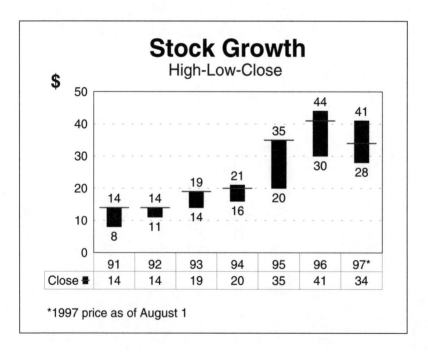

Stock Growth
High-Low-Close

Close ■	91	92	93	94	95	96	97*
	14	14	19	20	35	41	34

*1997 price as of August 1

86

American International Group, Inc.

70 Pine Street
New York, NY 10270
212-770-7000

Chairman and CEO: Maurice R. Greenberg
President: Thomas R. Tizzio

Earnings Growth	★ ★	Dividend Growth	★ ★
Stock Growth	★ ★ ★	Consistency	★ ★ ★ ★
Dividend Yield		Shareholder Perks	
NYSE—AIG		**Total**	**11 points**

When C. V. Starr opened a small insurance agency in China in 1919, Shanghai was the bustling commercial center of China and East Asia. But because of political unrest, Starr relocated his agency to New York in 1939, where it adopted its current name. Now American International Group (AIG) writes insurance that covers the world. The company offers policies in about 130 companies.

As a sign of the times, AIG reestablished a presence in Shanghai in 1992. The same year, AIG opened an office in Moscow, the first American insurance company to do so.

Overseas operations account for about 35 percent of AIG's net premiums written and 50 percent of the company's total revenue. In the U.S. market, AIG is the largest underwriter of commercial and industrial insurance polices.

AIG's mainstay is property and casualty insurance, which accounts for about 56 percent of its annual revenue. Life insurance accounts for 33 percent of the company's revenue and financial services and other types of insurance account for 11 percent.

AIG recently entered the personal auto insurance market.

The company has been growing steadily in recent years, and the pace is expected to continue as AIG aggressively pursues opportunities in the largely underinsured foreign markets. The recent ratification of the NAFTA and GATT treaties will help spur international growth.

The company has 33,000 employees and about 10,000 shareholders.

EARNINGS-PER-SHARE GROWTH ★ ★

Past 5 years: 90 percent (14 percent per year)
Past 10 years: 327 percent (16 percent per year)

STOCK GROWTH ★ ★ ★

Past 10 years: 594 percent (21 percent per year)
Dollar growth: $10,000 over 10 years (including reinvested dividends) would have grown to $73,000
Average annual compounded rate of return (including reinvested dividends): 22 percent

DIVIDEND YIELD (no points)

Average dividend yield in the past 3 years: 0.4 percent

DIVIDEND GROWTH ★ ★

Increased dividend: 10 consecutive years
Past 5-year increase: 86 percent (13 percent per year)

CONSISTENCY ★ ★ ★ ★

Increased earnings per share: 12 consecutive years

SHAREHOLDER PERKS (no points)

The company does not offer a dividend reinvestment and stock purchase plan, nor does it provide any other shareholder perks.

AIG AT A GLANCE

Fiscal year ended: Dec. 31
Revenue and net income in $ millions

	1991	1992	1993	1994	1995	1996	Avg. Annual (%)	Total (%)
							5-Year Growth	
Revenue ($)	16,883	18,388	20,068	22,358	25,874	26,545	9	57
Net income ($)	1,553.0	1,657.0	1,938.8	2,175.5	2,510.4	2,897.3	13	87
Earnings/share ($)	3.24	3.47	4.07	4.58	5.30	6.15	14	90
Div. per share ($)	.21	.23	.26	.29	.32	.39	13	86
Dividend yield (%)	.5	.6	.4	.5	.4	.4	—	—
Avg. PE ratio	12	13	14	13	15	16	—	—

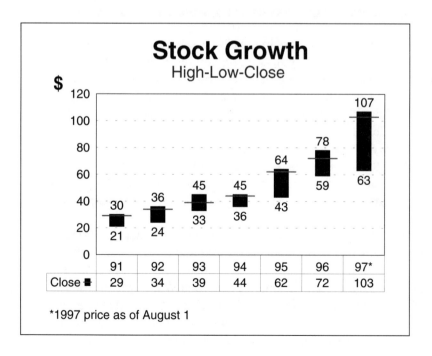

Stock Growth
High-Low-Close

	91	92	93	94	95	96	97*
Close	29	34	39	44	62	72	103

*1997 price as of August 1

Carnival Corp.

3655 N.W. 87th Avenue
Miami, FL 33178-2428
305-599-2600

Chairman and CEO: Micky Arison

Earnings Growth	★ ★	Dividend Growth	★
Stock Growth	★ ★ ★	Consistency	★ ★ ★ ★
Dividend Yield	★	Shareholder Perks	
NYSE—CCL		**Total**	**11 points**

This is a company with some very impressive assets. Its *Carnival Destiny,* for instance, is the world's largest ocean-going resort ship with a 3,400-guest capacity and a 1,050-member crew. First launched in 1996, the *Destiny* is valued at $400 million and weighs more than 100,000 tons. It towers more than 200 feet above the water and spans a length of nearly three football fields.

The *Destiny* is one of 22 Carnival cruise ships, with an aggregate capacity of 30,837 passengers. Carnival also owns 50 percent of Seabourn Cruise Line, which operates two ships, and it holds a 29.5 percent share of Airtours, a leisure travel company with two cruise ships marketed primarily in Europe.

The Miami-based operation has seven new ships under construction that should be seaworthy within the next three years.

Carnival is the world's largest cruise company. Its main lines are the Carnival Cruise Lines, Holland America Line, and Windstar Cruises. The company's main cruise locations are the Caribbean and Alaska areas, although its ships also sail through a number of other areas around the world. In all, the company hosted about 1.76 million cruise passengers in 1996.

In addition to its cruise ships, Carnival operates a tour business that markets sight-seeing tours and cruises to Alaska. It also operates 16 hotels in Alaska and the Canadian Yukon, two luxury day boats offering tours of the glaciers of Alaska and the Yukon River, and 290 motor coaches used for sight-seeing and charters in Washington and Alaska. It also operates 12 private domed railcars on the Alaskan railroad between Anchorage and Fairbanks.

Along with its cruise-line revenues, the company earns extra revenue from onboard activities such as casino gaming, liquor sales, gift shop sales, shore tours, and promotional advertising by merchants located in ports of call. The on-ship casinos feature slot machines, blackjack, craps, roulette, and stud poker.

Carnival Cruise lines began humbly in 1972 when its only ship, the *Mardi Gras,* shoved off from the port of Miami for its maiden voyage and quickly ran aground on a sandbar. By 1974, the company was deeply in debt and near bankruptcy. The original parent company, American International Travel Service, sold the cruise line to Ted Arison for $1 and an assumed $5 million debt. Arison, who is considered the Carnival founder, turned the company around and added a second ship in 1975 and a third ship in 1978. It's been clear sailing for Carnival ever since.

The company has about 18,000 employees, including corporate staff and ship crew members, and 3,500 shareholders.

EARNINGS-PER-SHARE GROWTH   ★ ★

Past 5 years: 110 percent (16 percent per year)
Past 10 years: 333 percent (16 percent per year)

STOCK GROWTH   ★ ★ ★

Past 9 years: 420 percent (18 percent per year)
Dollar growth: $10,000 over 10 years (including reinvested dividends) would have grown to $62,000
Average annual compounded rate of return (including reinvested dividends): 20 percent

DIVIDEND YIELD ★

Average dividend yield in the past 3 years: 1.3 percent

DIVIDEND GROWTH ★

Increased dividend: 9 consecutive years
Past 5-year increase: 52 percent (9 percent per year)

CONSISTENCY ★ ★ ★ ★

Increased earnings per share: 10 consecutive years
Increased sales: 10 consecutive years

SHAREHOLDER PERKS (no points)

The company provides no dividend reinvestment and stock purchase plan.

CARNIVAL CORP. AT A GLANCE

Fiscal year ended: Dec. 31
Revenue and net income in $ millions

	1991	1992	1993	1994	1995	1996	5-Year Growth Avg. Annual (%)	Total (%)
Revenue ($)	1,404.7	1,473.6	1,556.9	1,806.0	1,998.2	2,212.6	10	58
Net income ($)	253.8	281.8	318.2	381.8	451.1	566.3	18	123
Earnings/share ($)	0.93	1.00	1.13	1.35	1.59	1.95	16	110
Div. per share ($)	0.25	0.28	0.28	0.29	0.32	0.38	9	52
Dividend yield (%)	2.3	2.0	1.5	1.2	1.4	1.4	—	—
Avg. PE ratio	11	14	17	17	14	15	—	—

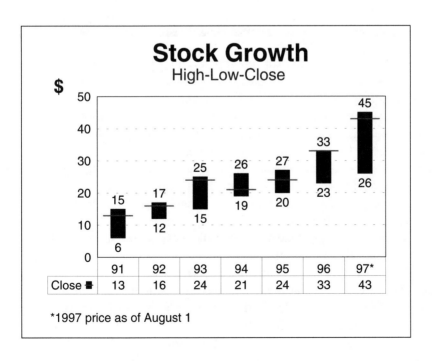

Stock Growth
High-Low-Close

	91	92	93	94	95	96	97*
Close ■	13	16	24	21	24	33	43

*1997 price as of August 1

88

W. W. Grainger, Inc.

W.W. GRAINGER, INC.

455 Knightsbridge Parkway
Lincolnshire, IL 60069-3620
847-793-9030

Chairman: David W. Grainger
President and CEO: Richard L. Keyser

Earnings Growth	★	Dividend Growth	★ ★ ★
Stock Growth	★ ★	Consistency	★ ★ ★ ★
Dividend Yield	★	Shareholder Perks	
NYSE—GWW		**Total**	**11 points**

W. W. Grainger supplies 700,000 different parts and supplies to commercial and industrial customers, and has access to another 3 million products through its Grainger Integrated Supply Operations.

Grainger markets a broad array of electric motors, gas engine–driven power plants, heating equipment and controls, hydraulic equipment, janitorial supplies, and lighting fixtures and components.

It also sells pumps, material-handling and storage equipment, motor controls, office equipment, outdoor equipment, plant and office maintenance equipment, power and hand tools, power transmission components, safety products, and shop tools.

Grainger markets its products through its network of 527 stores in all 50 states, Canada, Puerto Rico, and Mexico.

Grainger sells primarily to contractors, service shops, industrial and commercial maintenance departments, manufacturers, hotels, and health care and educational facilities. In all, the company has about 1.1 million small-business customers and 200,000 large-business customers. The large businesses account for about two-thirds of Grainger's $3.54 billion in annual revenue.

The company offers an innovative "electronic catalog" for customers. The catalog uses PC-based software and CD-ROM technology. Customers can call up Grainger products on the computer, complete with specifications, prices, and pictures. More than 26,000 copies of the electronic catalog are currently in use. The firm recently put the catalog on the World Wide Web (http://www.grainger.com).

Founded in 1927, Grainger has about 12,000 employees and 2,100 shareholders.

EARNINGS-PER-SHARE GROWTH ★

Past 5 years: 70 percent (11 percent per year)
Past 10 years: 213 percent (26 percent per year)

STOCK GROWTH ★ ★

Past 10 years: 283 percent (14 percent per year)
Dollar growth: $10,000 over 10 years (including reinvested dividends) would have grown to $44,000
Average annual compounded rate of return (including reinvested dividends): 16 percent

DIVIDEND YIELD ★

Average dividend yield in the past 3 years: 1.4 percent

DIVIDEND GROWTH ★ ★ ★

Increased dividend: 25 consecutive years
Past 5-year increase: 61 percent (10 percent per year)

CONSISTENCY ★ ★ ★ ★

Increased earnings per share: 11 consecutive years
Increased sales: 13 consecutive years

SHAREHOLDER PERKS (no points)

The company offers no dividend reinvestment and stock purchase plan, nor does it offer other shareholder perks.

GRAINGER AT A GLANCE

Fiscal year ended: Dec. 31
Revenue and net income in $ millions

	1991	1992	1993	1994	1995	1996	5-Year Growth Avg. Annual (%)	5-Year Growth Total (%)
Revenue ($)	2,077.2	2,364.4	26,298	3,023.1	3,276.9	3,537.2	11	70
Net income ($)	127.7	137.2	149.3	127.9	186.7	208.5	10	63
Earnings/share ($)	2.37	2.58	2.88	2.50	3.64	4.04	11	70
Div. per share ($)	.61	.65	.71	.78	.89	.98	10	61
Dividend yield (%)	1.1	1.1	1.2	1.3	1.5	1.4	—	—
Avg. PE ratio	18	20	20	18	17	18	—	—

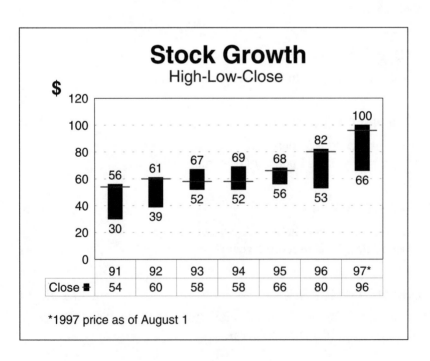

Stock Growth
High-Low-Close

	91	92	93	94	95	96	97*
Close	54	60	58	58	66	80	96

*1997 price as of August 1

89

Xerox Corp.

800 Long Ridge Road
P.O. Box 1600
Stamford, CT 06904

Chairman and CEO: Paul A. Allaire

Earnings Growth	★ ★ ★ ★	Dividend Growth	
Stock Growth	★	Consistency	★
Dividend Yield	★ ★ ★	Shareholder Perks	★ ★
NYSE—XRX		**Total**	**11 points**

There once was a time long, long ago when Xerox was one of the hottest stocks in America. But that was during the 1970s. In the 1980s, Xerox was ambushed by a barrage of competition from low-priced Japanese copiers. The company's earnings dropped 40 percent in the decade from 1980 to 1990, and its stock price dropped by almost 70 percent.

But a new direction, a broad new line of products and services, and a tighter rein on costs—including a work-force reduction of more than 12,000 employees—has helped bring back Xerox from the dead. Its earnings have nearly doubled in the past five years, and its stock price has grown nearly 500 percent since its 1990 low.

Xerox makes a full line of both color and black-and-white copy machines, and other document processing and printing equipment.

The company's leading product line continues to be its black-and-white copiers, which account for 58 percent of its $17.4 billion in annual revenue. Xerox markets the broadest line of black-and-white copiers and duplicators in the industry, ranging from a three copies-per-minute personal copier to a 135-copies-per-minute duplicator to special copiers designed for large engineering and architectural drawings of up to four feet long.

The Stamford, Connecticut, operation holds about a 29 percent share of the $35 billion black-and-white copier market.

Xerox also manufactures a family of DocuTech digital publishing systems. The systems can scan hard copy and convert it into digital documents, or accept digital documents directly from networked personal computers or workstations. DocuTech prints high-resolution pages at up to 135 impressions per minute, and the in-line finisher staples completed sets or finishes booklets with covers and thermal-adhesive bindings.

Xerox has been a pioneer in electronic laser printing, which combines computer, laser, communications, and xerographic technologies. The company markets a line of electronic printers with speeds ranging from five pages per minute to 420 pages per minute.

The company entered the digital color copier market in 1991 and currently offers several high-end color copiers. Its publishing products (such as color copiers and digital printers) account for 25 percent of its revenue. Paper and other products account for 17 percent.

Xerox is worldwide in scope, generating about 51 percent of the company's total revenue through foreign sales.

The company has about 85,000 employees and 69,000 shareholders.

EARNINGS-PER-SHARE GROWTH ★ ★ ★ ★

Past 5 years: 179 percent (23 percent per year)
Past 10 years: 131 percent (9 percent per year)

STOCK GROWTH ★

Past 10 years: 161 percent (10 percent per year)
Dollar growth: $10,000 over 10 years (including reinvested dividends) would have grown to $57,000
Average annual compounded rate of return (including reinvested dividends): 14.5 percent

DIVIDEND YIELD ★ ★ ★

Average annual dividend yield in the past 3 years: 2.6 percent

DIVIDEND GROWTH   (no points)

Increased dividend: Increased in 1996 for the first time since 1980
Past 5 years: 12 percent (2 percent per year)

CONSISTENCY   ★

Increased earnings per share: 7 of the past 10 years
Increased sales: 9 of the past 10 years

SHAREHOLDER PERKS

Dividend reinvestment and stock purchase plan: voluntary cash contributions of $10 up to $5,000 per month.

XEROX AT A GLANCE

Fiscal year ended: Dec. 31
Revenue and net income in $ millions

	1991	1992	1993	1994	1995	1996	5-Year Growth Avg. Annual (%)	5-Year Growth Total (%)
Revenue ($)	13,438	14,298	14,229	15,088	16,611	17,378	5	29
Net income ($)	454	−1020	−126	794	1,076	1,273	23	180
Earnings/share ($)	1.25	1.74	−0.84	2.24	3.07	3.49	23	179
Div. per share ($)	1.00	1.00	1.00	1.00	1.00	1.12	4	12
Dividend yield (%)	5.3	4.0	3.8	3.0	2.5	2.3	—	—
Avg. PE ratio	11	15	16	16	14	15	—	—

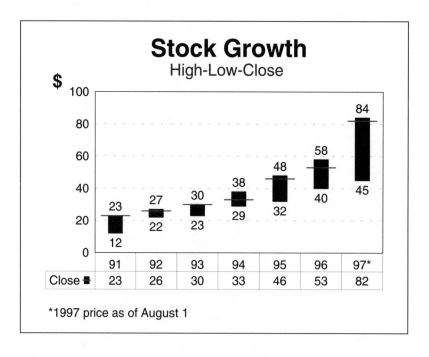

Stock Growth
High-Low-Close

	91	92	93	94	95	96	97*
Close	23	26	30	33	46	53	82

*1997 price as of August 1

90

International Flavors & Fragrances, Inc.

521 West 57th Street
New York, NY 10019-2960
212-765-5500

Chairman and President: Eugene P. Grisanti

Earnings Growth		Dividend Growth	★ ★ ★
Stock Growth	★	Consistency	★ ★ ★
Dividend Yield	★ ★ ★	Shareholder Perks	
NYSE—IFF		**Total**	**10 points**

True to its name, International Flavors & Fragrances is an international producer and marketer of flavors for foods and beverages and of fragrances for cosmetics, soaps, and other products. The New York–based manufacturer spends about $100 million a year in researching and developing new flavors and fragrances at 28 laboratories in 22 countries.

IFF has operations in more than 50 countries, drawing about 70 percent of its $1.4 billion in annual revenue from outside North America.

The company sells its flavor products primarily to the food, beverage, and tobacco industries for use in a wide variety of foods, beverages, dairy products, drink powders, pharmaceuticals, alcoholic beverages, cigarettes and other tobacco products, toothpaste and other oral care products, meats, and pet foods.

The company also produces extracts, concentrated juices, and concentrates derived from various fruits, vegetables, nuts, herbs, and spices. Flavors account for 43 percent of IFF's total revenue.

The other part of IFF's business is its fragrances, which account for 57 percent of its total revenue. It sells its scents primarily to manufacturers of consumer products such as soaps, detergents, cosmetic creams, lotions and powders, lipsticks, after-shave lotions, deodorants, hair preparations, air fresheners, perfumes, and colognes.

The company produces thousands of compounds, with new compounds being added constantly. Most of the new compounds are produced for the exclusive use of a specific client. Its products are sold in solid or liquid form, and in amounts ranging from a few pounds to many tons.

The company makes its products from both synthetic and natural compounds such as flowers, fruits, and other botanical and animal products.

Founded in 1909, IFF has about 4,700 employees and 5,500 shareholders.

EARNINGS-PER-SHARE GROWTH   (no points)

Past 5 years: 16 percent (4 percent per year)
Past 10 years: 125 percent (8 percent per year)

STOCK GROWTH   ★

Past 10 years: 224 percent (12 percent per year)
Dollar growth: $10,000 over 10 years (including reinvested dividends) would have grown to $40,000
Average annual compounded rate of return (including reinvested dividends): 15 percent

DIVIDEND YIELD   ★ ★ ★

Average dividend yield in the past 3 years: 2.8 percent

DIVIDEND GROWTH   ★ ★ ★

Increased dividend: 36 consecutive years
Past 5-year increase: 66 percent (11 percent per year)

CONSISTENCY   ★ ★ ★

Increased earnings per share: 9 of the past 10 years
Increased sales: 9 of the past 10 years

SHAREHOLDER PERKS   (no points)

The company offers no dividend reinvestment plan, nor does it provide any other special perks for its shareholders.

INTERNATIONAL FLAVORS & FRAGRANCES AT A GLANCE

Fiscal year ended: Dec. 31
Revenue and net income in $ millions

	1991	1992	1993	1994	1995	1996	5-Year Growth Avg. Annual (%)	5-Year Growth Total (%)
Revenue ($)	1,017	1,126.4	1,188.6	1,315.2	1,439.5	1,436.1	7	41
Net income ($)	168.7	176.7	202.5	226	248.8	189.9	5	13
Earnings/share ($)	1.47	1.53	1.78	2.03	2.24	1.71	4	16
Div. per share ($)	0.83	0.93	1.02	1.12	1.27	1.38	11	66
Dividend yield (%)	3.0	2.6	2.7	2.6	2.8	2.9	—	—
Avg. PE ratio	19	22	21	20	22	24	—	—

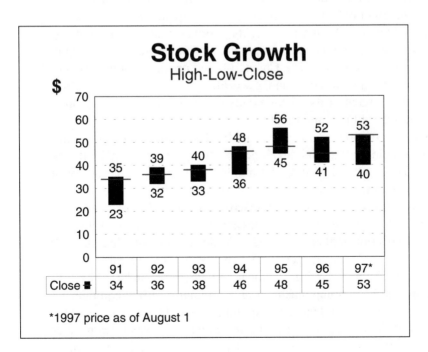

Stock Growth
High-Low-Close

	91	92	93	94	95	96	97*
Close	34	36	38	46	48	45	53

*1997 price as of August 1

Molex, Inc.

2222 Wellington Court
Lisle, IL 60532
630-969-4550

Chairman and CEO: Fredeick A. Krehbiel
President: John H. Krehbiel, Jr.

Earnings Growth	★ ★ ★	Dividend Growth	★ ★
Stock Growth	★ ★	Consistency	★ ★ ★
Dividend Yield		Shareholder Perks	
Nasdaq—MOLX		**Total**	**10 points**

Molex helps link the world together. The company makes electronic, electrical, and fiber optic interconnection products and systems, switches, and related products. Molex markets its goods to manufacturers in the automotive, computer, business equipment, consumer products, and telecommunications industries. The Chicago-based operation is the second-largest connector manufacturer in the world.

About 67 percent of its revenue comes from products manufactured and sold outside of the United States.

Molex was founded in 1938 in Brookfield, Illinois, as a manufacturer of a plastic-molding material developed by company founder, Frederick Krehbiel. Trademarked Molex, the material was used for a variety of products, including toy guns and clock castings.

A few years later, the company discovered that its Molex plastic had excellent electrical-insulating properties and began using it for a variety of electrical connection applications. Today, Molex offers more than 100,000 products, including elecstric terminals, connectors, planer cables, cable assemblies, backplanes, and mechanical and electric switches. The firm also manufactures crimping machines and terminal-inserting equipment.

Sales to computer and business equipment manufacturers account for 36 percent of the company's $1.38 billion in annual revenue; consumer products account for 28 percent; automotive, 15 percent; telecommunications, 13 percent; and other industries such as medical equipment, electronic, vending machines, and security equipment account for the other 8 percent.

Molex has 46 manufacturing facilities in 21 countries on six continents. It has sales organizations in Japan, Hong Kong, Germany, India, England, Australia, China, Mexico, France, and 17 other countries.

Molex has about 10,000 employees and 10,600 shareholders.

EARNINGS-PER-SHARE GROWTH ★ ★ ★

Past 5 years: 116 percent (17 percent per year)
Past 10 years: 230 percent (13 percent per year)

STOCK GROWTH ★ ★

Past 10 years: 302 percent (15 percent per year)
Dollar growth: $10,000 over 10 years (including reinvested dividends) would have grown to $40,000
Average annual compounded rate of return (including reinvested dividends): 15 percent

DIVIDEND YIELD (no points)

Average dividend yield in the past 3 years: 0.13 percent

DIVIDEND GROWTH ★ ★

Increased dividend: 17 consecutive years
Past 5-year increase: 500 percent (from 1 cent to 6 cents; 44 percent per year)

CONSISTENCY ★ ★ ★

Increased earnings per share: 9 of the past 10 years

SHAREHOLDER PERKS (no points)

The company offers no dividend reinvestment or stock purchase plan.

MOLEX AT A GLANCE

Fiscal year ended: June 30
Revenue and net income in $ millions

	1991	1992	1993	1994	1995	1996	5-Year Growth Avg. Annual (%)	5-Year Growth Total (%)
Revenue ($)	707.9	776.2	859.3	964.1	1,197.7	1,382.7	14	95
Net income ($)	64.6	67.5	71.1	94.9	124.0	145.6	18	125
Earnings/share ($)	0.67	0.69	0.76	0.96	1.24	1.45	17	116
Div. per share ($)	.01	.01	.02	.02	.03	.06	44	500
Dividend yield (%)	.1	.1	.1	.1	.1	.2	—	—
Avg. PE ratio	19	24	24	24	22	23	—	—

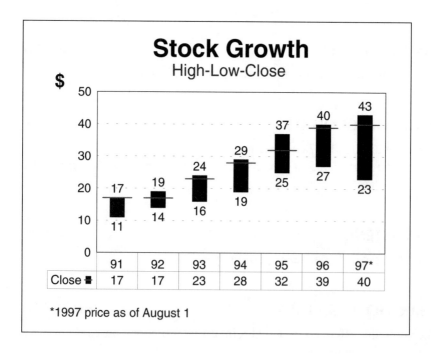

Stock Growth
High-Low-Close

	91	92	93	94	95	96	97*
Close	17	17	23	28	32	39	40

*1997 price as of August 1

Kellogg Company

One Kellogg Square
Battle Creek, MI 49016-3599
616-961-2000

Chairman, President, and CEO:
Arnold G. Langbo

Earnings Growth		Dividend Growth	★ ★
Stock Growth	★	Consistency	★ ★
Dividend Yield	★ ★	Shareholder Perks	★ ★ ★
NYSE—K		**Total**	**10 points**

For 90 years, Kellogg has continued to broaden its selection of product offerings, but it has never lost sight of its primary focus. From the introduction of its first product in 1906—Toasted Corn Flakes—the company that invented ready-to-eat breakfast cereal continues to concentrate almost entirely on the breakfast food market. In addition to its broad line of cereals, Kellogg also offers such breakfast favorites as Eggos waffles, Pop-Tarts, and Nutri-Grain frozen waffles.

Its lineup of cereals continues to grow. Leading brands include All-Bran, Apple Jacks, Apple Raisin Crisp, Apple Cinnamon Rice Krispies, Cocoa Krispies, Corn Flakes, Froot Loops, Frosted Flakes, Frosted Bran, Frosted Mini-Wheats, Fruity Marshmallow Krispies, Just Right, Low Fat Granola, Mueslix, Nut & Honey Crunch, Product 19, Raisin Bran, Rice Krispies, and Special K.

Kellogg's growth has come not only through brand extension but also through foreign expansion. The company continues to forge new markets around the world, attempting to convert foreign consumers from their traditional breakfast fare to the American-style ready-to-eat cereals. The company's success has come slowly but steadily. Kellogg now dominates the foreign cold cereal market, holding a 52 percent market share outside the United States.

Foreign sales account for 43 percent of the company's $6.68 billion in annual sales. Kellogg products are now produced in 18 countries and sold in more than 160 countries. Of the top 15 selling cereals in the world, 12 are Kellogg brands.

Kellogg brands account for 37 percent of the U.S. cereal market.

The company was founded by W. K. Kellogg who first test-marketed his toasted flake cereals in the late 1880s on the patients of the Battle Creek Sanitarium. The cereal was such a hit with patients that many of them wrote the sanitarium after their release to ask where they might buy more of Kellogg's flakes.

Kellogg, recognizing a classic market opportunity when he saw one, founded the Battle Creek Toasted Corn Flake Company in 1906.

While W. K. Kellogg will be remembered most for his pioneering efforts in the development of cold cereals, it was his shrewd, aggressive marketing efforts that set his company apart from the competition. A full-page ad in the *Ladies Home Journal* shortly after the company opened in 1906 helped propel Corn Flakes sales to 2,900 cases a day. By 1911, Kellogg's advertising budget had swelled to more than $1 million a year. And in 1912, the company erected the world's largest sign on Times Square in New York City—an 80-foot high, 100-foot wide "Kellogg's."

Kellogg introduced 40% Bran Flakes in 1915 and All-Bran in 1916. Rice Crispies first began to snap, crackle, and pop on American breakfast tables in 1928.

The company has about 16,000 employees and 23,000 shareholders.

EARNINGS-PER-SHARE GROWTH   (no points)

Past 5 years: 22 percent (5 percent per year)
Past 10 years: 129 percent (8 percent per year)

STOCK GROWTH   ★

Past 10 years: 190 percent (11 percent per year)
Dollar growth: $10,000 over 10 years (including reinvested dividends) would have grown to about $36,000
Average annual compounded rate of return (including reinvested dividends): 13.5 percent

DIVIDEND YIELD

Average dividend yield in the past 3 years: 2.4 percent

DIVIDEND GROWTH

Increased dividend: 40 consecutive years
Past 5-year increase: 50 percent (9 percent per year)

CONSISTENCY

Increased earnings per share: 8 of the past 10 years
Increased sales: 51 of the past 52 years (sales declined in 1996 for the first time in half a century)

SHAREHOLDER PERKS ★ ★ ★

Good dividend reinvestment and stock purchase plan: voluntary stock purchase plan allows contributions of $25 to $25,000 per year.

All new shareholders of record receive welcome kits with brochures and reports on the company along with coupons for free grocery products such as cereal, frozen waffles, or one of Kellogg's newer products.

Those attending the annual meetings in Battle Creek also receive product samples. At a recent meeting, shareholders received Kellogg's Honey Crunch Corn Flakes, Cocoa Frosted Flakes, and Lender's Bagels.

KELLOGG AT A GLANCE

Fiscal year ended: Dec. 31
Revenue and net income in $ millions

	1991	1992	1993	1994	1995	1996	5-Year Growth Avg. Annual (%)	5-Year Growth Total (%)
Revenue ($)	5,786.6	6,190.6	6,295.4	6,562	7,003.7	6,676.6	9	15
Net income ($)	606	657	680.7	705.4	762.3	651.1	3	7
Earnings/share ($)	2.51	2.86	2.94	3.15	3.48	3.07	5	22
Div. per share ($)	1.08	1.20	1.32	1.40	1.50	1.62	9	50
Dividend yield (%)	2.1	1.9	2.3	2.6	2.2	2.3	—	—
Avg. PE ratio	20	23	19	17	19	23	—	—

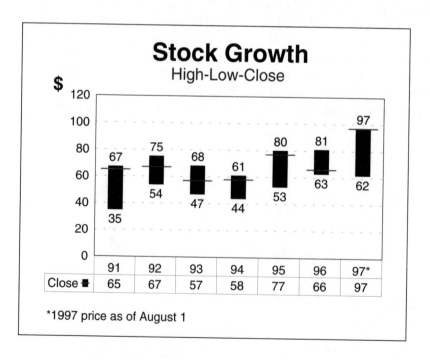

Stock Growth
High-Low-Close

Close	91	92	93	94	95	96	97*
	65	67	57	58	77	66	97

*1997 price as of August 1

93

Torchmark Corp.

2001 Third Avenue South
Birmingham, AL 35233
205-325-4200

Chairman, President, and CEO:
R. K. Richey

Earnings Growth		Dividend Growth	★
Stock Growth	★	Consistency	★ ★ ★
Dividend Yield	★ ★ ★	Shareholder Perks	★ ★
NYSE—TMK		**Total**	**10 points**

In an industry as unpredictable as the insurance business, Torchmark has managed to carve out one of the most consistent growth records in American business.

Torchmark operates several insurance subsidiaries, including Liberty National, and owns the nationwide financial planning company, Waddell & Reed. Waddell & Reed operates 165 offices with about 2,500 agents. Along with a full line of mutual funds, Waddell & Reed offers institutional investment management services and individual financial planning services.

Liberty National, which sells both life and health insurance, has about 2,400 full-time sales representatives working out of 115 district offices located primarily in the Southeastern United States.

Other key subsidiaries include:

- **United American Insurance Company.** Through 51,000 independent agents in the United States, Canada, and Puerto Rico, United sells senior life and health care, including individual renewable Medicare Supplement coverage and long-term care policies.
- **Global Life and Accident Insurance Company.** The unit specializes in individual life and health insurance, including Medicare Supplement, long-term care, and special senior life coverage.

- **United Investors Life Insurance Company.** This Torchmark subsidiary offers individual life insurance and annuities.
- **Family Service Life Insurance.** Using 1,000 independent agents, the company sells individual life insurance to fund prearranged funerals.
- **American Income Insurance Company.** Using 1,400 agents, the firm sells individual life and health insurance to union and credit union members.

Life insurance premiums account for about 37 percent of the company's $2.2 billion in annual revenue. Health insurance and other premiums account for about 38 percent, net investment income makes up 18 percent, and financial services fees bring in about 7 percent.

The Birmingham, Alabama, operation has about 2,900 corporate employees, 2,900 sales agents, and 61,000 independent agents and brokers. Torchmark has about 8,000 shareholders.

EARNINGS-PER-SHARE GROWTH   (no points)

Past 5 years: 43 percent (7 percent per year)
Past 10 years: 154 percent (10 percent per year)

STOCK GROWTH   ★

Past 10 years: 153 percent (10 percent per year)
Dollar growth: $10,000 over 10 years (including reinvested dividends) would have grown to $34,000
Average annual compounded rate of return (including reinvested dividends): 13 percent

DIVIDEND YIELD   ★ ★ ★

Average dividend yield in the past 3 years: 2.7 percent

DIVIDEND GROWTH   ★

Increased dividend: 45 consecutive years
Past 5-year increase: 16 percent (3 percent per year)

CONSISTENCY

Increased earnings per share: 9 of the past 10 years (and 44 of the past 45 years)

SHAREHOLDER PERKS

Good dividend reinvestment and stock purchase plan: voluntary stock purchase plan allows contributions of $100 to $3,000 eight times per year.

TORCHMARK AT A GLANCE

Fiscal year ended: Dec. 31
Revenue and net income in $ millions

	1991	1992	1993	1994	1995	1996	5-Year Growth Avg. Annual (%)	Total (%)
Revenue ($)	1,907.4	2,045.8	2,176.8	1,875.3	2,067.5	2,205.8	3	16
Net income ($)	255.3	277	280	268.9	270.6	314.5	4	23
Earnings/share ($)	3.13	3.58	3.76	3.71	3.80	4.47	7	43
Div. per share ($)	1.00	1.07	1.09	1.11	1.13	1.16	3	16
Dividend yield (%)	2.8	2.2	2.2	3.0	2.8	2.5	—	—
Avg. PE ratio	11	13	15	11	11	11	—	—

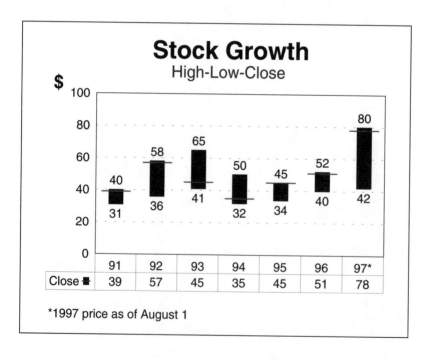

Stock Growth
High-Low-Close

	91	92	93	94	95	96	97*
Close	39	57	45	35	45	51	78

*1997 price as of August 1

Crompton & Knowles Corp.

One Station Place, Metro Center
Stamford, CT 06902
203-353-5400

Chairman, President and CEO: Vincent A. Calarco

Earnings Growth		Dividend Growth	
Stock Growth	★ ★ ★ ★	Consistency	★
Dividend Yield	★ ★	Shareholder Perks	★ ★
NYSE—CNK		**Total**	**9 points**

With a single business transaction, Crompton & Knowles nearly tripled its size. The Stamford, Connecticut, manufacturer of dyes, flavors, fragrances, food colorings, sweeteners, seasonings, and coatings, acquired the Uniroyal Chemical Corporation in 1996 through a stock-swap agreement. Prior to the acquisition, Crompton & Knowles had annual sales of $666 million, while Uniroyal had annual sales of $1.1 billion.

The addition of Uniroyal adds a broad range of new products to the Crompton & Knowles stable. Uniroyal has three core lines of business. Its chemicals and polymers are used for automotive, industrial, and construction applications. Its crop protection chemicals include miticides, seed treatments, growth regulants, and fungicides. And its specialty products are additives for plastics, petroleum, and petrochemical industries.

Traditionally, Crompton & Knowles had focused on dyes for clothing, carpeting, fabrics, upholstery, leather and paper products, and flavorings, fragrances, and coatings for beverages, prepared foods, pharmaceuticals, toiletries, perfumes, and other cosmetics.

The firm's dyes are marketed to a variety of industries, including garment and upholstery manufacturers, and paper, leather, and ink industries for use on stationery, towels, shoes, apparel, luggage, and other products.

Crompton & Knowles also manufactures flavorings and color additives for the food processing, bakery, beverage, and pharmaceutical industries. Its fragrances are sold to manufacturers of personal care and household products. The company's Davis-Standard division manufactures extrusion equipment for plastics and rubber, industrial blow-molding equipment, and related controls and equipment. Extrusion systems are used to mold plastics resins and rubber into such products as sports equipment, plastic furniture, appliances, home siding, furniture trim, and automotive parts.

With the addition of Uniroyal, about 27 percent of the company's total revenue comes from the sales of chemicals and polymers. Other leading segments include crop protection, 22 percent; specialties, 23 percent; dyes, 15 percent; and specialty ingredients, 5 percent.

Known originally as Crompton Loom Works, the company first opened for business in 1840. When Crompton joined with Knowles in 1898, the merged company became the world's largest manufacturer of fancy looms.

The company's loom business is long gone, but it continues to expand its presence in the fabrics industry. Crompton & Knowles sells its dyes and other specialty chemicals throughout the world. Foreign sales account for about 20 percent of its total revenue.

Crompton & Knowles has about 5,700 employees and 4,700 shareholders.

EARNINGS-PER-SHARE GROWTH (no points)

Past 5 years: 23 percent (5 percent per year)
Past 10 years: 429 percent (18 percent per year)

STOCK GROWTH

Past 10 years: 887 percent (26 percent per year)
Dollar growth: $10,000 over 10 years (including reinvested dividends) would have grown to $165,000
Average annual compounded rate of return (including reinvested dividends): 28.5 percent

DIVIDEND YIELD ★ ★

Average dividend yield in the past 3 years: 2.4 percent

DIVIDEND GROWTH (no points)

Increased dividend: 8 of the past 10 years
Past 5-year increase: 8 percent (1 percent per year)

CONSISTENCY ★

Increased earnings per share: 7 of the past 10 years
Increased sales: 10 consecutive years

SHAREHOLDER PERKS ★ ★

Good dividend reinvestment and stock purchase plan: voluntary stock purchase plan allows contributions of $30 to $3,000 per quarter.

CROMPTON & KNOWLES AT A GLANCE

Fiscal year ended: Dec. 31
Revenue and net income in $ millions

	1991	1992	1993	1994	1995	1996	5-Year Growth Avg. Annual (%)	5-Year Growth Total (%)
Revenue ($)	450.2	517.7	558.3	589.8	665.5	1,804	32	301
Net income ($)	35.9	34.5	52	50.9	40.5	64.6	13	80
Earnings/share ($)	.73	.87	1.00	1.00	.84	.90	5	23
Div. per share ($)	.25	.31	.38	.46	.52	.27	2	8
Dividend yield (%)	1.7	1.8	1.7	2.5	3.4	1.4	—	—
Avg. PE ratio	20	23	22	18	18	14	—	—

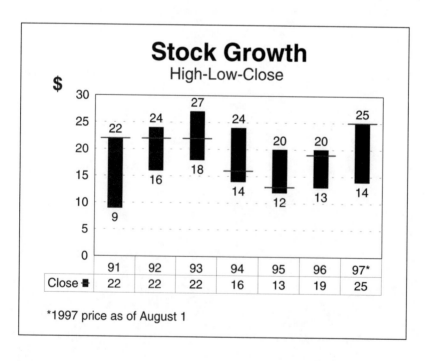

Stock Growth
High-Low-Close

Close ■	91	92	93	94	95	96	97*
	22	22	22	16	13	19	25

*1997 price as of August 1

Computer Sciences Corp.

2100 East Grand Avenue
El Segundo, CA 90245
310-615-0311

Chairman and CEO: William R. Hoover

Earnings Growth	★ ★	Dividend Growth	
Stock Growth	★ ★ ★	Consistency	★ ★ ★ ★
Dividend Yield		Shareholder Perks	
NYSE—CSC		**Total**	**9 points**

Computer Sciences helps companies get online and up-to-speed in the computer technology era. The company offers a broad array of professional computer services, including designing and developing complete information systems, and even operating all or a portion of a customer's technology infrastructure.

Founded in 1959, Computer Sciences originally did most of its business designing, installing, and servicing computer and communications systems for the U.S. government. But the El Segundo, California, operation has been steadily pushing into both the private sector and the international arena. Computer Sciences claims to be the nation's largest independent provider of information technology consulting, systems integration, and outsourcing to industry and government.

As recently as 1992, some 57 percent of its revenue came from U.S. government contracts. By 1996, that figure had slipped to just 37 percent of its $4.24 billion in annual revenue. The U.S. commercial customers account for 36 percent of its revenue, and global commercial accounts make up the other 27 percent of revenue.

For the federal government and many of its commercial customers, Computer Sciences designs, engineers, and integrates computer-based systems and communications systems, providing all the necessary hardware, software, training, and related elements. The company has special expertise in the development of software for aerospace and defense systems. It also provides engineering and technical assistance in satellite communications, intelligence, aerospace, and logistics.

In the commercial market, the company provides consulting and technical services in the development and integration of computer and communications systems, and comprehensive information technology services, including systems analysis, applications development, network operations, and data center management. Computer Sciences has about 34,000 employees and 8,000 shareholders.

EARNINGS-PER-SHARE GROWTH   ★ ★

Past 5 years: 85 percent (13 percent per year)
Past 10 years: 259 percent (14 percent per year)

STOCK GROWTH   ★ ★ ★

Past 10 years: 562 percent (21 percent per year)
Dollar growth: $10,000 over 10 years (including reinvested dividends) would have grown to $66,000
Average annual compounded rate of return (including reinvested dividends): 21 percent

DIVIDEND YIELD   (no points)

The company pays no dividend.

DIVIDEND GROWTH   (no points)

No dividend

CONSISTENCY   ★ ★ ★ ★

Increased earnings per share: 10 consecutive years
Increased sales: 15 consecutive years

SHAREHOLDER PERKS   (no points)

The company offers no dividend reinvestment and stock purchase plan, nor does it provide any other shareholder perks.

COMPUTER SCIENCES AT A GLANCE

Fiscal year ended: March 31
Revenue and net income in $ millions

	1991	1992	1993	1994	1995	1996	5-Year Growth Avg. Annual (%)	5-Year Growth Total (%)
Revenue ($)	1,737.8	2,113.4	2,479.8	2,582.7	3,372.5	4,242.4	20	144
Net income ($)	65.0	68.2	78.1	90.9	110.7	141.7	17	118
Earnings/share ($)	1.34	1.37	1.55	1.77	2.09	2.48	13	85
Div. per share ($)	–	–	–	–	–	–	–	–
Dividend yield (%)	–	–	–	–	–	–	—	—
Avg. PE ratio	12	17	15	17	22	26	—	—

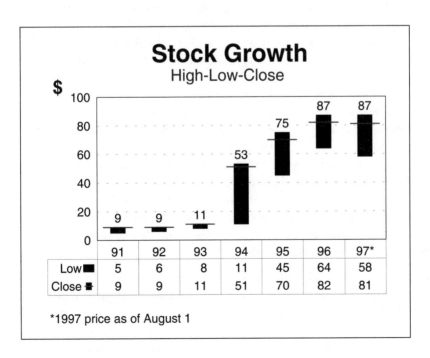

Stock Growth
High-Low-Close

	91	92	93	94	95	96	97*
Low	5	6	8	11	45	64	58
Close	9	9	11	51	70	82	81

*1997 price as of August 1

96

Tyco International, Ltd.

One Tyco Park
Exeter, NH 03833
603-778-9700

Chairman, President, and CEO:
L. Dennis Kozlowski

Earnings Growth	★	Dividend Growth	
Stock Growth	★ ★ ★	Consistency	★ ★
Dividend Yield	★	Shareholder Perks	★ ★
NYSE—TYC		**Total**	**9 points**

Tyco International is a diversified manufacturer that competes globally in several vastly unrelated markets. It makes disposable medical products, packaging materials, flow control products, and electrical and electronic components. It is also the world's largest manufacturer and installer of fire and safety systems.

Tyco operates in more than 50 countries around the world. Foreign sales account for 28 percent of the company's $5.1 billion in annual sales.

The company's leading segment is fire and safety products and services, which account for 39 percent of its total revenue. Tyco's Grinnell subsidiary, which was founded in 1850, is the largest manufacturer and installer of automatic fire sprinkler and alarm and detection systems in North America. Tyco's Wormald International subsidiary, founded in 1889, operates a major fire protection company, with contracting and manufacturing operations throughout Europe and the Asia–Pacific region.

Tyco's other key segments include:

- **Disposable and specialty products** (29 percent of revenue). Tyco makes products for wound care, vascular therapy, urological care, incontinence care, and anesthetic care. It also makes tapes, pressure-sensitive coated paper and films used for business forms and in printing applications, fax paper, and recording chart papers for medical and industrial instrumentation.

- **Flow control products** (23 percent of revenue). The company makes pipes, fittings, valves, meters, and related products that are used to transport, control, and measure the flow of liquids and gases.
- **Electrical and electronic products** (9 percent of revenue). Through several subsidiaries, Tyco makes underwater communications cable and cable assemblies, electrical conduit, and related components.

The New Hampshire–based manufacturer has about 40,000 employees and 24,500 shareholders.

EARNINGS-PER-SHARE GROWTH ★

Past 5 years: 68 percent (11 percent per year)
Past 10 years: 464 percent (19 percent per year)

STOCK GROWTH

Past 10 years: 545 percent (20.5 percent per year)
Dollar growth: $10,000 over 10 years (including reinvested dividends) would have grown to $70,000
Average annual compounded rate of return (including reinvested dividends): 21.5 percent

DIVIDEND YIELD ★

Average annual dividend yield in the past 3 years: 0.6

DIVIDEND GROWTH (no points)

Increased dividend: 6 of the past 10 years
Past 5-year increase: 11 percent (2 percent per year)

CONSISTENCY

Increased earnings per share: 8 of the past 10 years
Increased sales: 9 of the past 10 years

SHAREHOLDER PERKS

Good dividend reinvestment and stock purchase plan: voluntary stock purchase plan allows contributions of $25 to $1,000 per month.

TYCO INTERNATIONAL AT A GLANCE

Fiscal year ended: June 30
Revenue and net income in $ millions

	1991	1992	1993	1994	1995	1996	5-Year Growth Avg. Annual (%)	5-Year Growth Total (%)
Revenue ($)	3,107.9	3,066.5	3,919.4	4,076.4	4,534.6	5,089.8	10	64
Net income ($)	117.5	95.3	94.5	189.2	216.6	310.1	21	164
Earnings/share ($)	1.21	1.03	0.65	1.28	1.43	2.03	11	68
Div. per share ($)	.18	.18	.19	.20	.20	.20	2	11
Dividend yield (%)	1.0	.9	.7	.8	.6	.4	—	—
Avg. PE ratio	9	27	30	18	19	21	—	—

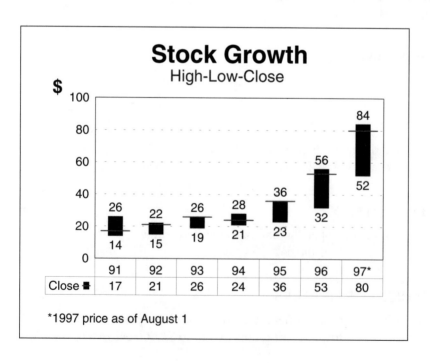

Stock Growth
High-Low-Close

	91	92	93	94	95	96	97*
Close	17	21	26	24	36	53	80

*1997 price as of August 1

Sealed Air Corp.

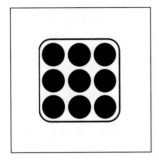

Park 80 East
Saddle Brook, NJ 07663-5291
201-791-7600

Chairman, President, and CEO:
T. J. Dermot Dunphy

Earnings Growth	★ ★ ★ ★	Dividend Growth	
Stock Growth	★ ★	Consistency	★ ★ ★
Dividend Yield		Shareholder Perks	
NYSE—SEE		**Total**	**9 points**

Sealed Air makes protective packaging for products of almost any size and shape, from cups and bowls to computers, telephones, and furniture.

The company's Instapak polyurethane foam–packaging systems are used by customers to tailor protective cushions for a broad range of products such as office and medical equipment, motors and compressors, books, office supplies, cosmetics, and other products.

The Instapak systems are sold primarily by manufacturers and distributors who buy both the packaging systems and the polyurethane chemicals used to create the packaging foam. One advantage of the Instapak system is the small storage space required for the packaging chemicals as compared to traditional paper-packing materials. The Instapak chemicals do not expand until they are mixed together, but once they are combined, the resulting foam expands almost instantly to 200 times the liquid volume of the chemicals.

Sealed Air's Instapak and other specialty polyethylene foams segment accounts for about 35 percent of its $790 million in annual sales.

The company's other product segments include:

- **Surface protection and other cushioning products** (48 percent of total revenue). The company makes cellular cushioning materials, protective and durable mailers and bags, thin polyethylene foams, paper-packaging products, and automated packaging systems.

- **Food-packaging products** (14 percent). The company makes absorbent pads, produce bags, and flexible films, bags, and pouches.
- **Other products** (3 percent). Sealed Air's other products include primarily specialty adhesive products, loose-fill polystyrene packaging, and recreation and energy conservation products.

Sealed Air sells its packaging products worldwide. Foreign sales account for about 39 percent of the company's total revenue.

The Saddle Brook, New Jersey, operation has about 4,000 employees and 1,200 shareholders.

EARNINGS-PER-SHARE GROWTH ★ ★ ★

Past 5 years: 270 percent (30 percent per year)
Past 10 years: 202 percent (12 percent per year)

STOCK GROWTH ★ ★

Past 10 years: 334 percent (16 percent per year)
Dollar growth: $10,000 over 10 years (including reinvested dividends) would have grown to $45,000
Average annual compounded rate of return (including reinvested dividends): 16 percent

DIVIDEND YIELD (no points)

The company pays no dividend.

DIVIDEND GROWTH (no points)

No dividend

CONSISTENCY ★ ★ ★

Increased earnings per share: 9 of the past 10 years
Increased sales: 10 consecutive years

SHAREHOLDER PERKS (no points)

The company offers no dividend reinvestment and stock purchase plan.

SEALED AIR AT A GLANCE

Fiscal year ended: Dec. 31
Revenue and net income in $ millions

	1991	1992	1993	1994	1995	1996	5-Year Growth Avg. Annual (%)	Total (%)
Revenue ($)	435.1	446.1	451.7	519.2	723.1	789.6	13	81
Net income ($)	16.2	20.8	25.9	37.2	52.7	69.3	34	328
Earnings/share ($)	0.44	0.54	0.66	0.94	1.25	1.63	30	270
Div. per share ($)	–	–	–	–	–	–	–	–
Dividend yield (%)	–	–	–	–	–	–	–	—
Avg. PE ratio	20	23	20	17	19	22	—	—

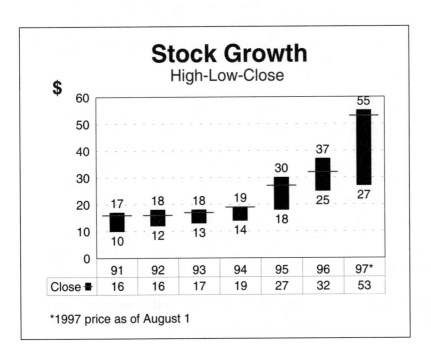

*1997 price as of August 1

98

Cincinnati Financial Corp.

6200 South Gilmore Road
Fairfield, OH 45014
513-870-2000

Chairman: John J. Schiff, Jr.
President and CEO: Robert B. Morgan

Earnings Growth			Dividend Growth		★ ★ ★
Stock Growth		★	Consistency		★
Dividend Yield		★ ★	Shareholder Perks		★ ★
Nasdaq—CINF			**Total**		**9 points**

Even as rising waters rushed through its home city of Cincinnati during the great flood of 1997, insurance giant Cincinnati Financial was able to calmly ignore the devastation—and the financial wreck and ruin that other insurers were encountering.

The reason: Cincinnati Financial doesn't offer flood insurance, and it manages to avoid most other types of disaster insurance that can sweep away its profits in one devastating act of nature. It writes most of its premiums close to home in the Midwest, where the ground never quakes and a hurricane's winds never blow.

What it does sell through its three property and casualty subsidiaries is tightly underwritten property and casualty, life and health, workers' compensation, and other policies.

Its strict underwriting standards are understandable, considering employees own a large stake of the company stock. Cost controls have helped keep Cincinnati Financial's productivity level in the upper ranks of the insurance industry and have allowed the firm to increase its dividend for 36 years in a row.

Cincinnati Financial's three property and casualty companies are Cincinnati Insurance, Cincinnati Casualty, and Cincinnati Indemnity. Life and health policies are written through the Cincinnati Life Insurance Company.

Cincinnati Financial invests heavily in the training of the 1,000 independent agents who sell its products. Training focuses on the theme of providing extraordinary customer service. Staff development ranges from computer training to claims and underwriting classes as well as self-study courses from the leading insurance institutes.

The company management believes that making it easier for local agents to conduct business through training and support pays off in the long run through the stronger customer and community relationships the agents can strike. Independent consumer surveys continue to rate Cincinnati Financial's claim service higher than any other agent-represented company.

A fifth subsidiary, CFC Investment Company, writes leases and loans on office and medical equipment, computers, vehicles, and other types of equipment. More than 90 percent of the company's premium income comes from property and casualty insurance, while life insurance makes up about 4 percent, and accident and health insurance accounts for less than 1 percent.

The company has 2,300 employees and 9,420 shareholders.

EARNINGS-PER-SHARE GROWTH (no points)

Past 5 years: 47 percent (8 percent per year)
Past 10 years: 151 percent (10 percent per year)

STOCK GROWTH ★

Past 10 years: 224 percent (12.5 percent per year)
Dollar growth: $10,000 over 10 years (including reinvested dividends) would have grown to $40,000
Average annual compounded rate of return (including reinvested dividends): 15 percent

DIVIDEND YIELD ★ ★

Average dividend yield in the past 3 years: 2.4 percent

DIVIDEND GROWTH

Increased dividend: 36 consecutive years
Past 5-year increase: 81 percent (13 percent per year)

CONSISTENCY ★

Increased earnings per share: 7 of the past 10 years
Increased premiums earned: 10 consecutive years

SHAREHOLDER PERKS ★ ★

Good dividend reinvestment and stock purchase plan: voluntary stock
purchase plan allows contributions of $25 to $5,000 per quarter. Partici-
pants are assessed a nominal fee of $1 to $3 per transaction.

CINCINNATI FINANCIAL AT A GLANCE

Fiscal year ended: Dec. 31
Revenue and net income in $ millions

	1991	1992	1993	1994	1995	1996	5-Year Growth Avg. Annual (%)	Total (%)
Revenue ($)	1,161.1	1,304.2	1,442.2	1,512.5	1,655.7	1,808.7	9	56
Net income ($)	146.3	171.3	202.2	201.2	227.4	223.8	9	53
Earnings/share ($)	2.66	3.07	3.57	3.55	3.99	3.92	8	47
Div. per share ($)	0.80	0.95	1.05	1.18	1.32	1.45	13	81
Dividend yield (%)	2.5	2.2	1.9	2.4	2.4	2.5	—	—
Avg. PE ratio	12	14	15	14	13	16	—	—

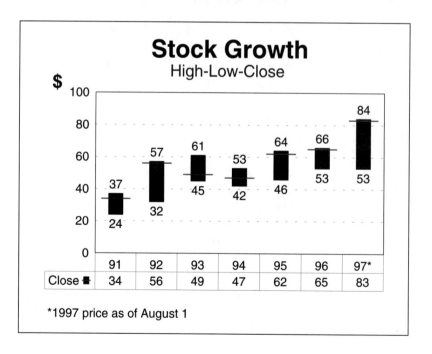

Stock Growth
High-Low-Close

Close ■	34	56	49	47	62	65	83
	91	92	93	94	95	96	97*

*1997 price as of August 1

99

Crown Cork & Seal Company

9300 Ashton Road
Philadelphia, PA
215-698-5100

Chairman and CEO: William J. Avery
President: Michael J. McKenna

Earnings Growth		Dividend Growth	
Stock Growth	★ ★ ★	Consistency	★ ★ ★
Dividend Yield	★ ★	Shareholder Perks	
NYSE—CCK		**Total**	**8 points**

No company in the world manufactures more containers than Crown Cork & Seal. The company had been a major player in both the U.S. and global markets, but with its acquisition in 1996 of Carnaud MetalBox, based in Paris, France, Crown Cork became the world's leading container company.

International sales for the Philadelphia-based operation account for about one-third of Crown Cork's $8.3 billion in annual revenue.

In all, the firm has 138 plants worldwide, including 70 plants in the United States and 68 in foreign markets. The company serves a broad base of clients in the food, citrus, brewing, soft drink, oil, paint, toiletry, drug, antifreeze, chemical, and pet food industries.

After 12 consecutive years of increased earnings, Crown Cork had an off year in 1995 during a major restructuring, but earnings bounced back in 1996.

Crown Cork not only manufactures metal and plastic containers, but it also manufactures and markets packaging and handling machinery. The production of metal cans is Crown Cork's mainstay (along with metal crowns, closures, and packaging machinery), generating about 75 percent of the company's annual revenue.

The sale of plastic containers and closures accounts for about 25 percent of the company's revenue. The 105-year-old operation has about 48,000 employees and 6,000 shareholders.

EARNINGS-PER-SHARE GROWTH   (no points)

Past 5 years: 43 percent (7 percent per year)
Past 10 years: 154 percent (10 percent per year)

STOCK GROWTH   ★ ★ ★

Past 10 years: 411 percent (18 percent per year)
Dollar growth: $10,000 over 10 years (including reinvested dividends) would have grown to $52,000
Average annual compounded rate of return (including reinvested dividends): 18 percent

DIVIDEND YIELD

Average dividend yield: 2.1 percent (The company paid a dividend for the first time in 1996.)

DIVIDEND GROWTH   (no points)

See above

CONSISTENCY

Increased earnings per share: 9 of the past 10 years
Increased sales: 9 of the past 10 years

SHAREHOLDER PERKS   (no points)

The company offers no dividend reinvestment plan, nor does it offer any other shareholder perks.

CROWN CORK AT A GLANCE

Fiscal year ended: Dec. 31
Revenue and net income in $ millions

	1991	1992	1993	1994	1995	1996	5-Year Growth Avg. Annual (%)	5-Year Growth Total (%)
Revenue ($)	3,807.4	3,780.7	4,162.6	4,452.2	5,053.8	8,331.9	17	119
Net income ($)	128.1	155.4	180.9	131.0	141.9	298.1	19	133
Earnings/share ($)	1.48	1.79	2.08	2.29	1.57	2.11	7	43
Div. per share ($)	–	–	–	–	–	1.00	–	–
Dividend yield (%)	–	–	–	–	–	2.1	—	—
Avg. PE ratio	17	19	18	16	27	21	—	—

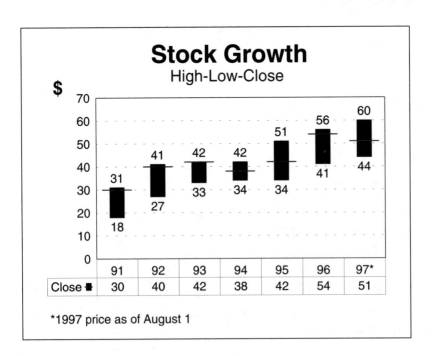

Stock Growth
High-Low-Close

	91	92	93	94	95	96	97*
Close	30	40	42	38	42	54	51

*1997 price as of August 1

Tyson Foods, Inc.

2210 West Oaklawn Drive
Springdale, AR 72762-6999
501-290-4000

Chairman and CEO: Leland E. Tollett
President: Donald E. Wray

Earnings Growth		Dividend Growth	★ ★
Stock Growth	★ ★	Consistency	★ ★
Dividend Yield		Shareholder Perks	
Nasdaq—TYSNA		**Total**	**6 points**

Why did the chicken cross the road?

To get to the Tyson processing plant, of course. Tyson is far and away the world's leading chicken production operation. It produces nearly three times the amount of chicken of its nearest competitor.

Tyson chicken is sold at 96 of the top 100 food-service chains. And its market share continues to grow. The company currently has a poultry production capacity of 36 million birds per week, and it is expanding that capacity to 44 million birds per week.

The Springdale, Arkansas, producer is also spreading its wings overseas, with sales in more than 40 countries. It exports more than 1.5 billion pounds of chicken per year. Foreign sales now account for about 13 percent of Tyson's $6.45 billion in annual revenue. Russia, Japan, Mexico, and China are among its leading markets. The company sells 175 million pounds of chicken paws per year to China.

Poultry sales account for about 78 percent of the company's total revenue, while beef and pork make up 5 percent, seafood accounts for 5 percent, Mexican foods comprise 5 percent, and other products make up the other 7 percent.

Tyson's stock-in-trade has been its ability to make strategic acquisitions of companies that can be easily integrated into its overall operation.

But Tyson's growth can be traced to more than just its aggressive acquisition strategy. The nation's appetite for poultry has grown dramatically over the past decade, as health-conscious consumers looked for alternatives to red meat. Poultry consumption is expected to continue to grow at a rate of 10 percent to 15 percent per year through the rest of this decade.

Tyson markets its fowl to grocery stores, restaurant chains, and institutional food services. About 50 percent of the company's revenue comes from the retail trade, while restaurants and food services account for the other 50 percent.

Tyson runs a fully integrated operation, processing its poultry through every phase of the production process. It operates a nationwide network of hatcheries, feed mills, and processing plants.

The company packages its fowl in many forms—fresh, frozen, mixed, and marinated, plus in more than 50 sizes, shapes, and styles of boneless breasts and breaded patties. These "value-enhanced" products make up about 85 percent of the poultry Tyson sells. "It significantly reduces our exposure to fresh or iced chicken, which is the least profitable, most volatile side of the poultry business," says Tyson Foods Founder Don Tyson. "By moving into value-enhanced products, we have more stable profits."

In all, the company offers more than 500 different meat products to the food-services market.

Tyson, which was founded in 1935 and first incorporated in 1947, has 58,000 employees and 37,000 shareholders.

EARNINGS-PER-SHARE GROWTH   (no points)

Past 5 years: –14 percent (–3 percent per year)
Past 10 years: 221 percent (9 percent per year)

STOCK GROWTH

Past 10 years: 304 percent (15 percent per year)
Dollar growth: $10,000 over 10 years (including reinvested dividends) would have grown to $41,000
Average annual compounded rate of return (including reinvested dividends): 15 percent

DIVIDEND YIELD   (no points)

Average dividend yield in the past 3 years: 0.4 percent

DIVIDEND GROWTH   ★ ★

Increased dividend: 5 of the past 10 years
Past 5-year increase: 300 percent (32 percent per year)

CONSISTENCY   ★ ★

Increased earnings per share: 8 of the past 10 years
Increased sales: 16 consecutive years

SHAREHOLDER PERKS   (no points)

The company does not offer a dividend reinvestment and stock purchase plan, nor does it offer any other perks.

TYSON FOODS AT A GLANCE

Fiscal year ended: Sept. 30
Revenue and net income in $ millions

	1991	1992	1993	1994	1995	1996	5-Year Growth Avg. Annual (%)	5-Year Growth Total (%)
Revenue ($)	3,922	4,169	4,707	5,110	5,511	6,454	11	65
Net income ($)	145.5	160.5	180.3	–2,120	219.2	86.9	–	–40
Earnings/share ($)	0.70	0.77	0.81	0.91	1.01	0.60	–	–14
Div. per share ($)	.03	.04	.04	.07	.08	.12	32	300
Dividend yield (%)	.2	.2	.2	.4	.3	.5	—	—
Avg. PE ratio	17	16	18	17	16	41	—	—

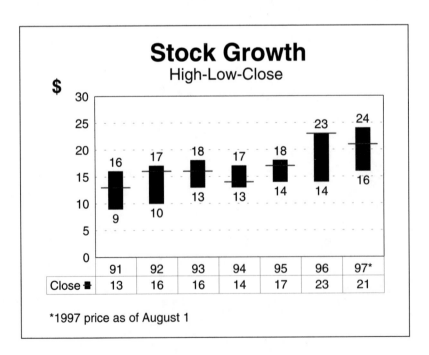

Stock Growth
High-Low-Close

	91	92	93	94	95	96	97*
Close	13	16	16	14	17	23	21

*1997 price as of August 1

The 100 Best by Industry

Industry	Ranking
Consumer Products	
Clorox	63
Colgate-Palmolive Company	34
The Gillette Company	3
The Procter & Gamble Company	30
Corporate Services	
Automatic Data Processing, Inc.	44
Cintas Corp.	31
Electronic Data Systems	51
Fiserv, Inc.	84
The Interpublic Group of Companies, Inc.	22
Electronics	
Federal Signal Corp.	13
Hubbell, Inc.	64
Molex, Inc.	91
Thermo Electron Corp.	85
Thermo Instrument Systems, Inc.	72
Entertainment	
Carnival Corp.	87
Walt Disney Company	73
Financial	
Banc One Corp.	40
Equifax	48
Fannie Mae	2
Fifth Third Bancorp	15
First Empire State	23
Franklin Resources	9
Norwest Corp.	4
SouthTrust Corp.	37
State Street Boston Corp.	24
SunTrust Banks, Inc.	26
Synovus Financial Corp.	10

Industry	Ranking

Food and Beverage Production

Campbell Soup	16
The Coca-Cola Company	7
ConAgra, Inc.	27
CPC International	59
H. J. Heinz Company	76
Hershey Foods Corporation	54
Kellogg Company	92
PepsiCo, Inc.	46
Sara Lee Corporation	33
Sysco Corporation	50
Tyson Foods, Inc.	100
William Wrigley, Jr., Company	8

Food and Drug Retail

Albertson's, Inc.	6
McDonald's Corporation	62
Walgreen Company	25

Health Care and Medical

Abbott Laboratories	36
American Home Products Corp.	74
Becton Dickinson	66
Bristol-Myers Squibb Company	67
Cardinal Health, Inc.	58
Johnson & Johnson	18
Medtronic, Inc.	1
Merck & Company	12
PacifiCare Health Systems, Inc.	82
Pfizer, Inc.	20
Schering-Plough Corp.	5
Sigma-Aldrich Corp.	75
Stryker Corp.	42
United HealthCare Corp.	71
Warner-Lambert Company	47

Industry	Ranking

Household and Commercial Furnishings

Emerson Electric Company	65
General Electric Company	21
Newell Company	29

Industrial Equipment

Carlisle Companies	53
Danaher Corp.	83
Donaldson Company, Inc.	45
Dover Corp.	60
W. W. Grainger, Inc.	88
Pall Corp.	56
Tyco International	96

Insurance

American International Group, Inc.	86
Cincinnati Financial Corp.	98
Jefferson-Pilot	52
Torchmark Corp.	93

Paper Products and Packaging

Bemis Company, Inc.	19
Crown Cork & Seal Company, Inc.	99
Kimberly-Clark	35
Sealed Air Corp.	97

Retail Department Stores

Dollar General	14
The Home Depot	17
The May Department Stores Company	55
Wal-Mart Stores, Inc.	39

The 100 Best by State

State	Ranking
Alabama	
SouthTrust Corp. (Birmingham)	37
Torchmark Corp. (Birmingham)	93
Arkansas	
Tyson Foods, Inc. (Springdale)	100
Wal-Mart Stores, Inc. (Bentonville)	39
California	
Cisco Systems (San Jose)	78
Clorox (Oakland)	63
Computer Sciences Corp. (El Segundo)	95
Walt Disney Company (Burbank)	73
Franklin Resources (San Mateo)	9
Hewlett-Packard (Palo Alto)	61
Intel Corp. (Santa Clara)	28
Oracle (Redwood Shores)	79
PacifiCare Health Systems, Inc. (Cypress)	82
Connecticut	
Crompton & Knowles Corp. (Stamford)	94
General Electric Company (Fairfield)	21
Hubbell, Inc. (Orange)	64
Pitney Bowes, Inc. (Stamford)	41
Xerox (Stamford)	89
District of Columbia	
Danaher (Washington)	83
Fannie Mae (Washington)	2
Florida	
Carnival (Miami)	87

State	Ranking

Georgia

The Coca-Cola Company (Atlanta)	7
Equifax (Atlanta)	48
Genuine Parts Company (Atlanta)	77
The Home Depot (Atlanta)	17
SunTrust Banks, Inc. (Atlanta)	26
Synovus Financial Corp. (Columbus)	10

Idaho

Albertson's, Inc. (Boise)	6

Illinois

Abbott Laboratories (Abbott Park)	36
Federal Signal Corp. (Oak Brook)	13
W. W. Grainger, Inc. (Skokie)	88
McDonald's Corp. (Oak Brook)	62
Molex (Lisle)	91
Newell Company (Freeport)	29
Sara Lee Corp. (Chicago)	33
Walgreen Company (Deerfield)	25
William Wrigley, Jr., Company (Chicago)	8

Massachusetts

Gillette Company (Boston)	3
State Street Boston Corp. (Boston)	24
Thermo Electron Corp. (Waltham)	85

Michigan

Kellogg Company (Battle Creek)	92
Stryker Corp. (Kalamazoo)	42

Minnesota

Bemis Company, Inc. (Minneapolis)	19
Donaldson Company, Inc. (Minneapolis)	45
Medtronic, Inc. (Minneapolis)	1
Norwest Corp. (Minneapolis)	4
United HealthCare Corp. (Minnetonka)	71
Valspar Corp. (Minneapolis)	32

State	Ranking

Missouri
Anheuser-Busch Companies, Inc. (St. Louis)	49
Emerson Electric Company (St. Louis)	65
The May Department Stores Company (St. Louis)	55
Sigma-Aldrich Corp. (St. Louis)	75

Nebraska
ConAgra, Inc. (Omaha)	27

New Hampshire
Cabletron (Rochester)	80
Tyco (Exeter)	96

New Jersey
American Home Products Corp. (Madison)	74
Automatic Data Processing, Inc. (Roseland)	44
Becton Dickinson (Franklin Lakes)	66
Campbell Soup (Camden)	16
CPC International (Englewood Cliffs)	59
Johnson & Johnson (New Brunswick)	18
Merck & Company (Rahway)	12
Schering-Plough Corporation (Madison)	5
Sealed Air (Saddle Brook)	97
Warner-Lambert Company (Morris Plains)	47

New Mexico
Thermo Instrument Systems, Inc. (Santa Fe)	72

New York
American International Group (New York)	86
Bristol-Myers Squibb Company (New York)	67
Carlisle (Syracuse)	53
Colgate-Palmolive Company (New York)	34
Computer Associates International (Islandia)	70
Dover (New York)	60
First Empire State (Buffalo)	23
International Flavors & Fragrances, Inc. (New York)	90

State	Ranking
New York (continued)	
The Interpublic Group of Companies, Inc. (New York)	22
Pall Corporation (East Hills)	56
PepsiCo, Inc. (Purchase)	46
Pfizer, Inc. (New York)	20
North Carolina	
Jefferson-Pilot (Greensboro)	52
Ohio	
Banc One Corp. (Columbus)	40
Cardinal Health, Inc. (Dublin)	58
Cincinnati Financial Corp. (Fairfield)	98
Cintas Corp. (Cincinnati)	31
Fifth Third Bancorp (Cincinnati)	15
Nordson Corp. (Westlake)	43
The Procter & Gamble Company (Cincinnati)	30
RPM, Inc. (Medina)	68
The Sherwin-Williams Company (Cleveland)	38
Oregon	
Nike (Beaverton)	57
Pennsylvania	
Crown Cork & Seal Company (Philadelphia)	99
H. J. Heinz Company (Pittsburgh)	76
Hershey Foods Corp. (Hershey)	54
U.S. Healthcare, Inc. (Blue Bell)	71
Tennessee	
Dollar General (Nashville)	14
Texas	
Compaq Computer (Houston)	81
Electronic Data Systems (Dallas)	51
Kimberly-Clark (Dallas)	35
Sysco Corp. (Houston)	50

State	**Ranking**

Washington

Microsoft Corp. (Redmond) — 69

Wisconsin

Fiserv, Inc. (Brookfield) — 84
Harley-Davidson, Inc. (Milwaukee) — 11

INDEX